atheism, ayn rand, and other heresies

george h. smith

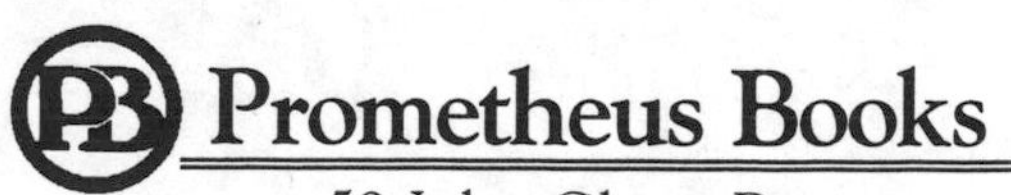

Prometheus Books
59 John Glenn Drive
Amherst, New York 14228-2197

To Greg Morris, the Magician

Published 1991 by Prometheus Books

 Inquiries should be addressed to Prometheus Books, 59 John Glenn Drive, Amherst, New York 14228–2197, 716–691–0133. FAX: 716–691–0137.

01 00 99 98 5 4 3 2

Library of Congress Cataloging-in-Publication Data

Smith, George H., 1949–
Atheism, Ayn Rand, and other heresies / George H. Smith.
p. cm.
Includes bibliographical references.
ISBN 0–87975–577–6
1. Atheism. 2. Rand, Ayn. 3. Religion and state—Controversial literature.
4. Smith, George H., 1949– . I. Title.
BL2747.3.S59 1990
211′.8—dc20 90–20656
CIP

Printed in the United States of America on acid-free paper

Contents

Part III: Other Heresies

Preface

This book contains a diverse collection of essays written over a period of two decades. Some have been published before, but most appear here for the first time.

The only theme that connects these essays is heresy in the broad sense; most of my interests and opinions fall well outside the orthodox mainstream. There should be something in this book to offend everyone.

I wish to thank the following individuals, heretics all, for their suggestions and encouragement: Wendy McElroy, Queen Silver, Jeff Riggenbach, Roy Childs, Gordon Stein, Ralph Raico—and a special thanks to Anne Regier.

Introduction
The Meaning of Heresy

The word "heresy" derives from the Greek word *hairesis*, meaning "choice."[1] In the New Testament, the word often denotes a party or sect of one's choosing—as when Paul refers to "the party of the Sauducees" (Acts 5.17), "the party of the Pharisees" (Acts 15.5), and "the sect of the Nazarenes" (Acts 24.5). No moral opprobrium was attached to this meaning of heresy, for choosing is part of life.

By the end of the New Testament period, heresy began to assume sinister connotations. It came to signify not a choice per se, but an incorrect and evil choice—a deviation from the true faith. Such deviations, according to the best theologians of the time, were promoted by Satan and his minions as part of their effort to splinter the Christian movement and impede its progress.[2]

Where we have heresy, we must also have orthodoxy—these are two sides of the same coin. Who decided which is which in the early Christian era? The historian Jeffrey Russell offers this explanation:

> The canon of the New Testament was still in flux. Under such circumstances radical differences of opinion arose within the

> community during the second century. The party that eventually won became orthodox—"right-thinking"—by reason of its victory, and its writers were given the name "apologetic fathers." Their defeated opponents came to be called heretics.[3]

This account is realistic and appealing, but it fails to explain why Christians were so concerned about heresy. If orthodoxy and heresy emerged only *after* doctrinal disputes had been settled, then what *caused* those disputes to begin with? Why did Christians fight bitterly among themselves over everything from canonical writings to the nature of the Trinity, unless they were already forging an orthodoxy and attacking heresies in the process? The distinction between the right-thinking of orthodoxy and the wrong-thinking of heresy was more a cause than an effect of conflict.

There is another problem with Professor Russell's account. If it is true that the victors branded the losers as heretics, it is also true that the losers rejected that odious label, proclaimed themselves paragons of the true faith (as demonstrated, perhaps, by their persecution), and denounced the victors as the real heretics. The so-called heretics of the early Christian era "were no less implacable than the orthodox in claiming that only their position was the correct one."[4]

To my knowledge, no unorthodox sect in Christian history has ever willingly embraced the label of heresy. Why? Because to confess heresy was to confess (at least) three things: first, error; second, *willful* (and therefore morally blameworthy) error; third, *dangerous* error—a threat to the foundations of social order.

The problem of heresy preoccupied the Christian Church throughout the Middle Ages. If we wish to understand the reason for this, we might profitably compare the medieval heretic to his secular analogue—the traitor. Treason is to the modern state what heresy was to the medieval Church.

Interestingly, the word "traitor" sprang from a religious controversy. *Traditores* ("handers-over") were those Christians who obeyed an edict of Diocletian (c. 303) to hand over Scriptures to the state so they could be destroyed.[5] These *traditores* caused a major schism in the Church, especially in Africa, as theologians wrangled over whether *traditores* should be restored to communion and whether bishops who had been *traditores* could perform valid ordinations.

Clearly, treason includes the notion of betrayal; the same is true of heresy. But one must belong to an organization before one can betray it. This is what distinguishes the heretic from the infidel. The infidel is an outsider, a nonmember who is incapable of betraying a church he never belonged to. Similarly, a foreign citizen cannot commit treason against any government but his own.

During the Middle Ages, the individual was inducted into the Church through baptism. Since this usually occurred during infancy, it could scarcely be called voluntary. Nevertheless, the godparents made promises on behalf of the child, thereby obligating him for life.[6]

The Christian, bound to the Church legally and irrevocably through baptism, was required to defer to official doctrine. Heresy was the sin committed by a Christian who "showed intellectual arrogance by preferring his own opinions to those who were specially qualified to pronounce upon matters of faith."[7] Heresy was more than a sin, however; it was also a crime. The heretic committed high treason against the political authority of the Church and endangered the theocratic foundation of government.[8]

Orthodoxy was regarded as the ideological bedrock of social and political order. Heresy, if left unchecked, would erode this foundation until "society itself would collapse."[9] We see, therefore, that the similarities between heresy and treason are more than superficial. Heresy was itself punishable as treason, because it subverted the authority of the Church from within.

The apologist Tertullian (c. 160-225), a formidable foe of heretics who became one himself, suggested that heresies are "instigated by philosophy."[10] Walter Kaufmann has made a similar claim, but he does so approvingly. According to Kaufmann, "one may view the history of philosophy as a history of heresy."[11] Philosophers, unlike theologians, are not concerned with authority or tradition, nor are they wedded to dogma. Consequently, Kaufmann questions whether medieval philosophy is worthy of the name:

> [M]edieval philosophy was so different from both Greek and modern philosophy that it is somewhat misleading to call it by the same name. And if philosophy were defined as a search for truth that involves following arguments and evidence, without recourse to authority, wherever they may lead, frequently arriving at unforeseen conclusions, then medieval philosophy would not deserve the name at all.[12]

As much as I sympathize with the spirit of Kaufmann's remarks, I cannot agree with his conclusions. The history of philosophy cannot be a history of heresy, because the notion of heresy, strictly construed, has no meaning whatever in a philosophic context. It is the history of religion that is a history of heresy.

Of course, this objection is a bit contentious, because it overlooks Kaufmann's central point. He wishes to stress that philosophy seeks truth without fear or favor, whereas theology typically defends an orthodox credo. In other words, philosophy, when viewed from a *religious* perspective, invariably breeds heresy.

There is merit in this claim, but I think it omits a crucial factor. If theology is viewed as a branch of philosophy that investigates the existence and attributes of a divine being, then it needn't be any more dogmatic than other branches of philosophy. Theologians can, and frequently do, function as philosophers. But complications arise when theologians join organizations, such as churches, and serve as propagandists for a cause. Theology has been traditionally affiliated with institutions—and this, I suggest, accounts for a good deal of the "dogmatism" that Kaufmann attributes to theology. (This is essentially what Thomas Paine and other freethinkers had in mind when they attacked *organized* religion.)

An organization must establish an identity by which to differentiate members from nonmembers. If an organization is ideological, then its identity will be defined by a credo—a set of beliefs or principles that determines the conditions of membership. The ability of the credo to withstand philosophic scrutiny is irrelevant here. Whether rational or irrational, a credo constitutes the "orthodoxy," the intellectual foundation, of an organization. An organization without an orthodoxy is an organization without ideas.

Thus understood, an orthodox credo is a feature of all ideological institutions, religious *and* secular. Because philosophy normally lacks institutional affiliations, it does not have credos, orthodoxies, heretics, and dissenters. This is the nature of the beast called philosophy, but it does not render philosophers inherently more noble, honest, or undogmatic than their theological cousins.

The dilemma of the theologian is that he is at once a church member and a philosopher, and those roles may conflict. If they do, then the theologian must choose between orthodoxy and heresy. If the philosopher joins an ideological organization and commits to its credo, then he too may experience the tension between orthodoxy and heresy—between loyalty to an organization and loyalty to the voice of reason. I see no evidence to suggest that philosophers, when confronted with this decision, will necessarily choose better than theologians.

When viewed in an institutional setting, the ideas of orthodoxy and heresy are neither irrational nor dangerous—so long, that is, as membership in an institution is *voluntary*. Dissenters are free to quit an organization or to never join at all. This was the case with the the early Christian movement before it became a state religion in the fourth century. Christianity was more than a theology; it was an *organization*, and as such it needed to forge an orthodoxy, an intellectual identity, a set of beliefs that unified its members.

Only after Christianity acquired the reins of state power and substituted *force* for *persuasion* did its notions of orthodoxy and heresy become dangerous. What had been orthodoxy for a single religious organization became, through the instrumentality of government, orthodoxy for *society as a whole*. "[T]he church," writes the distinguished medievalist R. W. Southern, "was a compulsory society in precisely the same way as the modern state is a compulsory society."[13] As the good of the Church became synonymous with the good of society, heretics became more than wayward members of an organization—they became threats to the foundations of social order. This transformation was caused, not by the notion of orthodoxy per se, but by the *politicizing* of orthodoxy.

Heretics were ferociously persecuted by ecclesiastical authorities at various times during the Middle Ages. Historians have long been aware that these persecutions often had political undercurrents. But these same historians offer a defense (of sorts) of the persecutors. We are told that rulers were generally more lenient and open-minded than the people they ruled. As Southern puts it: "[O]n the whole the holders of ecclesiastical authority were less prone to violence, even against unbelievers, than the people whom they ruled."[14] Another historian maintains that heretics "aroused intense feelings of fear and hatred among the mass of the people because they dissociated themselves completely from all the values on which society was based."[15]

This standard interpretation has been challenged by R. I. Moore in a brilliant and provocative book. Moore questions whether the masses feared and despised heretics as much as historians believe; indeed, he points out that heresies often attracted large segments of the population. Thus, contrary to the view that "medieval man" feared and resented any deviation from the Catholic faith, Moore argues that "the reason why preachers of heresy were denounced, pursued and extinguished by whatever means availed was precisely the fear that they would undermine the faith of the *simplices*, and with it the social order." Upon examining those cases where heretics appear to have been executed by public demand, Moore concludes that "on inspection their numbers shrink rapidly." We possess "no true evidence of general popular antipathy to heresy as such."[16]

Medieval persecutors, according to Moore, were not "agents of society at large, at least if our conception of society is one which includes the great majority of its members." Persecutors had their own agenda; heretics were a political threat, because they declared "their own independence of the structures of established power. They looked for their authority to those who heard them."[17]

Emerging bureaucratic regimes stigmatized and persecuted heretics—along with Jews, homosexuals, witches, and even lepers—as a means to justify and consolidate their power. Quoting Moore:

> The attacks on particular *loci* of communal power which are represented by these forms of persecution and allied processes are generalized in the campaigns of moral repression with which newly instituted regimes so often establish their legitimacy, proclaim their adherence to traditional values, discredit their enemies and consolidate their hold on the instruments of power. Such drives tend to be directed not only against recognized forms of moral laxity, like sexual pleasure or conspicuous consumption, but also against stereotypical public enemies who may serve as the focus of rhetoric and the object of attack.[18]

This account reinforces a central theme of this essay: the crucial difference between the voluntary orthodoxy of organizations and the politicized orthodoxy of governments. Orthodoxy will always exist in a free society, but this is a *pluralistic* system where innumerable groups and movements, each with its own orthodoxy, compete for adherents.

The heretic in a free society can advocate unpopular or offensive views without fear of punishment. But the heretic will still be shunned, despised, and perhaps demeaned by some orthodox segments of society. If the heretic cannot live with this liability, then he should conceal his heresy or capitulate to orthodoxy. A heretic who protests the social consequences of heresy is like a boxer who protests whenever he is punched. It comes with the job.

Coercive orthodoxy is another matter entirely. A government doesn't compete; it compels. Governmental sanctions against heresy—whether religious, social, or sexual—differ in kind from social sanctions. If this seems obvious, it isn't. Even John Stuart Mill confused the two in *On Liberty*, a classic defense of pluralism.

According to Mill, social sanctions against noncomformists can be as devastating in their effects as governmental sanctions. True enough, but this is like saying that losing money from gambling has the same result as being robbed at gunpoint, or that a person who is born without legs is as unable to walk as a person who is maimed by a sadist, or that a person who dies naturally is as dead as a person who is murdered.

In the long run, as Keynes pointed out, we are all dead. That is a matter of nature, but *how* we die is a matter of justice. Likewise, heretics will always suffer consequences—that is a matter of human nature—but *how* those consequences are inflicted is a matter of justice.

A free society, complete with orthodoxies and prejudices, is the best of all possible worlds for the heretic. Liberty permits the heretic to pit his beliefs against those of the orthodox majority and hope for the best. Suppose the heretic succeeds. Suppose his heresy wins the day and is transfigured into a new orthodoxy. What will the former heretic do then? Will he politicize the new orthodoxy or will he defend liberty?

Few heretics have ever been presented with this decision, and even fewer have decided in favor of liberty. Those few—the exceptional among the exceptions—are the history of liberty.

Notes

1. F. F. Bruce, *The Spreading Flame: The Rise and Progress of Christianity from its First Beginnings to the Conversion of the English* (Grand Rapids: Wm. B. Eerdmans, 1958), p. 249.
2. See Jeffrey Burton Russell, *Satan: The Early Christian Tradition* (Ithaca: Cornell University Press, 1981), pp. 35ff.
3. Ibid., p. 51.
4. Jaroslav Pelikan, *The Emergence of the Catholic Tradition (100-600)* (Chicago: University of Chicago Press, 1971), p. 69.
5. Roland H. Bainton, *Christianity* (Boston: Houghton Mifflin, 1964), p. 94.
6. R. W. Southern, *Western Society and the Church in the Middle Ages* (Harmondsworth: Penguin Books, 1970), p. 18.
7. Walter Ullmann, *The Individual and Society in the Middle Ages* (Baltimore: Johns Hopkins, 1966), p. 37.
8. Walter Ullmann, *Law and Politics in the Middle Ages* (Ithaca: Cornell University Press, 1975), pp. 146-7.
9. Ullmann, *The Individual and Society*, p. 37.
10. Tertullian in *The Ante-Nicene Fathers*, ed. A. Roberts and J. Donaldson (New York: Charles Scribner, 1905), vol. III, p. 246.
11. Walter Kaufmann, *The Faith of a Heretic* (Garden City: Anchor

Books, 1963), p. 15.

12. Ibid., p. 17.

13. Southern, *Western Society and the Church*, p. 17.

14. Ibid., p. 19.

15. Bernard Hamilton quoted in R. I. Moore, *The Formation of a Persecuting Society: Power and Deviance in Western Europe, 950-1250* (Oxford: Basil Blackwell, 1990), p. 107.

16. Ibid., pp. 114-16.

17. Ibid., pp. 123, 133.

18. Ibid., p. 135.

PART 1

Atheism

1
My Path to Atheism

It was late in 1971, and I was reassessing life in the big city. Earlier that year, at age twenty-one, I had moved from Tucson to Los Angeles seeking fame and fortune as a free-lance philosopher. Ten months of working in a warehouse, however, persuaded me to return to the University of Arizona and finish my degree.

I quit my job and packed up my books. Then, within a week of my scheduled departure, one Roy A. Childs, Jr., entered my life.

Roy had moved to Los Angeles from the East Coast. Our common intellectual interests brought us together, and we got along famously. But Roy faced a problem: I was due to leave Los Angeles, and he didn't want to lose his partner in conversation. He asked what would get me to stay.

"Nothing," I replied.

"What if I get you a contract to write a book on atheism?" (Roy knew of my interest in the subject.)

"Sure, Roy," I said. "I have no academic credentials, and I'm leaving Los Angeles in five days. Sure, get me a book contract, and I'll stay."

Roy called me the next day. "I've been talking to Ed Nash at Nash Publishing, and he wants you to call him about a book on atheism." (Unbeknownst to me, but not to Roy, Nash had been looking for someone to write a book on the subject.)

To make a short story even shorter: within days I had signed a book contract and canceled my travel plans. Thus, from a friend's desire to keep me in Los Angeles came *Atheism: The Case Against God.*

So how did a devoutly religious boy mend his ways and find the path to atheism? That is the subject of this memoir.

My home environment was not especially religious. My father showed no discernible religious convictions, and my mother called herself a "Universalist-Unitarian." I wasn't sure what that religion had to offer, except never having to go to church.

I was raised on Air Force bases where Protestant churches, although officially nondenominational, had a decidedly fundamentalist slant. This became my religion of choice. I attended Sunday school and church; believed in the Bible, heaven, and hell; and worked diligently for my "God-and-Country" Boy Scout merit badge by assisting in church services, mowing church lawns, and memorizing the names of biblical books.

I was a model military child. By all indications, I would grow into a religious, civic-minded citizen of the Pat Boone variety. Then, at age ten, I suffered my first epistemological crisis.

During Sunday school my teacher, Sergeant Watson (a zealous fundamentalist whom I greatly admired), announced that only one person in ten makes it to heaven; the rest go to hell.

Well, I knew that *I* was going to heaven, but what about my family? The odds didn't sound good. I pondered this dilemma while riding my bicycle. Then it hit me: Just where did this statistic come from? I posed this question to Sergeant Watson the following Sunday. I don't recall his answer, but it was clearly unsatisfactory. I was annoyed at being led astray. My faith in Christianity remained intact, but not my faith in *Christians.*

I recall another glimmer of skepticism from my boyhood. Looking through the family album, I saw my baby pictures, my older brother's baby pictures, and pictures of yet another baby unknown to me. This, my mother explained, was Susan, her first child and my older sister. Susan had died suddenly at age two. My mother, distraught with grief, was on the verge of a nervous breakdown when the base chaplain paid his expected visit. He explained that God had a mysterious purpose in taking my mother's baby. My mother was furious. "What kind of God would kill an innocent baby?" she screamed. "And why would that God put me through this torture?" She told the chaplain to leave and thereafter attributed her daughter's death to a random, natural occurence, without rhyme or reason.

That belief comforted my mother. At least Susan's death had not been planned by a conscious being—in other words, her baby had not been *murdered*. Looking back, I find this an interesting counter-example to the oft-repeated claim that belief in God consoles the grieving.

While I was in seventh grade, my family moved to Tucson, where, for the first time, I lived off-base with civilians. The effect was dramatic; it was like moving from a communist country to the free world. No more sea of uniforms, no more buildings painted gray or drab-green, no more waiting in long lines to get into the commissary on payday, and (perhaps most liberating for a boy of twelve) no more monopolistic PX with its inadequate selection of DC comics.

I don't know what caused it—maybe it was those seductive Arizona mornings that beckoned a boy to play—but I stopped going to church. I still considered myself a Christian, but I no longer prayed or read the Bible.

I didn't think much about religion until my first year in high school. I was packing up my saxophone after band practice one day, when I was accosted by an obnoxious trombone player who had recently found Jesus. As this born-again musician quizzed me on my religious beliefs, I found myself expressing doubts for the first time.

We continued our weighty deliberations while eating hamburgers. My opponent insisted that all great thinkers have believed in God. Neither of us had the knowledge to argue the point, but that didn't stop us. After returning home, I dug up some passages in which Freud theorizes that belief in God is rooted in an infantile father-longing.

Shortly thereafter I set my first intellectual trap. Armed with a page of Freud quotations, I lured my opponent into another encounter. I had him repeat and confirm his earlier argument that all great thinkers have believed in God. Then I asked him if Freud was a great thinker. After dragging a reluctant "yes" from my now-wary opponent, I sprang my quotations on him. Victory was mine.

But I wasn't about to let him off that easily. I badgered him with questions about his relationship with his father. Revenge was mine as well.

This encounter left me with a nagging guilt, as if I had trespassed into prohibited territory. I felt that, if I didn't attend church, I should at least read the Bible. So I rummaged through my closet, found my Bible, and began at the beginning. Within a few months, I had traversed from Genesis through Revelation.

Like many devout Christians, I had never read the entire Bible—only preselected excerpts, mainly from the New Testament and especially from the Gospel of John. Burrowing through the Old Testament's sensualism, violence, and ceremonial laws can be quite an eye-opener for a puritanical youngster. That experience, more than anything else, dissuaded me from Christianity.

While reading the Bible I became curious about its history, so I visited a nearby Christian bookstore; there I purchased the *Abingdon Bible Commentary*, followed by other commentaries, Bible dictionaries, and concordances. And so began the rather bizarre excursion of a high-school sophomore into the land of "higher criticism." Within a year I could deliver a credible little speech on the canonization of the New Testament—a feat that surely delighted my friends.

Soon I discovered two classics of American freethought: Robert G. Ingersoll's *Some Mistakes of Moses* and Thomas Paine's *Age of Reason*.

Paine, a writer of extraordinary power, had the greatest impact on me, and I was amazed to learn that one of America's founding fathers had written a scathing indictment of Christianity. Why hadn't I heard this before? More doubts surfaced, this time about my formal education.

In the first part of *Age of Reason*, Paine attacks the atheism of the French Revolution and defends Deism—the belief in a god of nature, a creator who practices *laissez faire.* That was my kind of god. I quickly embraced Deism and counted Paine, Jefferson, Franklin, and other founding fathers as my mentors.

As I discovered more freethought literature, I became something of an evangelist for the cause. Accompanied by a freethinking friend, Greg Morris, I attended religious meetings far more regularly than I ever did as a believer. The services ranged from Baptist to Mormon to Christian Science to Pentecostal. I also attended small study groups, including weekly meetings with Jehovah's Witnesses.

The Jehovah's Witnesses, despite their annoying habit of waking up entire neighborhoods on Sunday mornings, were an amiable lot. In Tucson, the JWs (as Greg and I called them) lived in trailer parks, where they could live inexpensively and close to fellow believers. My interaction with JWs is what first made me aware of the strong social and familial bonds that render the deconversion of cultish believers so difficult and improbable.

I have tremendous admiration for ex-Jehovah's Witnesses, ex-Mormons, ex-Pentecostals, ex-Amish, and the like. When I gave up Christianity, I lost a god, but I did not risk losing family and friends. Such is not the case with members of closely knit religious groups, for whom deconversion means certain ostracism by family and friends. To deconvert in these circumstances requires an extraordinary amount of courage and intellectual independence.

If I liked the JWs, I cannot say the same for the Pentecostals, or "Holy Rollers." During services they "spoke in tongues"—that is, they babbled incoherently. They also railed against "the Devil's box" (television) and other sundry evils. While listening to this gibberish, I could not help but feel sorry for the youngsters who were entombed in that hellish madhouse called a Pentecostal Church. What kind of life lay before them was anyone's guess.

I had trouble taking the Christian Scientists seriously. I recall one sweet old lady who gave her testimony. She explained that, while driving her car, she stopped at an intersection, looked carefully in both directions, and then pulled out. Suddenly, out of nowhere, a motorcycle hit her broadside and crashed, pinning its two riders underneath. The lady got out of her car and approached the injured motorcyclists who were groaning in pain. She explained to them that they were not really hurt, that their pain was an illusion. The sweet old lady did not include their response in her testimony, but I suspect she learned some new words on that day.

Why did I, a freethinker, frequent Christian meetings? Partly from curiosity, partly to raise hell, and partly because it was an enjoyable challenge. I quickly learned how to argue with Christians of various stripes. For example, I knew which biblical arguments would work with a Baptist but not with a Jehovah's Witness, and vice versa (not exactly essential knowledge, to be sure, but valuable training nonetheless for a high-school student who had hitherto displayed little interest in ideas).

Of course, every self-respecting freethinker should belong to an organization—something that will add stature to his crusade. In 1965, Greg and I formed such a group. Its name was snappy and to the point, if somewhat bizarre: "The Anti-Biblical League." Our motto, printed below the title on a business card, read: "For People Who Aren't Afraid to Think." The letters "Q.E.D." did *not* appear on the card, but they were there in spirit.

This organization had exactly two members: Greg Morris and George Smith. We never solicited additional members. We just liked to see the reaction of Christians when we presented our card and asked if they would like to talk to us.

During the formative stages of "The Anti-Biblical League," it appeared that our organization might suffer an early demise. Greg was moving to Phoenix, thereby threatening to cut membership of the ABL (as we insiders called it) in half. No problem—a quick change in our business card turned a liability into an asset. The upper-left corner of our card now read: "George H. Smith, Tucson Branch"; the lower-right corner read: "Greg Morris, Phoenix Branch." (This early display of organizational talent would later prove useful as I became involved with other radical groups.) Greg, it so happened, never moved to Phoenix. But, having invested in a thousand embossed, two-color cards, we used them anyway.

Of the many ministers I encountered during my years of free-thought combat, Baptists were the most entertaining. I came to suspect that joining the Baptist ministry was like joining the police force—one had to meet certain physical requirements. Curly hair seemed important, as did a ruddy complexion, a pot belly, a firm handshake, and the capacity to perspire and turn beet-red on demand. Also important were peculiar linguistic skills, such as the ability to transform one-syllable words into two-syllable words (with a dramatic accent on the first syllable). Thus, *save* became *sa'-ave,* and *heal* became *he'-eal.* The name *Jesus,* of course, was pronounced with four syllables—*J'-uh-ee'-sus.*

One particular Baptist minister fulfilled these requirements admirably. I first learned of the good reverend through his mimeographed essay, "Why Sen. Robert Kennedy Blasphemed When He Said, 'Suppose God is Black.' " This masterpiece bore the author's name and a string of redundant credentials: "Rev. William 'Bill' Bowler, A.B., B.D., Pastor."

Bowler's essay contained two distinct arguments. It argued that God is a spirit and therefore lacks color altogether. So far so good. But then the Reverend cited biblical passages about white lights, angels in white garb, etc.—and he suggested that *if* God did have a color, it would most certainly be white. Or perhaps he meant that, although God does not have a color, he does have a *favorite* color, which is white. Having mislaid this valuable document some years ago, I cannot attest to the correct interpretation.

It is difficult to recall when I abandoned Deism for atheism; certainly the transition was complete by the end of my third year of high school. The change occurred quietly and naturally as I read more freethought literature. My earlier transition from Christianity to Deism, if not traumatic, was at least difficult—not so my ascent from Deism to atheism. The death of the personal god of Christianity who listened to my prayers (but usually said no) was far more disturbing than losing the deaf, dumb, and blind god of Deism.

Agnosticism never appealed to me. I had believed in God; I no longer believed in God. I had been a theist; I was now an atheist. "Do you *believe* in God?"—that, for me, was the relevant question, not "Can you *know* whether or not God exists?"

In my experience, atheism is the path followed by most deconverted fundamentalists and Catholics. Those who know what it means to believe also know what it means to lose that belief. Agnosticism, on the other hand, is preferred by former Protestant "liberals" who were never too clear about their beliefs in the first place.

Throughout most of high school I remained in the freethought mainstream; that is to say, I focused on theological arguments and biblical criticism and paid little attention to broader philosophical issues. My first exposure to Ayn Rand, when I saw her on the Johnny Carson show in the late sixties, was destined to change this.

I remember what impressed me about Ayn Rand. When Carson asked about her atheism, she answered in a matter-of-fact way that, of course, she was an atheist—as if any other alternative was inconceivable. Many people are turned off to Rand because of her atheism, but she appealed to me for precisely that reason. Compared to the cranks and ignoramuses I had encountered on the fringes of freethought, Ayn Rand was a breath of fresh air.

I eagerly devoured Rand's ideas and, like many of her followers, spat them up undigested. I memorized passages and definitions from her writing, blamed altruism and Immanuel Kant for all that is wrong in the world, and adamantly proclaimed the existence of a world external to consciousness. (It was difficult to find anyone who would argue this last point with me.)

All this, perhaps, can be forgiven a high-school senior smitten with heroine worship. Rand's lasting influence was to convince me (and thousands of other young people) that ideas *matter.* She had an astonishing ability to make philosophy seem important and exciting—something most philosophy professors never manage to approach. That was the true legacy of Ayn Rand.

Upon entering college, Greg and I formed a "Students of Objectivism" club. A little later, there occurred the famous (now infamous) split between Ayn Rand and psychologist Nathaniel Branden, her "intellectual heir." That split, a lovers' quarrel, was a tonic for many of Rand's admirers who might otherwise have succumbed to cultish devotion, for Rand was now seen as "human, all too human." (After Branden moved to Los Angeles, we joked about the schism in the Objectivist Church: Eastern Orthodox versus Western Reformed.)

Despite the split, my faith (there is no other word for it) in Rand's ideas remained fairly intact. Then I experienced an abrupt deconversion from orthodox Randianism.

The war in Vietnam was in full swing, as was the antiwar movement. Of course, I toed the Randian line: Americans shouldn't be in Vietnam at all—our intervention was altruistic, and Rand despised altruism—but, so long as we were there, we should fight to "win" (however this term might apply to the butchery of war). Rand, a Russian immigrant, admired America tremendously; she believed it to be the only free country on the face of the globe.

I had heard about the atrocities allegedly committed by American soldiers in Vietnam, but, having been raised in a military family, I could not believe them. I had grown up around military folk, and those decent, hard-working people were obviously incapable of committing "atrocities." Moreover, the antiwar movement was run by hippies—long-haired, drug-crazed freaks who, according to my father, "should be lined-up against a wall and shot." Rand's view of the hippies, and of the antiwar movement generally, was somewhat better than my father's, but not by much.

Given my father's patriotism and Rand's intellectual reinforcement of that patriotism, it seemed no argument could possibly shake my faith in America. That supposition was correct: no argument shook my faith—it took a solitary photograph instead.

I remember the incident as if it occurred yesterday. While walking to my car near the University of Arizona campus, I stumbled across a leftist bookstore. I don't know what lured me inside, maybe it was the same kind of temptation that caused Eve to eat from the tree of knowledge. My fall into sin was caused by *I. F. Stone's Weekly*, an antiwar "rag" (as I then called any leftist publication).

While browsing among the intellectual ruins, I spotted Stone's paper prominently displayed in a newspaper rack. The front page featured a photograph of three smiling American soldiers, their left knees touching the ground and their right hands clutching rifles. Their left hands were grasping, by the hair, the decapitated heads of three North Vietnamese soldiers, and the severed hands of these Vietnamese soldiers were prominently displayed in the foreground.

I glanced, nervously turned away, and surveyed multiple copies of Lenin's collected works. A few minutes later—perhaps inspired by Oscar Wilde's advice that the best way to overcome temptation is to succumb to it—I returned to the newspaper rack. Stone's paper and its featured photograph were still there.

I looked more closely. "Surely," I reasoned, with impeccable paternal and Randian logic, "this photograph must be fake. No American could possibly pose for a picture like this." Those young American G.I.s were virtual prototypes of the decent Americans I had grown up with.

I wanted more time to assess the photograph, so, with the trepidation of an underage boy about to purchase his first *Playboy* magazine, I plunked down the money for Stone's paper.

I examined the photograph for at least an hour after returning home. The severed heads and hands were gruesome enough, but that is not what disturbed me most. The three baby-faced American soldiers could have come from the Iowa heartland, the birthplace of my father. That was the horror.

Moreover, I had seen this pose before—hunters displaying the head and hooves of their prey. My father, an avid sportsman, had hunted moose, caribou, and deer; and, like many hunters, he took photos of his trophies. I still possess a picture of him on one knee in our Alaskan front yard, rifle in hand, with the sawed-off head and hooves of a hapless moose prominently displayed.

Stone's photograph compelled me to face the obvious: at least three American soldiers in Vietnam, whatever the justice of their cause, saw the enemy as subhuman prey. I was confused. As a Randian, I was fully aware of the eternal Manichean struggle between good and evil, light and darkness. But even the righteous John Galt, after defeating his collectivist enemies, would never pose with their heads and hands for the folks back home. Rand seemed oblivious to the insidious dehumanization caused by war.

Jarred by Stone's photograph, I awoke from my dogmatic Randian slumbers, broadened my reading, and learned that opposition to war and imperialism was part and parcel of the free-market Classical Liberal heritage—the tradition of Thomas Paine, Richard Cobden, John Bright, Herbert Spencer, and others. My faltering American nationalism soon gave way to the Enlightenment motto repeated by Paine, "I am a citizen of the world."

This saga had a curious ending. The UA Students of Objectivism, to my knowledge, was the only Randian group to participate in the nation-wide moratorium march for peace. And this (along with our opposition to conscription) earned us the dubious distinction of a place on the F.B.I.'s list of subversive campus organizations.

Previously, my doubts about God had led me to atheism. Now, my doubts about government led me to anarchism. Indeed, belief in the legitimacy and wisdom of government seemed to require more blind faith than belief in God. I agreed with Nietzsche: the State is the coldest of all cold monsters that bites with stolen teeth. And this disbelief in the goodness of the State, the deity of modern man, made me a political atheist.

So, is that the way it all happened? Probably not, but that's the way I remember it.

2
Atheism and the Virtue of Reasonableness

Habits and Virtues

Atheists like to think of themselves as reasonable people. The principles of reason, we believe, impel us to embrace atheism, and we advocate the use of reason in all areas of life.

Having said this, what more needs to be said—at least to an audience of atheists? I submit that a good deal remains to be said. Reasonableness includes more than even many atheists realize, and I shall explore some of these implications in this presentation.

First, let's define our terms. What is atheism? It is simply the absence of theistic belief, i.e., belief in a god. An atheist is a person who does not believe in the existence of a god. If, to the question, "Do you believe in the existence of a god," you answer, "No"—then you are an atheist.

What is meant by the "virtue of reasonableness"?

Philosophers in the Aristotelian tradition define *virtue* as "a morally good habit." This may seem peculiar, because we customarily associate habits with undesirable actions, such as overeating or smoking. But habits can be good, bad, or indifferent, depending on the purposes they serve.

A habit is a learned and automatized pattern of action, physical or mental. When we do something repeatedly without thinking about it, we are acting from habit.

People are sometimes said to be creatures of habit. This does not mean that we are slaves to habit or that we cannot change undesirable habits. But we do undertake the vast majority of everyday actions from habit rather than from conscious deliberation.

Consider, for example, the many actions that go into driving a car. Working the pedals, steering, glancing in the rearview mirror—these and similar actions would be horrendously unmanageable if each had to be performed consciously.

Consider also how we learn to drive a car. We focus on basic maneuvers, and we repeat (practice) these maneuvers until they can be performed automatically. Then we proceed to more difficult tasks, repeating these actions until they, too, become automatic. As each new task is mastered so that it can be performed habitually, the conscious mind is able to focus on other concerns, such as watching for pedestrians or avoiding hazards.

Habits are sometimes called one's "second nature." We are not born with habits; they are not part of our "first nature." But habits can become so ingrained in our character and way of life that we refer to them as second nature.

Habitual actions have consequences. If the consequence is desirable, we call the habit "good"; if undesirable, we call the habit "bad"; if neither, we call the habit "indifferent."

A virtue is a good habit, but it is more: it is a *morally* good habit. A virtue promotes a morally good purpose—a good purpose, in other words, that has *moral significance.* This leads to an obvious question: What gives an action moral significance? I shall not attempt to deal with the intricacies of this venerable philosophic question. Instead, I shall summarize what I think is a plausible answer.

An action is morally significant if it involves issues that are fundamentally important to human life and well-being. What are the basic principles according to which one should live? How should one deal with other people? What is the role of reason in human life? These and similar questions are essential to human existence and thereby have moral significance. Their answers constitute the sphere of ethics, or moral philosophy. Habits that affect moral issues are called virtues or vices. Morally good habits are virtues, morally bad habits are vices.

Now, let's apply the preceding analysis to the subject of reasonableness.

Reasoning is a goal-directed mental process, and its goal is knowledge. (This distinguishes reasoning from thinking, a much broader category of mental activity.) The knowledge sought through reasoning may be practical or theoretical, trivial or significant, but, when you engage your mind in the quest for knowledge, you are engaged in the process of reasoning.

Knowledge is required for human survival, so everyone reasons to some extent. Even the most irrational people must reason, if only to provide themselves with food and shelter. Clearly, then, "the virtue of reasonableness" does not refer to the occasional or selective use of reason. Instead, "the virtue of reasonableness" refers to the *habitual* use of reason. A reasonable person displays an ingrained respect for reason in all areas of life, as if it were second nature.

Knowledge is essential to human life and happiness, so the acquisition of knowledge is inextricably linked to one's pursuit of the good life. Reasoning is the *method* by which knowledge is acquired; reasonableness is the fundamental *virtue* which makes the good life possible. It is the queen of virtues.

Virtuous Atheism

The virtue of reasonableness is the most potent weapon in the atheist's moral arsenal. Atheism has value only when it flows from reasonableness. There are irrational forms of atheism, and these are usually worthless. Suppose, to take an extreme case, that you deny the existence of everything. Nothing, you argue, can be known to exist. Naturally, this position will lead you to deny the existence of a god along with everything else. You are an atheist, but so what? The irrational and self-contradictory nature of the premise from which your atheism proceeds negates the value that your atheism might otherwise have.

Atheism is a *consequence*, not a *cause*, of reasonableness. There is nothing praiseworthy in atheism as such. Any fool can disbelieve; any idiot can proclaim to the world that God is an illusion. There is nothing inspiring in this, nothing to command respect. *That* one disbelieves in a god is unimportant, but *why* one disbelieves is supremely important.

To announce one's atheism is easy; to defend and communicate it reasonably are far more difficult. And to extend the critical, questioning method to all spheres of thought is even more difficult. A person who wears his atheism as a badge of intellectual independence, but who is slavishly orthodox in other areas, does not possess the virtue of reasonableness.

The message of rational atheism—our gospel, so to speak—is not that people will be better off if they abandon their religious beliefs. There is no evidence to suggest this. Rather, our gospel should stress the beneficial effects of reason.

Many atheists will agree with what I have said thus far. Few atheists will denigrate the value of reasonableness. But reasonableness carries implications that some atheists are unaware of, and it is to these that I shall now turn.

First, we should distinguish rational beliefs from correct beliefs. A belief can be rational (i.e., accepted for good reasons) and yet prove incorrect. As fallible beings, we sometimes entertain a plausible belief, only to uncover additional information that proves us wrong. All knowledge is contextual; as we encounter new information, evidence, and arguments, we change our beliefs accordingly.

If you adopt a belief because you believe it is reasonable, and if you have a genuine respect for the canons of reason, then no one can justly accuse you of irrationalism, however mistaken your belief may prove to be.

Some errors are beyond our control; we do not always end up in the right spot in our quest for knowledge. But we can choose to travel carefully, with reason as our guide.

The crucial distinction between "irrational" and "incorrect" applies to different schools of theistic belief. There are rational theists, just as there are rational atheists. Some schools of theism, notably Protestant fundamentalism, explicitly profess irrationalism. Other schools, however, display a genuine regard for reason. Foremost among these rational theists are modern Thomists—the followers of Thomas Aquinas.

Atheists do a great disservice to their adversaries (and to themselves) when they lump all theists together indiscriminately and brand the lot as irrational. This procedure tells us more about the ignorance of the atheist than it does about the irrationalism of theists. This stereotyping reveals a failure to study the history of philosophy and theology. It shows, to put it bluntly, that the atheist has not done his homework.

I do not claim that rational theists are in any sense correct. But I do claim that some theists are genuinely reasonable people, and that the belief in God, in their minds, is justified by rational standards.

If we could dismiss all theists as irrational, then we would not have to worry about dealing with them reasonably. Rather than engage in an honest discussion and debate, we could denounce them as mystics, irrationalists, or whatever, and then leave feeling morally superior. But, if rational theism is possible, this means that, in any given confrontation, we may be dealing with a rational theist. If atheists do not engage in honest dialogues with theists, if they treat them not as equals but as children to be reprimanded, then it is the atheists who betray the ideal of reasonableness.

The virtue of reasonableness has internal and external manifestations. By internal, I mean the skill of reasoning—the ability to use the rules of logic, standards of evidence, and so forth. By external, I mean how people present themselves and their arguments to others.

Many atheists, even those skilled in the internal aspects of reasoning, are deficient in its external aspects. Atheists may reason well, but they often fail to *persuade.* Let's consider this problem in more detail.

An argument, philosophically considered, is an intellectual interaction between two or more persons who disagree. The purpose of an argument is to resolve the disagreement, or at least to reach a common understanding.

An argument is not a zero-sum game, like chess, where one person wins only if another person loses. Ideally, an argument should be cooperative, not competitive—a common venture in pursuit of truth. If anything, the person who "loses" an argument gains more than the person who "wins," for the loser acquires new knowledge or a fresh perspective on an old problem. The winner, on the other hand, leaves the argument as he entered it. It is boring and unproductive to win all of one's arguments hands down.

Few persons, atheists included, know how to argue well. Argument is an art; it requires thought and practice. Having a thought firmly planted in your mind is no guarantee that you can communicate that thought effectively to other people. Communication skills need to be *learned.* The atheist must master the *external* aspects of reasonableness. Clear thinking is necessary but not sufficient for this. You may have an irrefutable argument, but, if you broadcast it with a bullhorn to your adversary three feet away, you display a notable deficiency of reasonableness.

But let's be more specific. It's easy to say that you shouldn't do this or that, but what *should* you do? How does one cultivate the external aspects of reasonableness? I shall offer a few suggestions.

The Presumption of Rationality

When beginning an argument, you should presume that your adversary is a rational person and treat him or her accordingly. I call this *the presumption of rationality.* Applied to theism, this means that an atheist should presume that a religious adversary cares about truth and is open to persuasion. This, remember, is a *presumption,* a starting point—

rather like the legal presumption that one is innocent until proven guilty. And, like the presumption of innocence, the presumption of rationality is *defeasible*; it can be (and often is) proven wrong as the argument proceeds. (Then, as we shall see, a different strategy applies.)

A reasonable person with no previous evidence of an adversary's irrationalism should always operate by the presumption of rationality and treat others with intellectual respect and courtesy—in other words, just as you want to be treated.

If you fail to convince rational people with valid arguments, the fault may lie not with them, but with you and your manner of presentation. Before engaging in an argument, I suggest that you ask yourself the following questions:

1. What purpose do I want to achieve in this argument?
2. Can I realistically hope to achieve this goal?
3. Is it worth my time and effort to engage in this argument?

When I recommend asking yourself these questions, I mean it literally. Before you engage in an argument, pause for a moment and think these questions to yourself *explicitly*. This technique can improve your communication skills dramatically.

1. *What purpose do I want to achieve in this argument?* Suppose you are about to argue for atheism, so you ask yourself, "What is my purpose? What do I hope to achieve in this argument?" Then comes your answer: "I will show my opponents the light of reason, cause them to abandon their most cherished beliefs, and convert them to atheism—all within twenty minutes."

If this is your purpose, you have two chances of success—fat and slim. Yet, as absurd as this goal sounds when stated openly, it is astonishing to observe how many atheists rush headlong into arguments *as if* this were their goal. So what happens when you seek an unattainable goal? You fail, of course. You leave the argument unsatisfied because you haven't accomplished anything. True, you may have dazzled, confused, or even humiliated your opponents. You may rejoice in the feeling, "Well, I showed them." But if your goal was communicate and persuade, then you failed, pure and simple.

Unrealistic goals are the main reason why atheists often leave arguments feeling unsatisfied and frustrated. Satisfaction flows from success, and to succeed means to achieve what you set out to do. If you set wildly improbable goals in arguments, you will fail time and again, regardless of the merit of your ideas.

2. *Can I realistically hope to achieve this goal?* Trim your purpose until it is attainable. A modest goal will make your argument more directed, more coherent, and less frustrating. Here are some achievable goals for the atheist: identify an incorrect assumption held by the theists; explain that they have the burden of proof; ask them to define their terms; persuade them to read one good book on philosophy, freethought, or atheism; isolate one of their arguments for critical examination.

If you cast doubt on one major tenet of the rational theists, this may cause them to reexamine their beliefs. But don't expect your adversaries to change their minds on the spot; give them something to think about and time to mull over your remarks. Above all, don't humiliate or embarrass. If the theist concedes a point, then give credit where credit is due, for such a theist displays intellectual honesty and integrity.

And remember: An argument between reasonable people is an argument between equals. You are not there to instruct the theists, but to reason with them. You cannot demand something from them unless you are willing to reciprocate in kind. If you expect them to take your arguments seriously, then you must take their arguments seriously; if you ask them to read a book of your choice, then you must be willing to read a book of their choice; if you expect them to acknowledge their doubts, then you must be willing to acknowledge your doubts.

3. *Is it worth my time and effort to engage in this argument?* If you answer yes to this question, then you enter an argument consciously and deliberately, rather than allowing yourself to be pulled in unawares. How often have you left an argument with a headache, feeling that nothing was accomplished and being unsure how (or why) you ever got into that argument in the first place? Such "headache arguments" can be avoided by deciding *beforehand* whether an argument is worthwhile.

Of course, whether or not to engage in an argument is a personal judgment call, but a word of caution is in order: Don't debase your intellectual currency, or, as the Bible puts it, don't cast pearls before swine. You have invested considerable time and effort in your ideas, reasoning ability, and communication skills. Never squander this intellectual capital by arguing with fools. Only fools argue with fools.

Establishing Credibility

Aristotle pointed out that personal character—especially one's credibility—plays a major role in the art of persuasion. In his words: "Persuasion is achieved by the speaker's personal character when the speech is so spoken as to make us think him credible. His character may almost be called the most effective means of persuasion he possesses."

Credibility, as Aristotle suggested, emerges during the course of an argument. Your intellectual character—your manner of presenting yourself and your arguments—will establish more credibility than a string of credentials.

What, then, is "credibility"? If an Air Force pilot sights what he believes is an alien spacecraft, his report might be dubbed "credible," thus distinguishing his account from that of a crank with a similar story. Because the pilot is a credible witness, his testimony deserves consideration and should not be dismissed out of hand.

Of course, credible people are often dead wrong, so credibility has nothing intrinsically to do with true beliefs or valid arguments. Credibility won't win an argument, but it will at least get your argument into court for a hearing.

Herein lies the most formidable obstacle confronting today's atheist: getting his "case against God" into the court of public opinion so it can receive a fair hearing. And this depends not on the validity of our arguments but on the credibility of our advocates. Many Americans, I am sorry to say, don't even listen to our arguments because they expect atheists to be cranks. Some apostles of atheism, I am even more sorry to say, live up to that expectation with flying colors.

Intellectual credibility is an exceedingly complex character trait with countless nuances, subtleties, and variations. Knowledge, reasonableness, communication skills, maturity, sincerity, honesty, integrity—all of these contribute to one's credibility. But we need to narrow the field somewhat.

If you wish to establish credibility during an argument, you need to fulfill these minimum requirements: First, you must know what you're talking about. Second, your opponent must perceive that you know what you're talking about. Third, you must not pretend to know more than you actually do.

The following tactics can also improve your credibility:

1. Express your doubts where appropriate. If you present an argument but are uncertain of it, say so. This way, when you do profess certainty, you will command more respect.

2. When discussing factual matters, discriminate among your sources of information—e.g., "I got this information from so-and-so's book"; or, "I haven't given this subject much thought lately, but I did investigate some years ago. Here's the conclusion I reached then."

3. Show interest in what your opponent has to say. If he knows something about the subject, ask him questions. Assume you may learn something from him, even if you disagree with his conclusions. If he makes a good point, acknowledge it—e.g., "That's an interesting point; I'll have to think about it."

4. Don't hammer your opponent when he slips up and says something inane. Let him off gracefully. There is a good reason for this: silly arguments are given undeserved respect when you devote excessive time and energy refuting them. To direct your sharpest weapons against a weak argument is like trying to cut through a cushion with a sword. In addition, if you insist on grinding your opponent under foot, you will be perceived (rightly) as more interested in humiliation than in truth. And that will establish your immaturity, not your credibility.

5. When *you* say something stupid (and you will), admit it. When you commit a blunder, acknowledge it. Then move on. If you refuse to admit an error, your opponent will focus the rest of the argument

on that error, the argument will bog down, and your major points will be lost in a morass of your own making. This is perhaps the most common and costly error that occurs during arguments.

Controlling the Argument

Thus far I have discussed argumentation among reasonable people, where the presumption of rationality holds up. But what should you do when the presumption fails, as it often does? Should you argue with an irrational person?

Here it is useful to distinguish between two kinds of irrationalists: aggressive and passive. An aggressive irrationalist embraces irrationalism openly and proudly as his normal mode of dealing with ideas. We often find this kind of irrationalism in "born-again" Christians, whose notion of an argument consists of ranting about sinners, quoting the Bible, and describing the torments of hell.

To argue with an aggressive irrationalist is usually a waste of time. As Thomas Paine said, to argue with a person who has renounced the use of reason is like administering medicine to the dead.

Passive irrationalists, on the other hand, are irrational by default. Having been raised in religious environments, they may be unfamiliar with logic, rules of evidence, and the components of a valid argument. They "argue" the only way they know how, but they may also be open to new ways. They are irrational, but not militantly so.

Some passive irrationalists can be saved from their folly, but this can be a long and arduous process. Here again, you need to ask yourself, "Is it worth my time and effort?" Perhaps the passive irrationalist is a friend or relative, so you may decide to invest your time and labor. Be forewarned, however: When arguing with such people, the presumption of rationality fails, so the argument is not among equals. You, the senior partner of reason, will have to carry more than your fair share. Before you can persuade, you will have to *teach* this person some basic philosophical principles. How can this be done without alienating the irrationalist so that he tunes you out altogether? This is one of the most difficult and subtle skills in the art of argumentation. Above all, you will have to *control* the argument. Here are some suggestions:

1. Establish the authority of reason *before* you begin the argument. You might say the following: "If I show that your belief is unfounded or contradictory, will this cause you to rethink your position? Or will you tell me that God works in mysterious ways or, perhaps, that faith transcends reason?"

If your adversary concedes that an appeal to faith is down the road, then discuss the nature of faith before proceeding. Take it step by step.

2. You should uncover the basic assumptions of the passive irrationalist. He probably won't know these himself, so you will have to tease them out by using well-directed and precise questions.

Skilled question-asking can force your adversaries to articulate their premises, define their terms, and identify the fallacies in their reasoning. In addition, this technique, if done gracefully, will not intimidate or alienate your opponents. You will be seen as assisting them, not lecturing to them.

3. Establish the need for defining terms. Ask the theists to define, or at least to describe, what they mean by "God." Tell them that the concept makes no sense to you, and that it is useless to debate the existence of "God" until you understand what they mean by it.

4. As the argument begins, establish a methodology, if only a primitive one. For example, if the argument concerns the existence of God, establish where the burden of proof lies: with the theist. Make it clear that the atheist is obliged to do nothing more than refute theistic arguments.

5. When your opponents veer from the topic (a common problem), don't let them ramble on. Guide them back to the issue at hand. You might say: "You raise an interesting point, and I am willing to discuss it. But let's settle the present controversy first."

6. Keep the argument on *fundamentals*, i.e., on the essential underpinnings of your adversaries' beliefs. If they veer to an unessential subject, you should reply: "I am willing to discuss this subject with

you, but I suspect that, even if I convince you that you're wrong, it won't affect your beliefs. What, in principle, would change your mind? Let's deal with that issue now."

Arguing with Aggressive Irrationalists

As stated previously, to argue with aggressive irrationalists is usually a waste of time—if, that is, one's purpose is to persuade them. Such arguments may be productive, however, when an audience is present (e.g., during a debate). These "third-party arguments" are directed not at your adversaries per se, but at the audience. By pointing out the absurdity of your opponents' beliefs, you may influence the beliefs of onlookers.

If you decide to argue with aggressive irrationalists, then gird yourself for battle. The only way to combat aggressive irrationalism is with aggressive rationalism. Most importantly, you must not allow your adversaries to control the argument or to set its agenda.

The purpose of control is not to take advantage of your opponents, but to prevent them from taking advantage of you. This is especially important when dealing with militant fundamentalists, who, as propagandists for their faith, are sometimes quite adept at seizing control of an argument. In addition, these fundamentalists can be ill-mannered, even rude, during their (supposedly beneficient) effort to save unbelievers from the torments of hell.

Here are some typical opening gambits of fundamentalists.

They will ask: "Have you accepted Jesus as your personal savior?" They will appeal to your "sinful" nature—"You know you're a sinner, don't you?" They will (in God's name) threaten you with eternal punishment—a kind of intimidation by proxy. They will exhibit mock caring: They worry about you and are praying for you. They will claim that you must first believe before you can understand. The variations are endless.

Such tactics are manipulative and should be blocked immediately. If you respond to them as phrased, then you are playing in the fundamentalists' court and by their rules. In short, you have surrendered control of the argument. Your response—any response—will only encourage similar gibberish.

You must gain control of the argument and place it in the court of reason. This can be accomplished (if it can be accomplished at all) with aggressive questions and counter-examples. Always remember that theists assume the full burden of proof. They have beliefs that they wish you to accept, so it is *their* responsibility to demonstrate their case. The above tactics seek to evade this responsibility.

Aggressive irrationalists can be so unpredictable and erratic that it is nearly impossible to frame general principles on how to respond to their assertions. They shoot from the hip at anything and everything. Therefore, if you decide to have a showdown with one of these intellectual outlaws, you, too, will have to engage in intellectual gunslinging. The following dialogue should illustrate what I mean.

Fundamentalist: "Have you accepted Jesus Christ as your personal savior?"

Atheist: "From what you've said, I assume that you believe in a god of some kind. I would like to know, first, what you mean by 'god,' and, second, how you justify your belief in this being."

Fundamentalist: "But don't you know that Jesus Christ died for your sins?"

Atheist: "Obviously, if I don't believe in a god, then I don't believe in a nonexistent son. Moreover, since *sin* is defined as disobedience to a god, I don't believe in sin either. I am not a sinner. Now please get to the point and answer my questions."

Fundamentalist: "But everyone is a sinner."

Atheist: "You maybe, but not me. You know nothing about me, yet you presume to judge me. That is rude and offensive. Now, are you going to behave yourself and answer my questions or not?"

Fundamentalist: "God will come into your heart if you ask him to."

Atheist: "I don't have room in there for anything else, thank you."

Fundamentalist: "But won't you even pray to God?"

Atheist: "If you explain what you mean by the word 'god' and explain how you know there is such a being, I might consider it. But you refuse even to explain what you're talking about. You're not doing your job, and your god, if he exists, won't like that."

Fundamentalist: "Don't you want to be saved?"

Atheist: "Saved? From *what?*"

Fundamentalist: "From eternal punishment in hell."

Atheist: "Really, this is becoming absurd. Tell me, why do you believe in hell?"

Fundamentalist: "It's in the Bible."

Atheist: "Do you believe everything you read?"

Fundamentalist: "I believe the Bible; it's God's word."

Atheist: "Oh, so this god of yours wrote a book! I tell you what: Have him autograph a copy and send it to me by angel express, or whatever. I assume he knows where to find me. All you need do is produce a signed copy of his book, and you've made your case. Since you won't give me any other reasons to accept your beliefs, that seems to be your only alternative."

Obviously this exchange (I hesitate to call it an argument) is going nowhere, but nowhere is the predictable destination when you discuss ideas with an aggressive irrationalist. Without the common ground of reason, there is no way to resolve a dispute.

If you wish to argue with an aggressive irrationalist, I suggest that you observe the following guidelines:

1. Insist on good manners. When fundamentalists harp on your supposed sins, they are being insufferably arrogant and rude, and you should point this out. *Do not excuse insults because they are draped in religious rhetoric.*

2. Fundamentalists will doubtless flaunt their religious fervor and tell you how Jesus has changed their lives. Here you may wish to give your own "testimony" and relate how *reason* has changed *your* life. You understand that fundamentalists have strong convictions, *but so do you*—so do millions of other people who subscribe to religious beliefs other than their version of Christianity. Strong convictions, needless to say (except to the fundamentalist), prove nothing.

3. When the fundamentalist asserts that belief in Jesus will "change

your life"—i.e., make you feel better—identify this ploy for what it is: a kind of intellectual *hedonism.* Then turn the tables on the fundamentalist. For example:

Atheist: "Are you telling me that I should do something because it feels good? Surely you aren't serious. I frankly don't believe that you would accept this as a guide in your own life. If someone wished you to engage in a particular sexual practice because it feels good, would you regard this as a compelling reason?"

Fundamentalist: "No."

Atheist: "Then you aren't a hedonist after all. You demand more than the possibility of pleasure in order to take an action or adopt a belief. So do I. You reject sexual promiscuity on moral grounds, regardless of the pleasure it may bring. Similarly, I reject *intellectual* promiscuity on *moral* grounds. My moral principles do not allow me to accept or to do just anything, just because it might feel good. You surely understand this, don't you?"

This tactic is a form of intellectual jujitsu, where, rather than clash head-on with your opponents, you redirect the premises of their own arguments to your advantage. You say, in effect, "You wouldn't expect me to do something that you yourself admit is wrong, would you? Of course not. Now let's move on."

Conclusion

The virtue of reasonableness depends as much on how we argue as it does on *what* we argue. Rational arguments are not enough, especially when defending an unpopular position like atheism. We need to develop the virtue of reasonableness in ourselves and encourage it in others. Then, even if we fail to persuade, we will at least command respect.

This, in my judgment, is the ideal atheist—not just a robot reciting the atheist catechism, but a reasonable person whose arguments may be rejected but never dismissed.

3
Defining Atheism

Prominent atheists have defended for many years the view that an atheist is a person who lacks theistic belief. Baron d'Holbach took this view when he argued, "All children are theists—they have no idea of God"[1] Charles Bradlaugh, Britain's most important crusader for atheism, upheld a similar position, noting that "no position is more continuously misrepresented" than atheism. Bradlaugh stated: "Atheism is *without* God. It does not assert *no* God."[2]

J.M. Robertson, the great historian of freethought, remarked on the negative atheism of Charles Southwell, who, in 1842, founded the *Oracle of Reason*, England's first avowedly atheistic periodical:

> [T]he *Oracle* pursued a logical course of confuting theism, and leaving "a-theism" the negative result. It did not, in the absurd terms of common religious propaganda, "deny the existence of God." It affirmed that God was a term for an existence imagined by man in terms of his own personality and irreducible to any tenable definition. It did not even affirm that "there are no Gods"; it insisted that the onus of proof as to any God lay with the theist, who could give none compatible with his definitions.[3]

The historian Edward Royle has also described the "negative atheism" of Carlile, Southwell, Cooper, Holyoake, and other nineteenth-century atheists:

> Logically, this kind of atheism did not prove that there was no God . . . . On the contrary, Southwell was typical in placing the *onus probandi* on those who affirmed the existence of God and Holyoake regarded himself as an atheist only in his inability to believe what the churches would have him believe. They were content to show that the Christian concept of the supernatural was meaningless, that the arguments in its favor were illogical, and that the mysteries of the universe, insofar as they were explicable, could be accounted for in material terms.[4]

As Royle indicates, negative atheism went hand in hand with the "onus-of-proof" principle. Annie Besant, who defined atheism as "without God," clearly explained the importance of this principle:

> If my interlocutor desires to convince me that Jupiter has inhabitants, and that his description of them is accurate, it is for him to bring forward evidence in support of his contention. The burden of proof evidently lies on him; it is not for me to prove that no such beings exist before my non-belief is justified, but for him to prove that they do exist before my belief can be fairly claimed. Similarly, it is for the affirmer of God's existence to bring evidence in support of his affirmation; the burden of proof lies on him.[5]

This negative definition of atheism carried over into the twentieth century, especially among British atheists. When a critic accused atheists of dogmatism for positively denying the existence of God, G.W. Foote challenged the critic "to refer me to *one* Atheist who *denies* the existence of God." Foote continued: "Etymologically, as well as philosophically, an ATheist is one without God. That is all the 'A' before 'Theist' really means."[6]

Joseph McCabe, author of dozens of books and articles pertaining to atheism, defined atheism as "the absence of theistic belief."[7] The same idea was put forcefully by Chapman Cohen, President of

Britain's National Secular Society and a prolific defender of atheism. Cohen wrote:

> If one believes in a god, then one is a Theist. If one does not believe in a god, then one is an A-theist—he is without that belief. The distinction between atheism and theism is entirely, exclusively, that of whether one has or has not a belief in God.[8]

Perceptive critics of atheism have also defended the negative definition. For example, the learned theologian Richard Watson wrote:

> ATHEIST, in the strict and proper sense of the word, is one who does not believe in the existence of a god, or who owns no being superior to nature. It is compounded of the two terms . . . signifying *without God*.[9]

That able defender of theism, Robert Flint, had no doubt about the proper definition of atheism. Flint declared:

> The atheist is not necessarily a man who says, There is no God. What is called positive or dogmatic atheism, so far from being the only kind of atheism, is the rarest of all kinds. . . . [E]very man is an atheist who does not believe that there is a God, although his want of belief may not be rested on any allegation of positive knowledge that there is no God, but simply on one of want of knowledge that there is a God.

Flint concluded, "The word atheist is a thoroughly honest, unambiguous term. It means one who does not believe in God, and it means neither more nor less."[10]

If so many atheists and some of their critics have insisted on the negative definition of atheism, why have some modern philosophers called for a positive definition of atheism—atheism as the outright *denial* of God's existence? Part of the reason, I suspect, lies in the chasm separating freethinkers and academic philosophers. Most modern philosophers are totally unfamiliar with atheistic literature and so remain oblivious to the tradition of negative atheism contained in that literature.

Perhaps the greatest confusion over atheism's definition was caused by A. J. Ayer in his classic presentation of logical positivism, *Language, Truth, and Logic.* In defending empirical verifiability as a criterion of meaning, Ayer rejected all "metaphysical" utterances, including theistic claims, as nonsensical. To say that God exists, according to Ayer, "is to make a metaphysical utterance which cannot be either true or false." The claim does not "possess any literal significance."

Ayer cautioned against confusing his noncognitivist position with atheism. Atheism, which Ayer construed positively as the denial of God's existence, presupposes that the concept of God has meaning. But "if the assertion that there is a god is nonsensical, then the atheist's assertion that there is no god is equally nonsensical, since it is only a significant proposition that can be significantly contradicted."[11]

Unfortunately, Ayer's treatment lacks historical perspective on what atheists have argued for many years. In introducing noncognitivism as a supposed alternative to atheism, Ayer misled a generation of philosophers, for noncognitivism has always been an important weapon in the atheist's arsenal.

For example, the importance of noncognitivism was discussed extensively in the seventeenth century by Ralph Cudworth, whose *True Intellectual System of the Universe* remains one of the most interesting critiques of atheism ever penned. Some philosophers adopt atheism, Cudworth noted, "because theists themselves acknowledging God to be incomprehensible, it may be from thence inferred, that he is a nonentity." The very notion of an infinite God, atheists maintain, "is utterly inconceivable." Atheists argue that the attributes of God are a "bundle of unconceivables and impossibilities, huddled up together . . . ."[12]

The atheist Baron d'Holbach argued that "what has been said of [God] is either unintelligible or perfectly contradictory; and for this reason must appear impossible to every man of common sense."[13] In *The System of Nature,* a masterpiece of Englightenment thought and perhaps the best defense of atheism ever written, Holbach devoted considerable space to the position that the term "God" is meaningless. He concluded:

> Can theology give to the mind the ineffable boon of conceiving that which no man is in a capacity to comprehend? Can it procure to its agents the marvellous faculty of having precise ideas of a god composed of so many contradictory qualities?[14]

The noncognitivist argument was commonly found in the writings of nineteenth-century atheists, as illustrated in this passage from Annie Besant's *Why I Do Not Believe in God:*

> Never yet has a God been defined in terms which were not palpably self-contradictory and absurd; never yet has a God been described so that a concept of Him was made possible to human thought.[15]

Many similar quotations could be given. Clearly, noncognitivism—the position that the term God is literally *meaningless*—has been standard atheist fare for centuries. Therefore, when Ayer argued for his version of noncognitivism, he was not, as he believed, offering a true alternative to atheism. Rather, Ayer's argument placed him squarely within a venerable atheistic tradition.

In a thoughtful discussion of atheism contained in *The Encyclopedia of Philosophy*, Paul Edwards proposes a definition of atheism that falls midway between the negative definition (the absence of theistic belief) and the positive definition (the outright denial of theism). An atheist, according to Edwards, is a person "who rejects belief in God" for whatever reason.[16] This definition allows Edwards to include as atheists those who maintain that the concept of God is incoherent or that the concept of God is incoherent or that the proposition "God exists" is meaningless and hence neither true nor false.

By classifying noncognitivism as a species of atheism, Edwards rehabilitated an important atheistic position. But Edwards wished to "preserve, at least roughly, the traditional battle lines" between atheists and theists—and the most common definition of an atheist, according to Edwards, is "a person who maintains that there is no God, that is, that the sentence 'God exists" expresses a *false* proposition."[17]

As we have seen, this positive definition of atheism is *not* the most common one, nor the traditional one—not, that is, if we consult what most atheists have *really* said rather than listen to uniformed critics who tell us what atheists *should* have said. The purely negative definition—atheism as the *absence* of theistic belief—has a better pedigree than either the positive definition of the compromise (the rejection of theistic belief) defended by Edwards.

A provocative discussion of atheism is found in Michael Scriven's book *Primary Philosophy*. Even if one rejects Scriven's conclusion, his treatment is significant as an effort to sketch a methodological framework for atheism.

Scriven accepts the positive definition of atheism, but he denies that the theist and the atheist share equally the burden of proof. The atheist, Scriven maintains, need not prove the nonexistence of God in order to say that God does not exist. Rather, the burden falls upon the theist to prove the existence of (at least one) god, and if he fails in this attempt, "there is no alternative to atheism."[18]

Scriven concedes that the existence of a god cannot be directly disproved, but belief in such a being can be shown to be wholly unfounded, and this is sufficient grounds for atheism.

What, according to Scriven, is an unfounded claim? It is one that lacks both particular and general evidential support. Consider, for example, the claim, "The Loch Ness Monster exists." This claim lacks particular evidential support, but it is not contrary to past experience (we have discovered previously unknown species before), nor does it invoke supernaturalism. Thus, we should not brand the claim as false from lack of evidence alone; we should suspend judgment instead.

The case is different, Scriven maintains, when a claim lacks not only specific evidence but general support as well. This occurs in supernatural claims that are without precedence in our experience. Given the radical nature of these claims, they demand a high quality of evidence, and when such evidence is lacking, not mere suspension of judgment but explicit disbelief is the appropriate response.

Scriven illustrates his argument using Santa Claus as an example. We are justified in saying that Santa Claus does not exist even though no one has positively disproved his existence. As we mature, we realize that there are no reasons to believe in the existence of this being—and this results, not in the suspension of judgment about Santa's existence (a kind of Santa agnosticism), but in the stronger claim that it is foolish even to believe in the likelihood of his existence. Because the belief in Santa lacks particular *and* general support, the proper alternative "is not mere suspension of belief, e.g., about Santa Claus; it is *disbelief*."[19] And so it goes, Scriven argues, withb elief in a god.

One of the few modern philosophers to embrace the negative definition of atheism is Antony Flew in his article, "The Presumption of Atheism." According to Flew, the prefix "a" in "atheism" should have the same negative meaning as in words like "amoral," "atypical," and "asymmetrical." "In this interpretation," Flew argues, "an atheist becomes: not someone who positively asserts the non-existence of God; but someone who is simply not a theist."[20]

Flew fears that this negative definition "may appear to be a piece of perverse Humpty Dumptyism, going arbitrarily against established common usage,"[21] so he presents compelling reasons to support what he sees as an unusual definition. Perhaps this was for the best, because the resulting article, "The Presumption of Atheism," is one of the finest pieces on atheism ever written. But Flew's negative definition is anything but perverse. On the contrary, it is a much-needed return to a grand tradition.

The technical problems of defining "atheism" may be divided into two categories: (1) etymological and (2) epistemological. (For the purpose of this discussion, I shall accept the common definiton of "theism" as "belief in a god or gods.")

1. It is sometimes claimed that the chief etymological problem in defining "atheism" is how to construe the prefix "a." Should we regard it as a term of privation meaning "without," or should we regard it

as a term of negation meaning "no"?

If we choose the privative meaning of "without," then "a-theism" will mean "without-theism"—i.e., "without (or lacking) belief in a god or gods." This clearly supports the definition of atheism as the absence of theistic belief.

What if we construe the prefix "a" negatively to mean "no"? This has been preferred by those who wish to define atheism as the outright denial of God's existence. But consider: even the negative sense of "a" doesn't, by itself, give us this definition. "A-theism," with the negative "a," translates into "no-belief in a god or gods." Here again, we have an essentially privative definition—atheism as the *absence* of theistic belief.

I suggest, therefore, that the real problem is defining "atheism" lies, not in the meaning of the prefix "a," but in determining precisely *where* that prefix should be inserted.

Atheism as outright denial can be achieved only if the negative "a" is used, not to qualify the entire meaning of "theism," but only part of it—i.e., "a-theism" means "belief in *no* god or gods." In this interpretation, atheism is construed, not as the absence of a belief, but as a particular *kind* of belief.

The case for atheism as a kind of belief—the belief in the nonexistence of God—was championed by no less a figure than J. M. Robertson, the great historian of freethought. Robertson argued that any "ism," including atheism, implies that we are dealing with a positive belief or doctrine, not a simple privation. Contrary to Robertson's view, "-ism" can mean something other than a doctrine or belief; it can mean "a state or condition" as well. Thus, the privative definition of atheism is still possible. Atheism as the absence of belief can denote an "ism"—a state of mind in which theistic belief is absent.

2 Linguistic arguments over the correct definiton of "atheism" will solve little, because—as philosophers like to remind us—questions of word-meaning are ultimately determined by conventional usage, not by the decrees of linguistic "experts." But conventional usage does not solve the problem either, for we may ask: whose usage? During the McCarthy era, for example, atheism was commonly linked to communism. What, then, were noncommunistic atheists to do?

Should they have stepped forward and defied conventional usage, thereby incurring the wrath of McCarthy, his goons, and philosophers?

Those philosophers who rely solely on "conventional usage," should recall that "atheism" has been used throughout history as a term of opprobrium, a veritable smear word. Indeed, until the eighteenth century, an "atheist" could be anyone who disagreed with one's own religious convictions—a person who denied the divinity of Roman emperors, or who disbelieved in witchcraft, or who denied the Trinity, or who rejected infant baptism, or who maintained that philosophers should be free to seek the truth, wherever it may lead them.

Perhaps atheists can find refuge from the tyranny of "conventional meaning" in what philosophers call "technical" definitions. Thus, biologists are permitted to offer their own definition of "life," for example, without being overly concerned whether laymen (the conventional majority) agree with, or even know of, their definition. Similarly, professed atheists may have the epistemological right to define atheism, in the technical sense, as the "absence of theistic belief," even if most laymen (i.e., theists) disagree with that definition.

Or perhaps atheists can fall back on the rule of fundamentality, which says that a definition should identify the fundamental, or *essential,* attribute of the concept being defined. Obviously, the absence of theistic belief is more fundamental than the denial of theism, for the latter is a subset of the former. (One who denies the existence of God also lacks belief, but the reverse is not necessarily true: one who lacks belief in God does not necessarily deny its existence.)

According to this reasoning, one who denies God's existence is a legitimate atheist, but he subscribes to a particular species of atheism. If, however, we construe atheism as the denial of God's existence, then the person who merely lacks theistic belief is not a real atheist, but an imposter. This exclusion by definition, it seems to me, is ungracious, and it shows ignorance of what important atheists have argued for many years.

Notes

1. Baron d'Holbach, *Good Sense*, 1772.
2. Charles Bradlaugh, *The Freethinker's Text-Book* (London, 1876).
3. J. M. Robertson, *A History of Freethought in the Nineteenth Century* (London, 1929).
4. Edward Royle, *Victorian Infidels* (Manchester, 1974).
5. Annie Besant, *Why I Do Not Believe in God* (London, 1887).
6. G. W. Foote, *What Is Agnosticism* (London, 1902).
7. Joseph McCabe, *A Rationalist Encyclopedia* (London, 1950).
8. Chapman Cohen, *Primitive Survivals in Modern Thought* (London, 1935).
9. Richard Watson, *A Biblical and Theological Dictionary* (London, 1831).
10. Robert Flint, *Agnosticism* (Edinburgh, 1903).
11. A. J. Ayer, *Language, Truth, and Logic* (London, 1936).
12. Ralph Cudworth, *True Intellectual System of the Universe*, 1678.
13. Holbach, *Good Sense*.
14. Baron d'Holbach, *The System of Nature*, 1770.
15. Besant, *Why I Do Not Believe in God*.
16. Paul Edwards, ed., *The Encyclopedia of Philosophy* (New York, 1973).
17. Ibid.
18. Michael Scriven, *Primary Philosophy*, (New York, 1966).
19. Ibid.
20. Antony Flew, *God, Freedom, and Immortality: A Critical Analysis*, "The Presumption of Atheism" (Buffalo, N.Y., 1984), p. 14.
21. Ibid.

4
Atheist Commentaries

Commentary 1

"The fool says in his heart, 'There is no God.' They are corrupt, they do abominable deeds, there is none that does good."

This famous biblical passage captures the essence of how the average religious person views atheism. Atheism is probably the least popular, and least understood, philosophical position in America today. The very word "atheist" often conjures up the image of an immoral, dangerous cynic—an apostle of destructive negativism.

Atheism, to put it simply, has suffered from bad press. Christians have spent a good deal of their 2,000-year history fretting over disbelievers, and a major weapon in their arsenal has been the portrayal of disbelief as the most horrendous of evils, deserving of the most severe punishment. Jesus, according to the New Testament, threatened that nonbelievers shall be thrown "into the furnace of fire" where "men will weep and gnash their teeth." The medieval theologian Thomas

---

Originally presented in 1979 on KPFK radio, Los Angeles.

Aquinas, perhaps the greatest mind in Catholic history, taught "the sin of unbelief is greater than any sin that occurs in the perversion of morals," and he recommended that the heretic "be exterminated from the world by death."

It has been common for centuries to label atheism a spiritual or moral disease. Typical of this trend is a book written in 1878, titled *The Natural History of Atheism*, wherein the author refers to "the atheistic disease" that results from a "moral disorder of the reasonable creature." The author divides atheists into two categories: "atheistic incapables" and "atheistic monsters," and he argues that these result from "the morbid atheistic pathology."

Can we dismiss such statements as the irrational ravings of a past age? Unfortunately, no. Similar sentiments, if not asserted in such extreme language, are found today among both Catholic and Protestant theologians. A Catholic priest, writing in 1971, refers to atheism as "the most serious spiritual affliction of modern man," as "a destructive, voracious parasite," and as a disease that is "rapidly becoming virulent." Similarly, a distinguished theologian representing the Protestant evangelical movement wrote a book recently in which he proclaims, "The essence of sin is unbelief." And what is the punishment for sin, according to the theologian? He lists: "guilt, death, hell, moral servitude, and spiritual blindness." Such, we are to believe, is the destiny of the atheist.

In these commentaries I shall examine various intellectual and social issues from an atheistic perspective. As my previous remarks indicate, however, an atheist is bound to encounter a great deal of prejudicial misinformation about his position. Therefore, in order to set the record straight from the beginning, I shall now address, as briefly as possible, some of the questions most commonly asked about atheism.

What is an atheist? An atheist is a person who does not believe in the existence of a god, i.e., in the existence of a supernatural being.

Why doesn't the atheist believe in a god? Quite simply, because belief in a god is unreasonable.

Can the atheist prove that a god does not exist? The atheist need not "prove" the nonexistence of a god, just as one who does not believe in magic elves, fairies, and gremlins does not have to prove their nonexistence. A person who asserts the existence of something assumes the burden of proof. The theist, or god-believer, asserts the existence of a god and must prove the claim. If the theist fails in this task, reasonable people will reject the belief as groundless. Atheists do not believe in a god because there is no reason they should.

But haven't philosophers proved the existence of a god? No. All such attempts have failed. Most philosophers and theologians now concede that belief in a god must rest on faith, not on reason.

Then why not accept the existence of a god on faith? Because to believe on faith is to defy and abandon the judgment of one's mind. Faith conflicts with reason. It cannot give you knowledge; it can only delude you into believing that you know more than you really do. Faith is intellectually dishonest, and it should be rejected by every person of integrity.

Isn't it possible for reason to err? Yes, reason is fallible, but this calls for a more diligent and conscientious use of reason, not its abandonment. Our eyesight may occasionally fail us or lead us astray, but this does not mean that we should blind ourselves or walk with our eyes closed.

But don't people need to believe in a god? No. First and foremost, a person needs to know the truth, for this is the basic means by which we function successfully in the world. To say that a person needs to believe in the irrational is a prescription for disaster.

Is atheism immoral? Far from it. An honest, carefully examined conviction can never be immoral. On the contrary, the scrupulous use of one's reason is a supreme virtue.

How can there be meaning and purpose to life without a god? This is a matter of personal responsibility. Only you, the individual, can decide whether to live your life with meaning and purpose. Pushing the responsibility onto a mysterious god is an escape, not a solution.

Why is atheism important? Atheism is important because it is reasonable, and reason is of crucial importance in human affairs. Atheism is an alternative to the morass of irrational, antimind doctrines found in various religions.

Why, then, should I consider atheism? Because you owe it to yourself to examine the issue of religious belief carefully and to reach the best judgment you can. Never, never doubt the efficacy of your mind. Never allow others, through pressure or intimidation, to cloud your judgment. If you decide that atheism is a reasonable position, then adopt it with pride and dignity. Always remember that your mind is your most precious characteristic. Do not abuse it through slavish conformity to religious doctrines.

Commentary 2

Media commentators have recently discovered a new pastime: explaining to a befuddled public the various ways in which a religion differs from a cult. The Jim Jones tragedy in Guyana focused unprecedented media attention on the cult phenomenon, bringing with it a new problem for the mass media. How can an investigator take a hard, critical look at cults and yet avoid stepping on orthodox toes? How can the media convey the message, "These cultists are misled dupes and fanatics," without suggesting that a similar charge might be leveled at conventional religions?

The problem was solved with a little verbal slight of hand. First, there is the essential distinction between a religion and a cult. A religion, you see, is good, whereas a cult—well, a cult is not so good. Religious people are sincere believers; cultists are fanatics. Religions instruct; cults indoctrinate. Religions teach devotion; cults demand obedience. Religions are based on faith; cults are based on programming. Ah, the magic of words. Simply attach derogatory labels to an unpopular group and watch the fun begin.

Theologians have attempted for centuries to differentiate religion from superstition, and their efforts resemble the current hobby of separating religion from cults. The philosopher Thomas Hobbes, writing in the seventeenth century, offered what is still the best dividing line between religion and superstition. "Fear of power invisible, feigned by the mind, or imagined from tales publicly allowed"—this, said Hobbes, is religion. The same thing when *not* publicly allowed—this, he said, is superstition.

This applies equally well to the subject of cults. A cult is basically an unpopular religion that falls outside the social mainstream. "Cult" is a term of opprobrium—a smear word by which the religious establishment places its competition in an unfavorable light. Except for this there is no important difference between a cult and a religion. They may peddle different products, but they do so by similar means. If anything, cults are closer to the ideals of the early Christian movement than the major churches today. Virtually every characteristic attributed to cults can be found in the New Testament. Here are some examples.

Cults are said to alienate young people from their families. Yet Jesus, according to the book of Matthew, said: "Every that hath forsaken houses, or brethren, or sisters, or father, or mother, or wife, or children, or lands, for my name's sake, shall receive an hundredfold, and shall inherit everlasting life."

Cult members are said to associate only with other cult members, isolating themselves from the outside world. In II Corinthians we read: "Be ye not unequally yoked together with unbelievers: for what fellowship hath righteousness with unrighteousness? and what communion hath light with darkness?"

Cults are intolerant. So was Jesus. "He that is not with me is against me," warned Jesus; "He that believeth not is condemned already. . . . The wrath of God abideth on him."

Cults, it is claimed, use devious means to accomplish their ends. The apostle Paul saw nothing wrong with deceit, however, if it served Christianity. He asked rhetorically, "If through my falsehood God's truthfulness abounds to his glory, why am I still being condemned as a sinner? And why not do evil that good may come?"

Cult leaders allegedly make false promises to their followers as a means of gaining their devotion. Jesus was a master of this. "If you have faith as a grain of mustard seed, you will say to this mountain, Move hence to yonder place,' and it will move; and nothing will be impossible to you." " If you ask anything in my name," Jesus promised,

"I will do it."

Cults allegedly use threats and intimidation to instill fear in their members. This has also been a stock-in-trade of Christianity. Jesus warned, "He that believeth not shall be damned," and Paul followed in his master's footsteps with, "He that doubteth is damned."

Given this common groundwork, it is not surprising that many cult members are recruited from the ranks of Christianity. Good Christians have the necessary prerequisites: they have learned to turn off their critical faculties and to believe in the absurd. This is part of the Christian heritage, after all. America, nurtured by a fertile Christian soil, produces a bumper crop of intellectual vegetables from which the cults harvest their share.

Teach children to revere that which they cannot understand. Teach them that to doubt is sin. Teach them that faith is superior to reason. Teach children these things if you will, but do not be surprised if they eventually replace your brand of irrationalism with some other. Without the guidance of a sharp, disciplined mind, they will be easy prey for whatever cult can capture their emotional fancy.

The religious establishment should end its hypocritical hand-wringing over cults. Cults will always exist in a society that prizes faith and religious belief. If religious leaders wish to alleviate the problem, they can launch a vigorous campaign to teach people the value of critical thinking in religious matters. Religious leaders could do this, but they won't, for they know this to be a greater threat to their position than the cults themselves.

If Christians truly wish to understand the fundamental cause of cult mania, they would do well to heed the advice of the wise Pogo: "We have have seen the enemy, and it is us."

Commentary 3

In recent years we have seen a resurgence of interest in Protestant fundamentalism. A literal belief in the Bible, faith healing, an emphasis on sin and salvation—these and other aspects of primitive Christianity are becoming more and more popular in American culture.

One indication of this revival is the popularity of Hal Lindsay's *The Late Great Planet Earth.* This book, first published in 1970, has sold nearly ten million copies, and the movie version recently made its rounds in Los Angeles. *The Late Great Planet Earth* purportedly documents the fulfillment of biblical prophecy in recent years. We are living in the last days, according to Hal Lindsay, and we shall soon witness the reappearance of Jesus on earth.

Of course, predictions of this kind are nothing new in Christian history. Jesus, according to the New Testament, taught the people of his generation that the coming of God's kingdom was imminent. "[T]here are some standing here," he said, "who will not taste death before they see the kingdom of God come with power." Jesus was mistaken, but his followers continued to believe that Armageddon, the final conflict between the forces of good and evil, was just around the corner. "The end of things is at hand," declared the author of I Peter; "Jesus was made manifest at the end of the times for your sake. . . ." Throughout the New Testament we see references to "these last days," and Paul warns, "The appointed time has grown very short."

Such predictions have continued to the present day, especially during periods of war, plague, and famine. Author Hal Lindsay has simply contributed his share to the long and dismal record of Christian prophecy.

The movie version of *The Late Great Planet Earth,* I should note, is a turkey that even the presence of Orson Wells as narrator cannot redeem. The book isn't much better, but it does provide a number of specifics, including a detailed account of World War III (which will culminate in Armageddon) complete with a map showing how various invasions will occur.

Lindsay predicts a Mideastern conflict involving Russia and her allies, a ten-nation European confederacy led by the Antichrist, and a Chinese army 200 million strong. After the destruction of the Russian army, the European alliance will confront Chinese forces in a massive nuclear war. As this war reaches its climax, Jesus will appear to save man from extinction and to institute a 1,000-year reign on earth.

The entrance of Jesus is dramatic, to say the least. He will descend from heaven to the Mount of Olives. As his foot touches the mountain, an earthquake will split it in two, creating a giant crevice. This will provide shelter for the many Jews who have converted to Christianity.

What happens to the born-again Christians during this tribulation period? Nothing, according to Lindsay, because God will have snatched them up before this occurs. Millions of fundamentalists will disappear without a trace. Think of it! A world without even one born-again Christian. Perhaps this is God's final blessing on the rest of mankind.

When can we expect Armageddon to take place? Very soon. The key was the reestablishment of Israel in 1948, and the author estimates that the tribulation will occur around forty years later—that is, by 1988.

This is the future as seen by Hal Lindsay. His crystal ball is an astonishing crazy quilt of passages from the Bible, especially from Isaiah, Jeremiah, Ezekial, and Daniel in the Old Testament, and the Book of Revelation in the New Testament. Lindsay does such violence to the spirit and context of the Bible as to make any biblical scholar flinch in acute embarrassment. Biblical passages are wrenched from their context, the reader is misinformed concerning the dates and authors of biblical books, and Lindsay engages in one flight of fancy after another. The interested reader need only consult a reputable Bible commentary to verify the many deceptions contained in *The Late Great Planet Earth.* (I recommend the twelve-volume *Interpreters Bible,* a work of prodigious scholarship, or the more modest *Abingdon Bible Commentary.*)

The Late Great Planet Earth would not be worth discussing were it not for two points. First, there is its possible, if unlikely, impact on foreign affairs. There is no way to tell how many of the readers of this book take it seriously—I'm not sure if even Lindsay does—but let's assume that many do. For these true believers, God has decreed a Mideastern conflict leading to World War III. To quote Lindsay, "The clearly predictable course of the Middle East will not be changed." The prospect of millions of God's little helpers cheering on a world war in the next decade is frightening indeed. And if some of these prophecy freaks should be in a position to influence governmental policy—well, I leave it to you to ponder the consequences.

Lastly, there is the intellectual significance of *The Late Great Planet Earth*. Its intellectual significance is that it doesn't have any. It typifies the intellectual depravity of which the born-again movement is capable. Those who regard the fundamentalist revival as a harmless return to religious values would do well to take a closer look. There is a deep, underlying revolt here—a rejection of the rationalism and humanism in modern society. Fundamentalists are the first to admit this, and they carry themselves with pride. Meanwhile their opposition remains silent, too busy or too embarrassed to comment on our backward march into the dark ages. It is time for the defenders of reason to come out of the closet and to articulate the values they hold dear. With the increasing influence of the born-again movement, such values can no longer be taken for granted.

Commentary 4

I previously noted the revival of Protestant fundamentalism in America today, particularly in the form of the evangelical, born-again movement. There is no doubt that the well-financed evangelical campaign has enjoyed spectacular success.

The average person's knowledge of the born-again movement comes through radio and television programs. Well-trained popularizers of fundamentalist theology—preachers, as they are called—entertain us with their melodramatic antics, testimonies of how they found Jesus, and their assembly-line versions of faith healing. But radio and television provide little in the way of discussion of the philosophical premises and implications of fundamentalism. For this information we must turn to the academic writings of professional theologians.

For an authoritative source on the theology of the born-again movement, I have consulted a book by Donald G. Bloesch, *Essentials of Evangelical Theology*, the first volume of which was published in 1978. Professor Bloesch's credentials are impressive: he is Professor of systematic theology at Dubuque Theological Seminary in Iowa, he has authored or edited a dozen books, and he has served as President of the Midwest Division of the American Theological Society.

The word "evangelical," Professor Bloesch explains, derives from the Greek signifying the "message of salvation through the atoning sacrifice of Christ." Evangelicalism is rooted in faith and in the Bible. It does not seek a natural knowledge of God—that is, knowledge gained through reason; rather, it seeks "the revelation of Jesus Christ given in Holy Scriptures."

What role does reason play in the process? Professor Bloesch is clear on this point. "In this perspective," he writes, "reason is not a stepping stone to faith but a useful instrument in the hands of faith." God, we are told, is enveloped in mystery; he cannot be comprehended by human reason. But this assertion creates serious difficulties. As an eighteenth-century atheist pointed out, if God is unknowable, the logical thing to do is not to think of him at all and to move on to more relevant matters. To escape this dilemma, Professor Bloesch pens one of the finest examples of theological double-talk that I have seen in recent years: "Mystery does connote obfuscation but an illumination that eludes rational assimilation."

This passage is on my list of favorite theological believe-it-or-not quotations, alongside such memorable sayings as that of a theologian of the seventh century, who wrote: "That mind is perfect which, through true faith, in supreme ignorance, supremely knows the supremely unknowable."

Returning to Professor Bloesch's book: an important section is the chapter titled "Total Depravity."

Bloesch concedes, somewhat grudgingly, that man is essentially good. Why? Because man is God's creation, and what God creates is good. Of course, no evangelical can stop here. The very concept of salvation—which is what fundamentalism offers us—hinges on a view of man as morally corrupt and irredeemable without God's grace. So we have what appears to be a logical chasm separating man's essential goodness on the one side from the theological need to condemn man as depraved on the other.

No theologian worth his salt would be stymied by such minor obstacles, and certainly Professor Bloesch isn't. He, like countless theologians before him, trots out original sin. Man's earthly nature, although originally pure, was corrupted by Adam's fall into sin. As Professor Bloesch puts it, "man's whole being is now marred by a deep-rooted perversity." This doctrine of total depravity, he emphasizes, "is integral to all Evangelical thought."

Humans, therefore, are mired in sin and moral depravity, from which only the grace of God can rescue them. This seems simple enough, but it becomes more complex in Chapter Eight. There, Professor Bloesch considers the question of whether we are saved by grace or by works. He argues that salvation is by grace; it is "a free gift of God that . . . cannot be earned or merited by good behavior." The implication, however, is that we have no control over whether we are saved or not, which seems a bit harsh on those souls condemned to eternal torment through no fault of their own. It is reasonable that people should get some credit for their own salvation, but this conflicts with the notion of grace as a free, undeserved gift. Professor Bloesch revels in one paradox after another, until he finally disposes of the problem with this astonishing declaration: "What is necessary to understand is that the act of salvation is a paradox or mystery which defies and eludes rational comprehension."

And here we have it: the punch line of 250 pages of detailed theological analysis. If the good professor contradicts himself, or if he cannot express himself intelligibly, or if he cannot defend his beliefs, we should by no means hold *him* accountable. What he says is incomprehensible, to be sure, but this is because he is dealing, he says, with incomprehensible truths. Professor Bloesch, by his own admission, frequently does not know what he is talking about. Usually we would not take such a person seriously. But in the topsy-turvy world of fundamentalist theology, it is considered a commendable act—indeed the key to being "born again"—to believe such professions on faith.

The born-again movement, in essence, represents an abdication of intellectual responsibility. This is the sum and substance of its doctrines.

Commentary 5

Professor Bloesch, you may recall, stresses the total depravity of man—a consequence of original sin. Man, whose "whole being is . . .marred by deep rooted perversity," depends entirely upon the grace of God to save him from his wretched condition. Man's "fall into sin" affects his nature in two basic ways. First, there is bondage of the will, which means that man "is not only unwilling but also unable to do the good. . . ." An unsaved person "may yearn for the good," argues Professor Bloesch, "but he is incapable of pursuing the good."

Secondly, sin results in "the impairment of man's reasoning." "Sin," to quote the author, "not only enslaves man's will but also blinds him to the truth about God and himself." In other words, the unregenerate disbeliever, if we are to believe this theologian, is unable to reason correctly and impartially about spiritual matters since his reasoning capacity is nothing more than a slave to his sinful nature.

Just as some Marxists evade arguments against their position by attributing them to "bourgeois logic," so the Christian can dismiss skeptical objections to God and Christianity by attributing them to "sinner reasoning." This is a convenient tactic indeed, as it relieves one of the responsibility to defend one's beliefs rationally.

Fundamentalism thus assaults the tradition of rationalistic humanism on two fronts: it denies that humans are naturally able to choose and pursue the good, and it attacks the ideal of an efficacious and impartial capacity to reason. Humans, without the grace of God, are reduced to moral and intellectual impotence.

These ideas are not new to Christian thought. On the contrary, they comprise one of the two major traditions of Christian theology, running from the writings of Paul in the New Testament, through St. Augustine in the early fifth century, and through the Protestant Reformation of the sixteenth century, especially in the works of Luther and Calvin. A merit of Professor Bloesch's book is that it delineates the heritage of these doctrines, and it candidly distinguishes them from the rationalist wing of Christian theology, as exemplified by Thomas Aquinas of the thirteenth century.

Figures like Augustine and Aquinas may seem a bit esoteric, but for one who wishes to understand the fate of reason in the history of Western civilization and is concerned about the future of reason in American culture, the distinction between Augustine and Aquinas could not be more significant. To put it simply, Augustine represents the worst that Christianity has to offer, and Aquinas represents the best that Christianity has to offer. Most of the doctrines that I have discussed thus far in conjunction with Professor Bloesch's book can be found in the writings of St. Augustine. Indeed, as Professor Bloesch points out, "It was Augustine who rediscovered the biblical doctrine of total depravity and gave it the recognition that it deserves."

Thomas Aquinas, in contrast, represents the fusion of Christianity with the rationalism of Aristotle. Although Aquinas believed in original sin, he attributed to it far less impact on human nature than did Augustine. Humans, for Aquinas, still retain their natural ability to discern and pursue the good, as revealed in natural law, and reason is essentially unimpaired by sin. Of course Aquinas was an orthodox Christian in most respects, and I don't wish to exaggerate his affinity with the rationalist tradition. But the historical record is clear. Augustine was the dominant intellectual force in Western civilization for at least six hundred years, and, under his tutelage, Europe experienced the period known as the Dark Ages, when the lights of philosophy and science were dim, if not extinguished altogether.

Aquinas, who liberated reason from its servitude to faith and theology, was a pervasive influence for hundreds of years after the thirteenth century—a span of time that, despite its superstitions and cruelties, included the Renaissance and the scientific revolution. Aquinas was not a complete rationalist, to be sure, but even a little reason goes a long way.

Protestant fundamentalism represents a return, not only to the Protestant reformation, but, more importantly, to the theology of St. Augustine. Most participants of the born-again movement are probably unaware of their forefathers, but academic theologians, such as Professor Bloesch, are well aware of theological history, and they consciously welcome this return to Augustine. But what of it? Does this really matter except, perhaps, to cloistered academics?

Yes, it matters tremendously. The evangelical movement, to the extent that it influences our society, will weave a predictable web spun from its basic premises. For example, a logical outgrowth of Augustine's theology was his intense condemnation of sexual pleasure. Augustine also believed that government was instituted by God as a punishment and remedy for sin. Now if sexual pleasure is a sin, and if the function of government is to punish sin, what do we get? We get the likes of Anita Bryant, and we get so-called courts of justice that are handing down pornography convictions with alarming frequency. The revival of fundamentalism portends another sexual dark age. Still think that an obscure intellectual who lived 1,500 years ago has no relevance to today? Think again.

Commentary 6

Since beginning these commentaries, I have often been asked: Why am I concerned about theological issues? More specifically, why have I emphasized the fundamentalist revival and its philosophical implications? Perhaps the atheist merely dignifies the absurdities of Christian fundamentalism when he grants them the undeserved respect of a reply. Perhaps the cause of reason would be served better by ignoring the opposition and by concentrating on more practical, day-to-day matters.

These comments make sense. After all, one cannot spend one's life battling every irrational belief that happens along. While acknowledging this fact, however, we must remember that religions have played a crucial role throughout history, and they will continue to do so. Why? Because the great religions address fundamental problems. Religions are successful, not because they provide the correct answers, but because they ask important questions—questions that concern every human being.

What is the nature of the universe? Is there a purpose, or plan, to human existence? Are right and wrong based on timeless, absolute standards? What is the role of reason? Are people inherently good, inherently depraved, or perhaps neither? How does one lead a good life? What is the proper role of sex in human relationships?

These and similar questions are of universal interest, and they are the questions with which religions have traditionally been concerned. Although religious answers range from inadequate, to mistaken, to disasterous, the genius of religious movements lies in the recognition that these questions are vital, and that people will always seek answers.

This is the key to the current success of Protestant fundamentalism. Liberal Christianity has been on the decline for many years, and the fundamentalist, with his back-to-basics program, has succeeded in breathing new life into a dying Christianity. Liberal theologians tried to make Christianity reasonable and relevant, and in so doing they gutted Christian doctrines of their significance. Christianity became so diluted and insipid that it lost its ability to inspire devotion. When asked, for example, whether Jesus was the Son of God, the typical liberal theologian would respond: "Well, yes, in a way. But then we are all children of God." But was Jesus more than a man? "Sort of, yes, but then all men have divine spark within them." But was Jesus resurrected from the dead? "Well, in a manner of speaking, yes—in a symbolic way, you see." And so went the liberal rhetoric in a desperate ploy to make Christianity appear reasonable.

The fundamentalist rejects these evasive maneuvers as theoretically and strategically unsound. Christianity, he points out, was never meant to be reasonable, and to force it into this mold is to destroy its very essence. The fundamentalist, whatever his faults, is at least willing to address crucial questions in a straightforward, unambiguous way. Is there purpose to human life? Certainly. There is God's purpose. Are people basically corrupt? Yes, thanks to original sin. Is there an absolute standard of right and wrong? You betcha. There is God's law, and he doesn't look favorably upon rebellion. There are no ifs, ands, or buts here, no wishy-washy evasions. The fundamentalist worldview resembles a 1930s Western on a cosmic scale. There are the good guys and the bad guys; they are easily distinguished, and the good guys win in the end.

Of course, the fundamentalist notion of what constitutes good is often dispicable. For instance, a Calvinist theologian, writing in 1973, advocated the death penalty for homosexuality. "God's penalty is death," he asserted, "and a godly order will enforce it." What of the charge that this is inhuman? This theologian does not flinch, he simply points out that God's law is to be obeyed, period. To base moral judgments on humanistic standards rather than on God's law is to defy the will of God.

Now, this is a bit stern even for a Calvinist, and most fundamentalists would not advocate the death penalty for sexual offenses. Perhaps twenty or thirty years in prison would suffice, as Anita Bryant suggested in her *Playboy* interview.

Even when fundamentalist doctrines are reprehensible, however, there is a certain boldness about them, a kind of crude simplicity. The evangelical movement stresses the importance of providing straightforward answers to important questions, and this emphasis has captured the attention of thousands of young people who have nowhere else to turn.

But is there an alternative? Is there some way to find answers other than by resorting to religious faith? Yes, there is philosophy, the purpose of which is to provide one with an integrated system of fundamental principles. Philosophy attempts to answer basic questions about the universe and the values proper to human life, and it seeks answers within the sphere of reason. This, at least, is the classical vision of philosophy, but it is an ideal which, I am sorry to say, has been seriously undermined by academic philosophers of the twentieth century.

Many professional philosophers, for reasons too complex to discuss here, have systematically isolated themselves from the general public; and they have refused to deal with the crucial questions outlined earlier. When was the last time you sought out a philosopher for advice? Or when was the last time you saw a philosopher interviewed on the news for his opinion on some important issue? In previous centuries, a philosopher was viewed as a sage, a repository of wisdom, from which one solicited knowledge and advice. The suggestion that one should seek out a philosopher for guidance today would be greeted in most circles with gales of laughter.

This, as I said, is largely the fault of philosophers themselves. The result of their self-isolation has been an intellectual and moral void that religions have attempted to fill. Fundamentalism will win one victory after another as long as it is the only contender in the arena of basic questions. Fundamentalists may provide irrational answers to these questions, but they will always have more appeal than the philosopher who refuses to deal with the questions at all.

Philosophy is important, not only for academics, but also for the average person. Philosophy provides a structure for reasoning, and, when that structure is not present, the influence of reason declines. This is what we have seen in the past several decades. The defenders of reason, therefore, must reintroduce philosophy into the public forum. This is a formidable task, but it is the only long-range solution to the problem of rampant irrationalism.

5
Christianity, Philosophy, and the Gods

Paul and Philosophy

Paul, "apostle to the Gentiles," was born in Tarsus, the principal city in the Roman province of Cilicia (in present-day Turkey). Tarsus was a stronghold of Greek learning, and Paul became fluent in both Greek and Aramaic. Paul's father was a Roman citizen (during a time when that privilege meant something) and a Pharisaic Jew. Thus, a young Paul—then called Saul; Paul was his Roman name—was sent to Jerusalem to study under Gamiliel, a renowned Pharisee and teacher.

Whether in Tarsus or in Jerusalem (perhaps in both), Paul acquired a working knowledge of Greek philosophy, especially Stoicism. After converting to Christianity, Paul made three famous missionary journeys. It was during his second journey (48–51) that he visited Athens and spoke before "Epicurean and Stoic philosophers." He even quoted Aratus, a Stoic poet (Acts 17.28).

Certain ideas in Paul's Athenian speech, notes one historian, "are wholly Stoic and cannot be understood at all without the help of Greek philosophy."[1] Paul failed to impress the philosophers; they "mocked" him and called him a "babbler" (Acts 17.18). Having won but few converts in Athens, Paul never returned to that city.

After his humiliating reception in Athens, Paul seems never again to have defended Christianity with philosophical arguments. And although his attitude toward Greek philosophy has been called "indecisive,"[2] he was, on the whole, clearly hostile. The Greeks "seek wisdom, but we preach Christ crucified . . ." (I Cor. 1.22,23). God has "made foolish the wisdom of the world" (I Cor. 1.20).

> Let no one deceive himself. If anyone among you thinks that he is wise in this age, let him become a fool that he may become wise. For the wisdom of this world is folly with God. (I Cor. 3.18,19)

Paul issued a similar warning to the Colossians (2.8):

> See to it that no one makes a prey of you by philosophy and empty deceit, according to human tradition, according to the elemental spirits of the universe, and not according to Christ.

Paul does not use philosophy to support his case for Christianity. He relies instead on revelation, especially on the revelation of Christ. Even when expressing his own opinion without a "command of the Lord," Paul attributes it to the "Spirit of God" (I Cor. 7.25,40). Paul's mission was to instill a faith based on the "power" and "wisdom" of God, rather than on the wisdom of men—that is, the wisdom gained through philosophy (I Cor. 2.4,5,7).

The Apologists

In the decades following Paul's death (c. 66), Christian theologians wrote primarily to instruct and counsel fellow Christians. These "apostolic fathers," as they are called, showed no inclination to enlist the aid of philosophy. This situation changed, however, around the middle of the second century.

Christians were a small minority in the Roman Empire—around fifty thousand in a population of sixty million[3]—but, as their numbers grew, they came to the critical attention of Greek, Roman, and Jewish writers. Various complaints were made against Christians—philosophical, political (they were said to be poor citizens), and moral (they were said to engage in incest, cannibalism, and sundry other practices).[4]

In response to such attacks, a new breed of Christian writers emerged—the "apologists" (from the Greek *apologia*, or speech for the defense).[5] The early apologists spoke Greek, and most had converted to Christianity from paganism. Some, such as Justin Martyr, had been trained in philosophy, and they used philosophical arguments both to attack pagan doctrines and to defend Christianity. The apologists were the first Christians to seek a reconciliation between philosophy and theology. They realized that, if Christianity was to progress beyond the status of a cult, it had to develop a more sophisticated arsenal of arguments.

Justin Martyr (c. 100–165) worked his way through a maze of pagan philosophies before converting to Christianity. He founded a school in Rome and was later martyred there. An admirer of Plato, Justin conscripted philosophy into the service of Christianity.

Justin and other apologists faced this problem: What was the status of persons who lived before the time of Jesus? Could they have possessed true knowledge? Yes, according to Justin. Christ "is the Word of whom every race of men were partakers; and those who lived reasonably are Christians, even though they have been thought atheists; as, among the Greeks, Socrates and Heraclitus, and men like them." Justin considered the moral teachings of the Stoics to be "admirable." Christians should appreciate and use the knowledge attained through philosophy: "Whatever things were rightly said among all men, are the property of us Christians. . . ." Justin concludes his *First Apology* with this appeal: "And if these things seem to you to be reasonable and true, honor them; but if they seem nonsensical, despise them as nonsense. . . ."[6]

Clement of Alexandria (c. 150–220), the head of an important school in Alexandria, has been called the "founder of speculative theology" and "the first Christian father who may be classified as a scholar."[7] For Clement, philosophy is "a preparatory discipline" for receiving the truths of Christianity. All philosophies, Hellenic and barbarian, contain germs of truth. "Let all, therefore, both Greeks and barbarians, who have aspired after the truth . . . produce whatever they have of the word of truth."[8]

Philosophy, says Clement, makes people virtuous, so it must be the work of God. Of course, the knowledge gained through divine revelation is more important than the knowledge gained through philosophy.

> But if at any time [the Christian] has leisure and time for relaxation from what is of prime consequence, he applies himself to Hellenic philosophy in preference to other recreation, feasting on it as a kind of dessert at supper.[9]

Clement points out that even the rejection of philosophy requires one to philosophize, because we must first know what philosophy is before we can condemn it—and this requires philosophic reasoning to determine.[10]

Enthusiasm for philosophy was by no means universal among the apologists. Even the pro-philosophy apologists demoted philosophy to a secondary position, because it deals with human wisdom rather than with divine wisdom. Pagan philosophy was admired only so far as it supported Christian ideas. Contrary to the Greek ideal of philosophy, no apologist advocated submitting all beliefs to the bar of critical reason.

Some of the hostility displayed by early Christians toward philosophy was caused by the rise of Gnosticism—a general name given to a diverse group of Christian "heresies." Gnostics (from the Greek for "knowledge" or "insight") generally stressed the need for a special kind of knowledge—sometimes inner knowledge of oneself—as the key to salvation, rather than faith in Christ. Some Gnostics blurred the line between philosophy and revelation so as to make them virtually indistinguishable.

Valentinus, the greatest Gnostic teacher of the second century, believed that Jehovah of the Old Testament was not the supreme god, but a lesser god—a kind of demiurge like that found in Plato's *Timaeus*.[11] Some Gnostics denied the physical resurrection of Jesus; they found the idea, in the words of one critic, "extremely revolting, repugnant, and impossible."[12] Instead, these Gnostics viewed the resurrection as a spiritual phenomenon or as a vision received in dreams and trances.

Whether in reaction to Gnosticism or for other reasons, some apologists were openly hostile to philosophy. One of the worst was Tatian, a second-century native of Assyria who studied under Justin Martyr in Rome.

In his *Address to the Greeks*, Tatian asks, "What noble thing have you produced by your pursuit of philosophy? Who of your most eminent men has been free from vain boasting?" Then he lists the flaws and follies of famous Greeks. Diogenes and Plato, he says, were gluttons. Aristotle, while tutor to the young Alexander, flattered the future conqueror with ridiculous praise. Moreover, the followers of Aristotle, in a confession of atheism, stupidly believe "that sublunary things are not under the care of Providence; and so . . . they themselves look after what is thus left uncared for."

Perhaps most amusing is Tatian's account of how Heraclitus ("self-taught and arrogant") supposedly tried to cure himself of dropsy: "he plastered himself with cow dung, which, as it hardened, contracted the flesh of his whole body, so that he was pulled in pieces, and thus died."[13]

Tatian exempts a few "just persons," including Socrates, from his ridicule, but, among the Greeks, "the bad will be found far more numerous than the good." Christians should follow the commands of God and "reject everything which rests upon human opinion." "It would be an excellent thing," Tatian tells the Greeks, "if your continuance in unbelief should receive a check," but Christians will remain loyal to God in any case. Then comes the threat, "Laugh, if you please; but you will have to weep hereafter."[14] The Catholic scholar Aloys Dirksen accurately describes Tatian as "an angry, scolding old man who rants and raves at everything Greek as valueless and productive only of evil and immorality."[15]

Tatian's diatribe against Greek philosophy is somewhat curious, considering that he studied with Justin, a man in love with Greek philosophy. But Tatian does agree with his master on some issues—for example, he claims that whatever wisdom the Greeks did possess was drawn from Moses, as "from a fountain."[16]

The argument that Greek philosophers borrowed (or stole) some of their ideas from Moses appears frequently in Christian apologetics. (It was first used by Jewish scholars.) Justin regarded Moses as the source of the creation story in Plato's *Timaeus.* Origen traced Plato's *Phaedrus* to the same source. Theophilus of Antioch maintained that Greek poets and philosophers "plagiarized from the Scriptures to make their doctrines plausible." Augustine, following Ambrose, speculated that Plato had become familiar with the Hebrew Scriptures while in Egypt.[17]

By tracing Greek ideas to Moses, the apologists sought to explain how pagans had been able to discern the truth without the benefit of revelation. This argument served another purpose as well. The Romans, like the Greeks, looked down their noses at non-Hellenic "barbarians." And Christianity, with its roots planted deep in Judaism, was clearly barbaric. (On several occasions, Tatian speaks defensively of the "barbaric philosophy" he has embraced.) Thus, by claiming that Plato and other Greeks had plagiarized from the barbarian Moses, the Christian apologists hoped to surmount a wall of prejudice.

Theophilus, who became Bishop of Antioch in Syria around 168, was another Greek-speaking apologist who spurned Greek philosophy. Like other apologists, Theophilus sets out to refute the false accusations leveled against Christians—namely, "that the wives of us all are held in common and made promiscuous use of; and that we even commit incest with our own sisters, and, what is most impious and barbarous of all, that we eat human flesh."[18]

Theophilus launches his defense with a vicious counterattack against Greek thinkers. Greek philosophers, not Christians, advocated "the eating of human flesh," including the eating of fathers by their children. (Zeno, Diogenes, and Cleanthes are mentioned in this absurd indictment.) The Greek philosopher Plato, not Christians, wanted communal wives. Epicurus and the Stoics, not Christians, "teach incest and sodomy, with which doctrines they have filled libraries. . . ."[19]

With this mixture of fact and falsehood (mainly the latter), Theophilus assails the Greeks for their "useless and godless opinions." Greek historians, philosophers, and poets did not personally witness what they wrote about, nor did they consult eyewitnesses, and "they who write of things unascertained beat the air." Ironically, this demand for eyewitnesses would later be used by freethinkers as they examined the Bible. This is also true of another criticism proffered by Theophilus: the Greeks gave inconsistent accounts of their gods, so "most of them demolished their own doctrines." Since conflicting reports cannot all be true, stories of Greek gods "are condemned by men of understanding."[20] Centuries later, freethinkers would say the same thing about conflicting accounts of Jesus.

Tertullian (c. 160–225), a founder of the Latin Church in Africa, is the most famous apologist who opposed philosophy. Tertullian was probably a lawyer who converted to Christianity around age forty, and he wrote voluminously against heresies. Ironically, Tertullian himself later embraced the Montanist heresy, which preached extreme asceticism, the imminent return of Jesus, and ongoing revelations from God transmitted through prophets (including women).

Tertullian takes his cue from Paul, who "expressly names *philosophy* as that which he would have us be on our guard against." Philosophy corrupts the truth and leads to heresy. "Indeed, heresies are themselves instigated by philosophy." Plato, Epicurus, Zeno (the founder of Stoicism), and Heraclitus asked the same dangerous questions as heretics: "Whence comes evil? Why is it permitted? What is the origin of man?" Aristotle, in particular, encouraged "unprofitable questions":

> Unhappy Aristotle! who invented for these [heretics] dialectics, the art of building up and pulling down; an art so evasive in its propositions, so far-fetched in its conjectures, so harsh, in its arguments, so productive of contentions—embarrassing, even to itself, retracting everything, and really treating of nothing.[21]

Tertullian asks, "What indeed has Athens to do with Jerusalem?" Christians should abandon all efforts to reconcile their faith with philosophy:

> Away with all attempts to produce a mottled Christianity of Stoic, Platonic, and dialectic composition! We want no curious disputation after possessing Christ Jesus, no inquisition after enjoying the gospel! With our faith, we desire no further belief. For this is our palmary faith, that there is nothing which we ought to believe besides.[22]

But what of the biblical injunction, "Seek and ye shall find"? This is true, Tertullian replies; one must seek the truth in order to find it. But after one has the truth, as Christians do, then seeking is no longer necessary—indeed, it indicates a lack of faith. In addition, all seeking must be done within the rule of faith. We should seek solely within the Scriptures and reject external sources.

> No man receives illumination from a quarter where all is darkness. Let our "seeking," therefore, be in that which is our own, and from those who are our own, and concerning that which is our own,—that, and only that, which can become an object of inquiry without impairing the rule of faith.[23]

These passages are from *The Prescription Against Heretics*. In Roman Law, a *praescriptio* was a charge that the opponent's case was out of order and should be dismissed without a hearing.[24] This was Tertullian's advice for dealing with heretics. Some heretics quote Scripture to prove their case, thereby trapping the unwary. Christians shouldn't engage in these controversies. Heretics "are not to be disputed with, but to be admonished." A controversy over the Scriptures "can, clearly, produce no other effect than help to upset either the stomach or the brain."[25]

Tertullian's most famous outburst of irrationalism appears in his treatise, *On the Flesh of Christ:*

> [T]he Son of God died, it is by all means to be believed, because it is absurd. And He was buried, and rose again; the fact is certain, because it is impossible.[26]

Some commentators claim that Tertullian was "not a blind irrationalist."[27] In a sense, this is true. He was an irrationalist with sight—a brilliant, if erratic, controversialist with a knack for isolating his adversary's weakest spot. The passage quoted above was directed against Marcion, a Christian who espoused "Docetism" (from the Greek for "I seem").[28]

Docetists viewed the humanity, suffering, and resurrection of Jesus as seeming, or spiritual, rather than as real. According to Marcion, the passion story, if taken literally, is "unworthy of God." In response, Tertullian points out that, when judged by this standard, *all* Christian beliefs can be dissolved into absurdity. None is reasonable, nor were they meant to be. Hence, the resurrection story "is certain, because it is imposssible"—that is to say, it meets the same criterion as all other Christian beliefs.

The Case Against the Gods

Early Christians were often accused of atheism, because they disbelieved in, or refused to worship, the pagan gods. As Justin Martyr observed: "[W]e are called atheists. And we confess that we are atheists, so far as gods of this sort are concerned, but not with respect to the most true God. . . ."[29]

Athenagoras (c. 177) also responded to the charge of atheism:

> [A]s to the . . . complaint that we do not pray to and believe in the same gods as the cities, it is an exceedingly silly one. Why, the very men who charge us with atheism for not admitting the same gods as they acknowledge, are not agreed among themselves concerning the gods. . . . When, therefore, they differ among themselves concerning their gods, why do they bring the charge against us of not agreeing with them?[30]

As Athenagoras suggests, every person, whatever his religion, disbelieves in the gods of competing religions—so, in that sense, *every* person is an atheist of some kind. (Modern Christians who proclaim the irrationality of atheism would do well to keep this point in mind, for such Christians presumably reject the existence of Zeus and countless other deities.) As Athenagoras put it:

> If, then, we are guilty of impiety because we do not practise a piety corresponding with theirs, then all cities and all nations are guilty of impiety, for they do not all acknowledge the same gods.[31]

Arnobius (c. 300) had this to say about the charge of atheism:

> Call us impious as much as you please, contemners of religion, or atheists, you will never make us believe in gods of love and war, that there are gods to sow strife, and to disturb the mind by the stings of the furies. For either they are not gods in very truth, and do not what you have related; or if they do the things which you say, they are doubtless no gods [at all].[32]

Surprisingly perhaps, most early Christians did not deny the existence of pagan gods. (Arnobius, quoted above, was a rare exception, as we shall see.) Rather, Christians considered the gods to be demons, or the work of demons; and this belief was grounded in Scripture.

The early Christian apologists read and spoke Greek, so they relied on a Greek translation of the Old Testament known as the Septuagint. That translation, however, rendered the Hebrew word for "idols" into the Greek word for "demons"—supernatural beings who inhabit an intermediate world between God and man. Thus, in the Septuagint version of Psalms 96.4f, the apologists read:

> Great is the Lord and highly to be praised, He is to be feared above all gods; for all the gods of the heathen are demons, but the Lord made the heavens.[33]

Even the modern "Revised Standard Version" says that heathens "sacrificed to demons which were no gods" (Deut. 32.17), and that disobedient Jews "sacrificed their sons and their daughters to the demons" (Psalms 106.37). Jesus, of course, was reported to have cast "demons" into a herd of swine (Matt. 8.28ff). And the apostle Paul left no doubt that "what pagans sacrifice they offer to demons and not to God" (I Cor. 10.20).

Given this background, it is understandable why Justin Martyr argued that Greco-Roman gods are demons, or evil spirits—the products of sexual intercourse between wayward angels and human women.[34] Tatian, a student of Justin, also discussed these "frenzied demons," which the Greeks mistook for gods. The Greeks, "profuse in words, but with minds strangely warped . . . follow demons as if they were mighty."[35]

The apologist Lactantius (c. 240–320) gives an account similiar to that of Justin. God sent angels "for the protection and improvement of the human race"; but the devil enticed these angels "and polluted them by intercouse with women." The offspring were demons, "neither angels or men, but bearing a kind of mixed nature. . . ." The fallen angels who fathered these demons were refused admission to heaven, so they became the devil's "satellites and attendants." Thus, according to Lactantius, "there came to be two kinds of demons; one of heaven, the other of the earth."[36]

> These contaminated and abandoned spirits . . . wander over the whole earth. . . . [T]hey fill every place with snares, deceits, frauds, and errors; for they cling to individuals, and occupy whole houses from door to door, and assume to themselves the name of genii; for by this word they translate demons into the Latin language.[37]

Christians attributed supernatural powers to these demons masquerading as gods; they were able to perform miracles. Augustine (354–430)—who thought that demons were fallen angels—mentions "phenomena which are quite evidently the result of the force and power of demons. . . ." And though Augustine claims that demonic miracles "are in no way comparable in power and grandeur with those performed . . . among the people of God," he concedes that demonic miracles "may seem in externals to equal many of those performed among true worshippers. . . ."[38]

Thus Augustine, like most of his predecessors, does not deny the reality of the pagan gods; he wishes only to relegate them to the lesser status of demons. As an eminent biographer of Augustine has written:

> [Demons] were usually conceived of at this time as being partly spiritual, though possessing bodies of a kind of volatile substance. They were immortal but subject to evil passions and were invisible as they haunted the world. In this view Augustine was at one with the best minds of the Church in his day, and like them he held that evil spirits had succeeded, over a period of centuries, in getting themselves or their creatures worshipped as gods, for men were convinced that the old gods really existed, whether they were human beings to whom the demons caused worship to be paid . . . or demons in the proper sense of the term.[39]

A rare exception to this standard explanation came from the pen of Arnobius, a North African rhetorician (c. 300) who wrote a century before Augustine. Arnobius does not demonize the gods; he denies their existence altogether. His is perhaps the most rationalistic account to be found in early Christian literature.

Arnobius admired Cicero's book *The Nature of the Gods* (written c. 51 B.C.), and he relied extensively on Cicero's arguments. This may partially explain why Arnobius was virtually ignored by other Christian writers (only Jerome mentions him). Cicero's critique of pagan religion was a double-edged sword that might be turned against Christianity. This was recognized by Lactantius, a disciple of Arnobius, who said that Cicero's book "altogether overthrows and destroys all religion."[40]

Cicero's book is cast in the form of a dialogue. The most skeptical discussant asks: "In this subject of the nature of the gods the first question is: do the gods exist or do they not?"[41]

Arnobius opens his lengthy case against the pagan gods with a similar question:

> [W]e demand, and ask you to tell us, whence you have discovered, or how you have learned, whether there are these gods, whom you believe to be in heaven and serve? For it may be that beings . . . of whose existence you feel assured, are found nowhere in the universe.[42]

According to Arnobius, defenders of the gods have "such tales about them as not merely to stain their honour, but, by the natures assigned to them, to prove that they did not exist at all."[43] Thus, Arnobius seeks to prove the nonexistence of the gods by exposing their absurd and impossible characteristics—a tactic that would later be used by atheists against the God of Christianity.

Arnobius ridicules the notion that gods are differentiated by gender. (Although we refer to the Christian God as "he," Arnobius insists that this is convention of language; God is not masculine.) If the gods are male and female, they must have generative organs with which to beget offspring. But if the gods are also immortal, then—given an eternity of begetting other gods—it follows that "the world should be full of gods, and that countless heavens could not contain their multitude."[44] If it is said that gods don't experience sexual desire, then why are they encumbered with useless organs? This, Arnobius suggests, does not befit the nature of divine beings.

Arnobius makes sport of the human form attributed to the gods. Do the gods have hair on their bodies? If so, does it grow, and do they need barbers to cut it? Do all the gods look alike? If so, how do they recognize each other? If not, do some have thick lips, moles, and snub noses? Are some fat, others thin, and others deformed? Again, however, it is the idea that gods have sexual organs that most offends the Christian sensibilites of Arnobius:

> Is not this really degrading, most impious, and insulting, to attribute to the gods the features of a frail and perishing animal? To furnish them with those members which no modest person would dare to

> recount, and describe, or represent in his own imagination, without shuddering at the excessive indecency?[45]

Arnobius is keenly aware of what has become known as "the anthropomorphic problem." If we ascribe human qualities to God, such as "goodness," then we must presuppose that God has human characteristics. Arnobius is unwilling to do this. He will not say that the Christian God is brave or wise, or that he has knowledge and forethought, or that he has purposes. These are good in man, "but who is so foolish, so senseless, as to say that God is great by [merely] human excellences?" According to Arnobius, we know only one thing about God—"that nothing can be revealed in human language concerning God."

> Whatever you say, whatever in unspoken thought you imagine concerning God, passes and is corrupted into a human sense, and does not carry its own meaning, because it is spoken in the words which we use, and which are suited [only] to human affairs.[46]

By the time Arnobius wrote, much of pagan religion had been explained through allegory.[47] For example, when Jupiter was said to have had sex with his mother, this, according to pagan philosophers, was an allegory in which Jupiter represents rain and his mother represents earth. And so with other stories, in which there supposedly "lurks a secret doctrine, and a dark profundity of mystery."[48]

Arnobius ridicules allegory as a ruse to "bolster up weak cases before a jury." They are "pretenses" used to rationalize disgusting and unbelievable stories. Critics of paganism need not inquire into supposedly hidden meanings, because the literal accounts are, in themselves, insulting to the deities.[49]

Once we resort to allegory, we cannot tell if our interpretation was actually intended by the original writer. Allegorical interpretation depends on the suppositions and biases of the interpreter: "it is open to everyone to put the meaning into it which he pleases."[50]

Must all of pagan religion be understood allegorically? Arnobius argues that this leads to insuperable difficulties. What of the claim that only some features should be understood allegorically? This "is refined subtlety, and can be seen through by the dullest." The interpreters can pick and choose to suit their purposes. There is no objective criterion to distinguish between what is to be taken literally and what is to be construed allegorically.

Arnobius gave us a brilliant critique of the allegorical method, but he seemed curiously unaware that the Bible itself had been subjected to allegorical interpretation by influential Christian theologians, especially those in Alexandria. These apologists were probably influenced by the brilliant Philo (c. 30 B.C.–A.D. 45). Known as "the Jewish Plato," Philo was the chief expositor of Judaism to the Hellenistic world; and this champion of the allegorical method exerted a powerful influence on Alexandria's intellectual life.[51] In particular, the allegorical method was adopted by two Alexandrian Christians: Clement (c. 150–220) and Origen (c. 185–254).

According to Clement, a true interpretation of Scripture entails looking beyond mere words to their "inner meanings." Clement, following Philo, variously described these inner meanings as secrets, mysteries, allegories, parables, and enigmas.[52] Clement believed that most biblical truths are presented in symbolic form. The prophets and apostles did not express themselves in philosophic terms, but their teachings contain a secret wisdom that can be discerned with the aid of philosophy.

According to Origen, "The Law has a twofold sense, one according to a literal meaning and the other according to an inner meaning. . . ."[53] When a critic ridiculed Christians for believing that God made Eve from Adam's rib, Origen replied that this story should be viewed figuratively, not literally. Pagans used allegory, and Origen believed that Christians should have the same privilege: "Are the Greeks alone at liberty to convey a philosophic meaning in a secret covering?"[54]

When Arnobius attacked the allegorical method, did he realize that his strictures applied to Christians as well as to pagans? Unfortunately, he didn't say.

Notes

1. Johannes Weiss, *Earliest Christianity*, trans. Frederick C. Grant (New York: Harper Torchbooks, 1959), vol. I, p. 241.

2. Harry Austry Wolfson, *The Philosophy of the Church Fathers*, 3rd ed. (Cambridge: Harvard University Press, 1970), vol. I, p. 7.

3. Robert L. Wilken, *The Christians as the Romans Saw Them* (New Haven: Yale University Press, 1984), p. 31.

4. On these charges, see Robert L. Wilken and Stephen Benko, *Pagan Rome and the Early Christians* (Bloomington: Indiana University Press, 1986).

5. See Karl Baus, *From the Apostolic Community to Constantine* (vol. I of *Handbook of Church History*, ed. H. Jedin and J. Dolan), p. 171.

6. *The Writings of Justin Martyr and Athenagoras*, trans. M. Dods, G. Reith, and B. Pratten (Edinburgh: T. and T. Clark, 1867), pp. 46, 66, 78, 83.

7. Aloys Dirksen, *Elementary Patrology* (St. Louis: B. Herder, 1959), p.73.

8. *The Writings of Clement of Alexandria*, trans. W. Wilson (Edinburgh: T. and T. Clark, 1867), vol. I, p. 389.

9. Ibid, vol. II, pp. 399, 401.

10. Ibid., vol II, p. 402.

11. Richard Kroner, *Speculation and Revelation in the Age of Christian Philosophy* (Philadelphia: The Westminster Press, n.d.), p. 55.

12. Quoted in Elaine Pagels, *The Gnostic Gospels* (New York: Vintage Books, 1981), p. 5. Pagels gives a sympathetic and very readable account of the Gnostics.

13. *The Writings of Tatian and Theophilus; and The Clementine Recognitions*, trans. B. Pratten, M. Dods, and T. Smith (Edinburgh: T. and T. Clark, 1867), p. 7.

14. Ibid., p. 36.

15. Dirksen, *Elementary Patrology*, p. 43.

16. *The Writings of Tatian*, p. 43.

17. See Jaroslav Pelikan, *The Emergence of the Catholic Tradition (100–600)* (Chicago: University of Chicago Press, 1971), pp. 33ff.

18. *The Writings of Tatian*, p. 18.

19. Ibid., p. 112.

20. Ibid., pp. 108, 109.

21. Tertullian in *The Ante-Nicene Fathers*, ed. A. Roberts and J. Donaldson (New York: Charles Scribner, 1905), vol. III, p. 246.

22. Ibid.

23. Ibid., p. 249.

24. See Justo L. Gonzalez, *A History of Christian Thought* (Nashville: Abingdon Press, 1970), vol I, p. 178.

25. Tertullian in *The Ante-Nicene Fathers*, p. 251.

26. Ibid., p. 525.

27. Gonzalez, *History of Christian Thought*, vol. I, p. 179.

28. See the entries under "Marcion" and "Docetism" in *The Oxford Dictionary of the Christian Church*, ed. F. L. Cross, 2nd ed. (Oxford: Oxford University Press, 1977).

29. *The Writings of Justin Martyr*, p. 29.

30. *The Writings of Justin Martyr*, p. 389.

31. Ibid., p. 390.

32. *The Seven Books of Arnobius Adversus Gentes*, trans. J. Bryce and J. Campbell (Edinburgh: T. and T. Clark, 1871), p. 32.

33. Quoted in Weiss, *Earliest Christianity*, vol. I., p. 248.

34. *The Writings of Justin Martyr*, p. 75.

35. *The Writings of Tatian*, p. 19.

36. *The Works of Lactantius*, trans. W. Fletcher (Edinburgh: T. and T. Clark, n.d.), p. 127.

37. Ibid., p. 128.

38. Augustine, *Concerning the City of God Against the Pagans*, trans. Henry Bettenson (Harmondsworth: Penquin Books, 1972), p. 395. Cf. Jeffrey Burton Russell, *Satan: The Early Christian Tradition* (Ithaca: Cornell University Press, 1981).

39. F. Van Der Meer, *Augustine the Bishop*, trans. B Battershaw and G. R. Lamb (New York: Harper Torchbooks, 1965), pp. 67-8.

40. *The Seven Books of Arnobius*, p. 47.

41. Cicero, *The Nature of the Gods*, trans. Horace McGregor (Harmondsworth: Penquin Books, 1972), p. 94.

42. *The Seven Books of Arnobius*, pp. 151-2.

43. Ibid., p. 153.

44. Ibid., p. 156.

45. Ibid., p. 160.

46. Ibid., p. 163.

47. See Pelikan, *The Emergence of the Catholic Tradition*, p. 28.

48. *The Seven Books of Arnobius*, pp. 256-7.

49. Ibid., p. 257.

50. Ibid., p. 258.

51. See Harry Austryn Wolfson, *Philo* (Cambridge: Harvard University Press, 1947), vol I, pp. 115ff.

52. Harry Austryn Wolfson, *The Philosophy of the Church Fathers*, vol I., p. 47.

53. Quoted in ibid., pp. 57-8.

54. *Contra Celsum* in *The Writings of Origen*, trans. F. Crombie (Edinburgh: T. and T. Clark, 1869), vol. II, p. 203.

6
Philosophies of Toleration

Early Christian Views

Early Christians faced sporadic persecution by the Roman State, so some of them defended toleration in an effort to stem the flow of blood. Tertullian (c. 145–225), a former pagan who converted to Christianity late in life, wrote:

> [I]t is a fundamental human right, a privilege of nature, that every man should worship according to his own convictions: one man's religion neither harms nor helps another man. It is assuredly no part of religion to compel religion—to which free will and not force should lead us. . . .[1]

This interesting passage contains both secular and religious assertions. Freedom of religion, according to Tertullian, is a natural right—"a privilege bestowed by nature," rather than by human authority. Moreover, one's religion "neither harms nor helps another man," so governments should not interfere. Thomas Paine could scarcely have put it better.

Tertullian also touches on a religious argument that was destined to play a major role in the toleration controversy: "free-will and not force should lead us" to religion. The idea here is that faith, an act of will, must be given freely if it is to be meritorious.

Lactantius (c. 240–320) also called for religious freedom. If pagans wish to convert Christians, they should use arguments, not coercion.

> [I]f they have any confidence in philosophy or in eloquence, let them arm themselves, and refute these arguments of ours if they are able; let them meet us hand to hand, and examine every point.[2]

According to Lactantius, coercion is useless in religious matters.

> There is no occasion for violence and injury, for religion cannot be imposed by force; the matter must be carried on by words rather than by blows, that the will may be affected. . . . Torture and piety are widely different; nor is it possible for truth to be united with violence, or justice with cruelty.[3]

Like Tertullian, Lactantius believes that faith must be given freely, because this is the source of its moral value. A coerced religion is a contradiction in terms.

> [I]f you wish to defend religion by bloodshed, and by tortures, and by guilt, it will no longer be defended, but will be polluted and profaned. For nothing is so much a matter of free-will as religion; in which, if the mind of the worshipper is disinclined to it, religion is at once taken away, and ceases to exist.[4]

Lactantius dismisses a rationale for persecution that, ironically, would later be used by Augustine. Perhaps the beneficiaries of persecution are the victims themselves. Perhaps the true interest of Christians is served when they are compelled to sacrifice to the pagan gods.

The response of Lactantius to such claims is brief but suggestive: "that is not a kindness which is done to one who refuses it." Then comes the persecutor's rejoinder: "But we must consult [the Christians'] interests, even against their will, since they know not what is good." Lactantius easily disposes of this lame excuse. If Romans really care about Christians, then why "do they so cruelly harass, torture, and weaken them . . . ?" Why do Romans destroy "those whose welfare they wish to promote?" True concern for the welfare of others is never manifested in violence.[5]

Lactantius considers another justification for persecution: that it serves the pagan gods who rightfully demand sacrifice as a token of loyalty, gratitude, and esteem. (This argument, appropriately modified, would later become a mainstay of Christian persecutors.)

According to Lactantius, "that is not a sacrifice which is extorted from a person against his will." Unless a sacrifice is offered "spontaneously" and "from the soul," it is nothing more than a "curse" extracted "by injuries, by prison, by tortures."

But what if a god actually demands sacrifices made under the threat of injury, prison, or torture? Lactantius, anticipating the reaction of modern freethinkers, is outraged. A god who demands cruelty is himself cruel, and unworthy of our worship.

> If they are gods who are worshipped in this manner, if for this reason only, they ought not to be worshipped, because they wish to be worshipped in this manner: they are doubtless worthy of the detestation of men, since libations are made to them with tears, with groaning, and with blood flowing from all the limbs.[6]

Augustine (354–430), a bishop in North Africa, defended religious liberty during his early years as a Christian. But, as conflicts intensified with a large group of schismatics known as Donatists, Augustine shifted his ground. Indeed, he shifted so far as to become the premier theorist of persecution in the history of Christendom. (We should note, however, that Augustine, unlike his successors, opposed putting heretics to death.) If one wishes to understand the theoretical background of persecution, one must understand the mind of Augustine.

In a letter to the Donatist Bishop Vincentius (408), Augustine explains why he changed his mind about persecution. While responding to the claim that "no one should be compelled to follow righteousness," Augustine defends "righteous persecution," i.e., persecution that supposedly benefits its victims.

> Let us learn, my brother, in actions which are similar to distinguish the intentions of the agents. . . . In some cases . . . both he that suffers persecution is in the wrong, and he that inflicts it is in the right. . . . In all these cases, what is important to attend to but this: who were on the side of truth, and who on the side of iniquity; who acted from a desire to injure, and who from a desire to correct what was amiss?[7]

What of Augustine's earlier conviction that "no one should be coerced into the unity of Christ, that we must act only by words, fight only by arguments, and prevail by force of reason"? And what of Augustine's famous saying, "No one can or ought to be constrained to believe"?

According to Augustine, "this opinion of mine was overcome not by the words of those who controverted it, but by the conclusive instances to which they could point." In other words, Augustine was confronted with many instances where, contrary to his expectations, heretics had been "brought over to the Catholic unity by fear."[8]

Clearly, persecution worked in these cases, but how? Augustine still denies that beliefs *per se* can be compelled, at least directly. But, as he explains to Vincentius, the threat of force *can* break "the heavy chains of inveterate custom." Some heretics were "too listless, or conceited, or sluggish, to take pains to examine Catholic truth." Others feared reprisals from fellow heretics. Others were raised as heretics and never knew any better. Others intended to embrace orthodoxy, but were afflicted with procrastination.

In such cases, Augustine holds that persecution, though unable to compel belief, can (and often does) change the heretic's mental attitude by breaking the bonds of bad habits, indifference, and sloth. Thus, even if force cannot impart truth, it can *prepare* the heretic to hear and receive the truth. Consider this passage from Augustine's *Treatise on the Correction of the Donatists* (417):

> It is indeed better (as no one ever could deny) that men should be led to worship God by teaching, than that they should be driven to it by fear of punishment or pain; but it does not follow that because the former course produces the better men, therefore those who do not yield to it should be neglected. For many have found advantage (as we have proved, and are daily proving by actual experiment), in being first compelled by fear or pain, so that they might afterwards be influenced by teaching, or might follow out in act what they had already learned in word.[9]

Augustine had a point: Punishment cannot change a person's beliefs *directly*, but it can influence them *indirectly*. This has been proved, as Augustine says, "by actual experiment," and only those blind to empirical evidence can deny it.

Thus does Augustine challenge the tolerationist argument that beliefs cannot (and therefore ought not) be compelled. But his argument is not yet complete. Even if force can influence beliefs, it does not follow that we *should* persecute in the name of truth.

Augustine puts his moral case as follows: Suppose two men live in a house that we know "with absolute certainty" to be on the verge of collapse. If these men ignore our warning to leave, what should we do? Should we "rescue" them against their wills, and reason with them afterward? Yes, says Augustine: "I think that if we abstained from doing it, we should well deserve the charge of cruelty."[10]

Next, suppose we find many people in a large house that is near collapse, and, as we undertake our forcible rescue, all occupants except one resist and kill themselves by jumping out of windows. Should we blame ourselves for these deaths? No, says Augustine:

> [W]e should console ourselves in our grief for the loss of the rest by the thoughts of the safety of the one [who was rescued]; and we should not allow all to perish without a single rescue, in the fear lest the remainder should destroy themselves.[11]

Having laid the foundation of his argument, Augustine proceeds to its predictable and logical conclusion. If "true reason and benevolence" demand that we forcibly secure the safety of people "for the brief space of their life on earth," then it follows that we should also compel them "in order that men may attain eternal life and escape eternal punishment." Thus, the righteous persecution of heretics is nothing less than a "work of mercy to which we ought to apply ourselves."[12]

If skeptics smirk at this argument, it is probably because they don't believe in hell and exclusive salvation (the tenet that heaven is reserved exclusively for those with correct beliefs). But if skeptics reject the *factual* assumptions of righteous persecution, what about its *moral* premise, as illustrated by Augustine's story of a dangerous house?

Today, many Americans would agree with Augustine's moral reasoning. Indeed, American law is strewn with prohibitions of self-endangering activities—living in condemned buildings, consuming illegal drugs, practicing voluntary euthanasia, and the like. Thus, before dismissing Augustine as an evil fanatic, we should realize that many Americans embrace the moral axiom of righteous persecution: They, like Augustine, are willing to coerce recalcitrant people for their own good.

If it is morally proper to force *earthly* benefits upon others, then why not force *heavenly* benefits upon others as well? Of course, we may disbelieve in hell and exclusive salvation, but this doesn't challenge the *principle* of righteous persecution. Mere disbelief is a precarious support for toleration, because it leaves the door open for persecution when the stakes are high enough, i.e., when one *does* believe in the relevant cause. (A similar point was made by Catholics who insisted that toleration stems from "indifference," or a lack of interest in religion altogether. As these critics observed, it is easy to tolerate something that one doesn't care about.)

If people believe in exclusive salvation, must they also endorse righteous persecution? This interesting question was answered in the affirmative by W. E. H. Lecky, the great nineteenth-century Irish historian.

Lecky's book, *A History of the Rise and Influence of the Spirit of Rationalism in Europe* (1865), contains a fascinating discussion of persecution. Augustine, according to Lecky, "became the framer and the representative of the theology of intolerance." Augustine consolidated "the whole system of persecution," and upon him "rests the responsibility of this fearful curse."[13]

For Lecky, Augustine's theory of persecution was simply "the direct practical result" of his belief in exclusive salvation. Quoting Lecky:

> If men believe with an intense and realising faith that their own view of a disputed question is true beyond all possibility of mistake, if they further believe that those who adopt other views will be doomed by the Almighty to an eternity of misery . . . these men will, sooner or later, persecute to the full extent of their power.[14]

Lecky's account is vulnerable on two fronts, factual and theoretical. Factually, it is untrue that believers in exclusive salvation have always advocated persecution—as we have seen, for example, with Lactantius (whom Lecky praises). Many other counterexamples suggest themselves: sixteenth-century Anabaptists, seventeenth-century Independents, eighteenth-century Baptists and Congregationalists, nineteenth-century Catholics, and English Dissenters. Prominent representatives of these groups managed to combine belief in exclusive salvation with strong protoleration views.

Theoretically, exclusive salvation does not necessarily entail a theory of persecution. There are five basic reasons for this. First, a salvationist may deny that beliefs can be compelled, thereby rejecting persecution as futile. Second, a salvationist, even one who concedes that force can influence beliefs, may contend that faith must be given freely if it is to have value. Third, a salvationist might believe that the Bible expressly prohibits persecution. Fourth, a salvationist, working from a theory of natural rights, might argue that persecution is unjust, whatever its supposed benefits. Fifth, a salvationist might argue that an open society, a society with freedom of religion, is far more conducive to the spread of Christian ideas and values than is a closed society. All of these arguments would contribute to the Christian defense of toleration.

Thomas Aquinas on Heresy

After Christianity became the state religion in the fourth century, Christian voices in favor of toleration were rarely heard. This is understandable, for the hare is more likely than the hound to abhor bloodsports. There were exceptions, however. In 365, St. Hilary of Poitiers condemned the Church's new role as persecutor:

> The Church terrifieth with threats of exile and dungeons; and she, who of old gained men's faith in spite of exile and prison, now brings them to believe in her by compulsion. . . . She, who was propagated by hunted priests, now hunts priests in her turn. . . .[15]

When the Emperor Charlemagne (c. 742–814) decreed that Saxon heathens must choose between baptism or death, he was opposed by Alcuin, his religious and educational advisor.

> Faith is a matter of will, not of necessity. How can you force a man to believe what he does not believe? One can force baptism on people, but not faith. Man, an intelligent being, reasons; disposition, and desire for truth ought to bring him to recognize the truth of our holy faith. And prayer, above all, ought to bring down upon him the mercy of Almighty God; for argument echoes in vain, if the dew of grace does not wet the heart of the hearer.[16]

The twelfth century was a time of intellectual ferment and relative liberalism in Europe—perhaps because the more bloodthirsty Christians were off in distant lands, butchering infidels for Christ. During this period, the right of erring conscience was recognized by a few prominent theologians, including Abelard and Peter Lombard, who said that the Church needs heretics, "because they stimulate us as Catholics in our search for truth and for a proper understanding of everything in the world."[17]

When heretics were massacred in Cologne, St. Bernard protested to the Pope that "faith is a work of persuasion, and cannot be imposed by force."[18] Unfortunately, Bernard, a champion of the bloody Crusades, was less understanding of Moslem infidels: "The Christian glories in the death of the pagan, because Christ is thereby glorified."

The thirteenth century was a heyday for persecutors, beginning in Southern France with the wholesale massacre of heretics known variously as Cathari (from the Greek meaning "pure"), Bulgari (from their origin in the Balkans), and Albigenses (from the French town of Albi, where they were especially numerous).

The cruelties of the Albigensian crusade almost defy belief. As crusaders laid seige to the Albigensian headquarters at Beziers (1209), the papal legate was asked whether upon taking the town orthodox Catholics should be spared. His answer lives in infamy: "Kill them all, for God knows his own." The sorting process must have occupied God for some time, because thousands of men, women, and children were put to the sword. Upon hearing this good news, Pope Innocent III gave thanks for a double blessing: The wicked were being killed, and their killers were that much closer to attaining salvation.

> God hath mercifully purged His people's land and the pest of heretical wickedness . . . is being deadened and driven away. . . . Wherefore we give praise and thanks to God Almighty, because in one and the same cause of His mercy, He hath deigned to work two works of justice, by bringing upon these faithless folks their merited destruction, in such a fashion that as many as possible of the faithful should gain their well-earned reward by the "extermination" of these folk.[19]

When the castle of Brom was taken, the victors, according to a contemporary account, "tore out the eyes of more than 100 of the defenders, and cut off their noses, leaving only one eye to a single one of the crew, that he might lead all the rest to Cabaret in mockery of our enemies."[20] When Minerve surrendered, 140 stubborn Cathari were burned alive in a "plentiful fire." At Lavaur, the gallows collapsed after the first hanging, so around eighty knights were slain "forthwith on the spot." After the lady of this castle had been dumped in a well and buried with stones, "our Crusaders burned innumerable heretics with prodigious joy." Another sixty were torched at Casses. And so it went, as thousands died for unacceptable beliefs.

W. E. H. Lecky had such atrocities in mind when he wrote that "the Church of Rome has shed more innocent blood than any other institution that has ever existed among mankind. . . ."[21] Perhaps Lecky was fortunate to have died in 1903, before Hitler, Stalin, and others of their ilk proved that persecution and mass murder—on a scale unimaginable to the medieval Church—are not the prerogatives of religion.

As the Church went about killing heretics, intellectuals rallied to her defense. Thomas Aquinas (c. 1224–74) discussed heresy in his voluminous *Summa Theologica*, and his views profoundly influenced Church policy. (In 1542, when Pope Paul III reconstituted the Holy Office of the Inquisition in Rome, he used the arguments of Aquinas.)

Aquinas, like theologians before him, distinguishes unbelief from heresy. Pure unbelievers are those who have never accepted the Christian religion, such as Jews and Moslems. These unbelievers should be punished if they blaspheme or commit other sins, but they should not be forced to accept Christianity.

Heretics, however, are a different matter, because heresy is a special kind of unbelief "pertaining to those who profess the Christian faith, but corrupt its dogmas."[22]

Unlike pure unbelievers, heretics should be compelled to accept the correct doctrines. Why? Because heretics, having pledged themselves to God, "should be submitted even to bodily compulsion, that they may fulfill what they have promised, and hold what they at one time received."[23]

The heretic betrays his pledge to God and so corrupts the very religion he professes to accept. This affront to God, Aquinas explains, deserves the death penalty.

> Heretics deserve not only to be separated from the Church by excommunication, but also to be severed from the world by death. For it is a much graver matter to corrupt the faith which quickens the soul, than to forge money, which supports temporal life. Therefore, if forgers of money and other evil-doers are condemned to death at once by the secular authority, much more reason is there for heretics, as soon as they are convicted of heresy, to be not only excommunicated, but even put to death.[24]

Although heretics deserve death for their first offense, the Church, merciful as always, should not inflict this penalty until the second relapse into heresy. This reasoned barbarism of Aquinas surpasses even that of Augustine, who had favored mere fines and banishment.

Protestant Persecution, Pro and Con

The Catholic Church regarded sixteenth-century Protestants as heretics worthy of death, and many of them paid that price. It is hardly surprising, therefore, that some Protestant leaders called for toleration (for themselves, at least).

In 1523, shortly after Martin Luther had split from the Catholic Church (and while his life was still in danger), he published a defense of toleration. Luther cites "the well-known saying, found also in Augustine, 'No one can or ought to be constrained to believe.' " He then summarizes this time-honored argument: "[I]t is useless and impossible to command or compel any one by force to believe one thing or another. It must be taken hold of in a different way; force cannot accomplish it."[25]

Luther thus proclaims the inability of persecution to accomplish its goal: "Heresy can never be prevented by force." If God's word does not correct heretics, "the end . . . will remain unaccomplished through secular power, though it fill the world with blood."[26]

Luther admits that persecution can compel conformity "by word and deed," but such outward conformity, when it does not flow from inner conviction, is sheer hypocrisy. Persecutors "cannot constrain [the heart], though they wear themselves out trying. For the proverb is true, Thoughts are free'."[27]

For Luther, salvation is a gift freely bestowed by God. This is another reason why persecution is futile.

> Faith is a free work, to which no one can be forced. Nay, it is a divine work, done in the Spirit, certainly not a matter which outward authority should compel or create.[28]

If Luther had written nothing else on toleration, he might have received accolades from succeeding generations, believers and unbelievers alike. But (as sympathetic biographers might say) Luther was a complex and tormented man who advocated different policies at different times. Or (as unsympathetic biographers might say) an older Luther—ensconced in power, his life and future secure—betrayed his principles and turned from persecuted to persecutor.

There is no doubt about it: after aligning with sympathetic German princes (who were concerned more with power and loot than religion) Luther became a fierce advocate of persecution. We see this in his attitude toward the Anabaptists ("rebaptizers")—those Protestants who believed in adult baptism and mocked infant baptism as "the Popish bath." Anabaptists were savagely persecuted by both Catholics and Protestants, and many thousands were cruelly tortured and slain. (Protestants, in a display of grotesque humor, liked to "baptize" Anabaptists by drowning them in rivers.)

Luther initially defended freedom for Anabaptists ("Let every one believe what he likes"), but he later called for the extermination of all heretics, along with Catholics who did not acknowledge themselves enemies of Christ and the Emperor.

> Heretics are not to be disputed with, but to be condemned unheard, and whilst they perish by fire, the faithful ought to pursue the evil to its source, and bathe their hands in the blood of the Catholic bishops, and of the Pope, who is a devil in disguise.[29]

Jews also felt the sting of Luther's hateful intolerance:

> Burn the synagogues; take away their books, including the Bible. They should be compelled to work, denied food and shelter, preferably banished. If they mention the name of God, report them to the magistrate or throw Saudreck [pig dung] on them. Moses said that idolators should not be tolerated. If he were here he would be the first to burn their synagogues.[30]

If Martin Luther provided erratic support for toleration, another Reformer, the Frenchman John Calvin, provided none at all. Calvin rejected Catholicism, but he did not reject the Catholic theory of persecution: "Because the Papists persecute the truth, should we on that account refrain from repressing error?"

Calvin believed in predestination, so he recognized that persecution is powerless to win converts. But Calvin believed that heresy and blasphemy insult the supreme majesty of God, and should be punished for that reason. Punishment vindicates the honor of God.

Calvin was the hardest among hard-liners. Under no circumstances should secular authorities tolerate heretics and blasphemers. Indeed, "Those who would spare heretics and blasphemers are themselves blasphemers." Such "implacable severity" is required because "devotion to God's honor should be preferred to all human concerns." And, in pursuit of this end, we "should expunge from memory our mutual humanity" as we exterminate heretics with righteous zeal.[31]

Calvin proved as good as his word. In 1553, he engineered the gruesome execution of the Spaniard Michael Servetus, a brilliant philosopher, scientist, and physician. Servetus was adjudged a criminal for two reasons, each punishable by death in Roman law: he rejected the Trinity as a needless, incomprehensible doctrine, and he denied the efficacy of infant baptism.

While hiding in France under an assumed name, Servetus sent a manuscript copy of his last book (*The Restoration of Christianity*) to Calvin in Geneva. Servetus apparently hoped the great Reformer would view the book sympathetically—a naive and fatal miscalculation.

Calvin never returned the manuscript; he had a better use for it. He gave four incriminating pages to a colleague, Guillaume Trie, who forwarded them to a Catholic correspondent in France. Trie also revealed the true identity of "Villanovanus," the pseudonym used by Servetus. The Protestant Trie chided Catholics for tolerating this heretic in their midst:

> You suffer a heretic, who well deserves to be burned wherever he may be. I have in mind a man who will be condemned by the Papists as much as by us or ought to be. . . . Where I'd like to know is the zeal which you pretend? Where is the police of this fine hierarchy of which you so boast?[32]

The tactic of Calvin and Trie almost worked. Servetus was convicted of heresy, but, before he could be roasted over a slow Catholic fire, he managed to escape and head for Italy. Unfortunately, Servetus chose a route that took him through Calvin's Geneva, where he was recognized, charged with thirty-nine counts of heresy and blasphemy, and sentenced to death for trying "to infect the world with [his] stinking heretical poison."

On October 27th, 1553, Servetus was bound to a stake with a rope twisted around his neck, his book tied to an arm, and a Protestant fire stirring below. It took thirty minutes for Servetus to die, thereby vindicating the honor of Calvin's God.

The execution of Servetus marked a turning point in the history of toleration. True, disposing of heretics was nothing new to Protestants, but their previous judicial murders had been defended primarily on political grounds. (Some Anabaptists, for example, displayed anarchist, socialist, or—worst of all—polygamist tendencies.) Servetus threatened no one politically; that brilliant intellectual was burned solely for heresy, and fellow Protestants had lit the fire. This spectacle appalled a handful of Protestant humanists, including the Frenchman Sebastian Castellio.

Sadly, Castellio is virtually unknown today, except to scholars. Yet, if we engage in the decidedly value-laden search for heroes from the past, and if we rank candidates based on their contributions to liberty, then Castellio towers above Augustine, Aquinas, Luther, Calvin, and other familiar names. If anyone deserves to be called a founding father of toleration, that person is Castellio.

While in that mini-police state called Geneva, Castellio quarreled with Calvin over doctrine. This could prove dangerous to one's health, so Castellio moved to Basel, where he eventually became a professor of Greek.

Basel (by sixteenth-century standards) was a bastion of tolerance and liberalism—thanks largely to the influence of the Catholic humanist Erasmus, who had lived there for seven years. Many Protestants, suffocating from the oppressive atmosphere in their native lands, fled to Basel in search of more tolerant air.[33]

Castellio protested Servetus's murder with *Concerning Heretics*, a book filled with protoleration passages from early Church fathers and others. The task of responding to this thinly veiled attack on Calvin fell to his faithful henchman, Theodore Beza, who called Servetus "of all men that have ever lived the most wicked and blasphemous." Toleration, Beza exclaimed, is a diabolical doctrine, and its defenders are "emissaries of Satan."

Castellio retaliated with another book; this time he attacked Calvin directly:

> If it is not blind rage to torture in the flames a man who is calling on the name of Christ, and not only is not convicted but is not even accused of any crime, then there is no such thing as blind rage.[34]

Castellio argued that Calvin had no right to execute Servetus for his beliefs:

> To kill a man is not to protect a doctrine, but it is to kill a man. When the Genevans killed Servetus, they did not defend a doctrine, but they killed a man. To protect a doctrine is not the Magistrate's affair (what has the sword to do with doctrine?) but the teacher's. But it is the magistrate's affair to protect the teacher, as it is to protect the farmer, and the smith, and the physician and others

> against injury. Thus if Servetus had wished to kill Calvin, the Magistrate would properly have defended Calvin. But when Servetus fought with reasons and writings, he should have been repulsed by reasons and writings.[35]

Other Protestants followed Castellio's lead and condemned the burning of Servetus. "The dogs," Calvin complained, "are yelping at me from every quarter. . . . Every slander that can be invented is being heaped upon me."

Various Reformers clustered around Castellio in Basel and subsequently carried the torch of toleration throughout Europe. After the Italian scholar Acontius left Basel, he wrote *Satan's Strategems*, an extraordinary analysis of intolerance. Mino Celso quoted liberally from Castellio in his defense of toleration. The former Franciscan Benardino Ochino, a friend of Castellio's, argued that "it is not needful to use sword or violence" when driving Satan from the hearts of men. Castellio's writings also influenced Faustus Socinus, a founder of Unitarianism and a strong voice for toleration in Poland.

Many Polish students attended the University of Basel and returned home thoroughly imbued with Castellio's spirit. During the 1570s, under Catholic rule, Poland became the first country to establish a policy of toleration. Poland's grand chancellor, John Zamoyski, remarked: "I would give half my life to bring back to Catholicism those who have abandoned it, but I would give my whole life to prevent them from being brought back by violence."[36] Castellio's works were also admired in Holland—a country destined (after considerable bloodshed) to become a showcase for the beneficial effects of toleration.

The English Controversy

During the 1640s, England witnessed the climax of decades of hostility between the Stuart monarchy and its opponents, resulting in the English civil wars, the beheading of Charles I, a short-lived Commonwealth, and the Protectorate (i.e., dictatorship) of Oliver Cromwell.

Enemies of the Stuart monarchy are sometimes called Puritans, because they wished to purify the Church of England of its Catholic rituals. But the term "Puritan" is misleading, because it suggests a uniformity of opinion that was by no means present. Revolutionaries included the intolerant Presbyterians and the more tolerant Independents (later called Congregationalists), who stressed the voluntary nature of church membership.

Then there were the "sectaries," a bewildering array of fringe groups. These included Ranters, Seekers, Quakers, Muggletonians, Socinians, Anabaptists, Brownists, Fifth-Monarchy Men—the list seems endless. These sects were often steeped in mysticism and millenarianism, and some of their political beliefs flirted with anarchism.

Government contol of the press broke down during the 1640s, thereby opening the floodgates for radical literature. This decade, one of the most fascinating in modern history, produced an astonishing variety of opinions—from extreme irrationalism to religious skepticism. Indeed, as Christopher Hill, Keith Thomas, and other historians have shown, anti-Christian views, and even atheism, found advocates among the "lower classes."

Clergymen who complained of rampant "atheism" may not have been exaggerating. In 1616, a Worcestershire man said that the word of God was simply man's invention. In 1633, Richard Sharp was accused of saying that "there is no God and that he hath no soul to save." From Durham in 1635 came the case of Brian Walker who, when asked if he did not fear God, replied, "I do not believe there is either God or Devil; neither will I believe anything but what I see."[37]

The religious establishment, whether Anglican or Presbyterian, responded to dissent with predictable handwringing. Of course, the issue here was as much political as religious, because a state church was supposed to instill the virtue of passive obedience. As King Charles I said, "Religion is the only firm foundation of all power." Bishop Goodman agreed, "The church and state do mutually support and give assistance to each other." Or, in the words of an astute observer, "The state pays the clergy, and thus they have dependence upon the state." To challenge the state religion was to challenge the political status quo.

Various radicals challenged the English status quo during the 1640s, thereby sparking the great debate on religious liberty, indeed, on liberty of all kinds. The case for toleration was broadened and placed on firmer ground, as radicals proclaimed religious liberty to be a natural right that should fall beyond the reach of government. We see this in the political platform of the Levellers, extreme individualists who advocated religious liberty for everyone, Catholics and atheists included. This proposal was so unusual that even John Milton and John Locke (decades later) did not endorse it.

In their first "Agreement of the People" (1647), the Levellers called liberty of conscience a "native right." Human authorities should have nothing to say in matters of belief and worship, "because therein we cannot remit or exceed a title of what our Consciences dictate to be the mind of God, without willful sin. . . ."[38]

This position rested on the classical argument expounded by Tertullian, Lactantius, and others. Beliefs, as such, cannot be willed in and out of existence, so they cannot be altered by coercion. As the Leveller William Walwyn put it in 1644:

> Of what judgment soever a man is, he cannot choose but be of that judgment. . . . [N]ow where there is necessity there ought to be no punishment, for punishment is the recompense of voluntary actions, therefore no man ought to be punished for his judgment.[39]

John Locke reiterated this argument nearly fifty years later in *A Letter Concerning Toleration:* "it is absurd that things should be enjoined by laws, which are not in men's power to perform; and to believe this or that to be true, does not depend upon our will."[40]

The Levellers regarded liberty of conscience as part of one's "self-propriety" or, as John Locke later phrased it, "property in one's person." The Leveller Richard Overton, writing in 1646, stated this premise thusly:

> To every individual in nature, is given an individual property by nature, not to be invaded or usurped by any: for every one as he is himself, so he hath a self propriety, else could he not be himself, and on this no second [person] may presume to deprive any of, without manifest violation and affront to the very principles of nature, and of the rules of equity and justice between man and man. . . .[41]

As part of this right of self-proprietorship, "every man by nature [is] Priest and Prophet in his own natural circuit and compass. . . ." In other words, according to Overton, every person is a self-owner and so has the fundamental right to determine his own religious beliefs and practices. Other persons, including those in government, cannot justly interfere with the exercise of this right "but by deputation, commission, and free consent from him, whose natural right and freedom it is."[42]

Here, with the Leveller argument from self-proprietorship, we have the essence of what later theorists (James Madison, for example) called "property in one's conscience," i.e., the natural right to believe as one sees fit. This became a standard argument used by eighteenth-century proponents of religious liberty in Europe and America. And it was this argument from natural rights that broke the back of Augustine's theory of righteous persecution. Rights establish boundaries to the interference of others, even when that interference is undertaken for supposedly good motives. Thus, a theory of righteous persecution cannot gain a foothold in a regime of natural rights.

We see this in John Locke's *Letter Concerning Toleration*. For Locke, "liberty of conscience is every man's natural right," and governments should protect this right. When a man minds his own business, others should leave him alone, even if his behavior is self-destructive. Quoting Locke:

> The care of every man's soul belongs unto himself, and is to be left unto himself. But what if he neglect the care of his soul? I answer, what if he neglect the care of his health, or of his estate; which things are nearlier related to the government of the magistrate than the other? Will the magistrate provide by an express law, that such an one shall not become poor or sick? Laws provide, as much as

> is possible, that the goods and health of subjects be not injured by the fraud or violence of others; they do not guard them from the negligence or ill-husbandry of the possessors themselves. No man can be forced to be rich or healthful, whether he will or no. Nay God himself will not save men against their wills.[43]

What of another popular argument for persecution: that governments should stamp out sin? Locke will have none of this:

> Idolatry, some say, is a sin, and therefore not to be tolerated. If they said it were therefore to be avoided, the inference were good. But it does not follow, that because it is a sin it ought therefore to be punished by the magistrate. For it does not belong unto the magistrate to make use of his sword in punishing everything, indifferently, that he takes to be a sin against God. Covetousness, uncharitableness, idleness, and many other things are sins, by the consent of all men, which yet no man ever said were to be punished by the magistrate. The reason is, because they are not prejudicial to other men's rights, nor do they break the public peace of societies.[44]

With the rise of the natural rights school, the demand for toleration expanded to a more radical demand for liberty of conscience. Thomas Paine, referring to the French Constitution of 1791, put the distinction this way:

> The French constitution hath abolished or renounced *Toleration*, and *Intolerance* also, and hath established UNIVERSAL RIGHT OF CONSCIENCE.
>
> Toleration is not the *opposite* of Intolerance, but is the *counterfeit* of it. Both are despotisms. The one assumes to itself the right of withholding Liberty of Conscience, and the other of granting it.[45]

Social Arguments for Toleration

Social arguments for toleration—those that stress its beneficial effects on society—generally fall into two categories.

Tolerationists in the first category desired uniformity of belief *in theory,* but they did not wish to impose uniformity *in practice* because of its staggering social costs—massive compulsion, civil wars, and social chaos. Perhaps the best known advocates of this approach were the *politiques*—French moderates (mainly Catholic) who grew sick of the incessant wars between Catholics and Calvinists (Huguenots) in sixteenth-century France.

The politiques were more concerned about social stability than religious doctrine, and they recommended toleration as the only way to restore peace. Fortunately for France, two assassinations and an accident of heredity raised the politique Henry of Navarre to the French throne as Henry IV, first of the Bourbon dynasty.

Henry had been a Huguenot chieftan, but as king he acted with the savvy of a true politique: He abjured Calvinism and embraced Catholicism, thereby placating the Catholic majority. Then, in 1598, sensible Henry forced the Edict of Nantes down the throat of his stubborn countrymen. This established a broad range of religious and political liberties for the Huguenot minority and brought internal peace to a war-torn France.

Some historians attribute the rise of toleration more to the politique way of thinking than to strictly ideological arguments. Practical men, sickened by the bloodshed and turmoil caused by religious conflict, opted for toleration as the only realistic solution.

This is true, to a point, but we should not underestimate the role of ideology. So long as men believed in the *desirability* of religious uniformity as an abstract goal, there remained the possibility that the toleration granted for political reasons could be rescinded for the same reasons. Indeed, we see this with the Edict of Nantes. In 1685, when Louis XIV no longer regarded the Huguenots as a significant threat, he revoked the Edict of Nantes, thereby causing many Huguenots to seek refuge in other countries. This illustrates the point raised by Thomas Paine: what the state gives the state can also take away.

Some theorists, of course, defended toleration in principle, while underscoring its practical necessity. The philosopher Spinoza belongs to this camp. An eloquent spokesman for liberty of conscience, Spinoza also believed, "it is imperative that freedom of judgment should be granted, so that men may live together in harmony, however diverse, or even openly contradictory, their opinions may be."[46]

The relationship between toleration and social harmony was not just an abstract notion in Spinoza's mind; he could point to seventeenth-century Amsterdam, one of the most prosperous *and* tolerant cities in Europe.

> The city of Amsterdam reaps the fruit of freedom in its own great prosperity and in the admiration of all other people. For in this most flourishing state, and most splendid city, men of every nation and religion live together in the greatest harmony, and ask no questions before trusting their goods to a fellow-citizen. A citizen's religion and sect is considered of no importance: for it has no effect before the judges in gaining or losing a cause, and there is no sect so despised that its followers, provided that they harm no one, pay every man his due, and live uprightly, are deprived of the protection of the magisterial authority.[47]

During the 1720s, while a young Voltaire was living in exile, he made a similar observation about England's religious toleration. Compared to France, England was a breath of fresh air. Why was this so?

Voltaire knew that toleration in England was a product of complex forces. Ideas were important, as was the embodiment of ideas in law. But there was more: England lacked the rigid class structure of his native France. The English nobility was small compared to France's, and it did not possess the same legal privileges. Upward mobility was common in England, thanks to the strong and industrious middle class. Business and commerce, spurned by the French aristocracy, were greatly admired in England. If England was "a nation of shopkeepers," this was for Voltaire no insult but the source of England's prosperity and liberty. "The English sell themselves," he wrote, "which is a proof that they are worth something; we French do not sell ourselves, probably because we are worth nothing."

Central to Voltaire's analysis was his belief that Britain's developing market economy was a key to its religious liberty. When individuals engage in trade for mutual benefit, their beliefs become irrelevant. The desire for profit is stronger than religious prejudice. Wrote Voltaire:

> Go into the London Stock Exchange—a more respectable place than many a court—and you will see representatives from all nations gathered together for the utility of men. Here Jew, Mohammedan and Christian deal with each other as though they were all of the same faith, and only apply the word infidel to people who go bankrupt. Here the Presbyterian trusts the Anabaptist and the Anglican accepts a promise from the Quaker. On leaving these peaceful and free assemblies some go to the Synagogue and others for a drink, this one goes to be baptized in a great bath in the name of the Father, Son and Holy Ghost, that one has his son's foreskin cut and has some Hebrew words he doesn't understand mumbled over the child, others go to their church and await the inspiration of God with their hats on, and everybody is happy.[48]

Karl Marx would later attack the market economy for its impersonal nature; a market exchange reduces human labor to the level of commodities. Ironically, the impersonal nature of the market was for Voltaire (and others of his time) the source of its greatness. The ability to deal with others impersonally, to deal with them solely for mutual profit, means that personal characteristics, such as religious belief, become largely irrelevant.

During the 1650s, when Oliver Cromwell readmitted Jews to England for the first time in centuries, he was motivated by their skill as merchants. Holland, England's chief commercial rival, did not indulge in such prejudice, and neither could England if she wished to compete in international markets. When commerce was despised, when charging interest on loans was condemned as usury, Jews could be persecuted. But as economic views changed, so did the need for toleration.

This brings us to the second category of arguments for toleration. Proponents of this approach extolled the benefits of religious pluralism *in theory*. They believed that, as different beliefs compete in a marketplace of ideas, truth (or its closest approximation) will eventually emerge triumphant.

The argument that truth will emerge from the free interplay of ideas became common during the seventeenth-century, especially among English theorists. The preeminent defense of this view was John Milton's *Aereopagitica* (1644). The quest for knowledge, Milton argues, is an ongoing process that should not be obstructed by laws.

> Well knows he who uses to consider, that our faith and knowledge thrives by exercise, as well as our limbs and complexion. Truth is compared in scripture to a streaming fountain; if her waters flow not in a perpetual progression, they sicken into a muddy pool of conformity and tradition.[49]

Milton was a sincere Protestant, but he did not believe that the Reformation had ended with the teachings of Calvin. Rather, the Reformation is a progessive gathering of knowledge that will continue until the return of Jesus. Truth "may have more shapes than one," so religious pluralism is necessary if the various pieces of knowledge are to be discovered and integrated.

> To be still searching what we know not by what we know, still closing up truth to truth as we find it (for all her body is homogeneal and proportional) this is the golden rule in theology as well as in arithmetic, and makes up the best harmony in a church; not the forced and outward union of cold, and neutral, and inwardly divided minds.[50]

According to Milton, religious diversity, far from being undesirable, is a sign of intellectual vigor.

> Where there is much desire to learn, there of necessity will be much arguing, much writing, many opinions; for opinion in good men is but knowledge in the making.[51]

If we wish truth to succeed, we need only allow it to compete in a free marketplace of ideas.

> [T]hough all the winds of doctrine were let loose to play upon the earth, so truth be in the field, we do injurously by licensing and prohibiting to misdoubt her strength. Let her and falsehood grapple; who ever knew truth put to the worse, in a free and open encounter. Her confuting is the best and surest suppressing.[52]

Milton distrusts those who favor coercion over persuasion in the battle of ideas. If a man believes he posseses the truth, then let him convince others by argument, not compel them by threats. Error alone relies on force:

> For who know not that truth is strong next to the almighty; she needs no policies, nor strategems, nor licensing to make her victorious; those are the shifts and the defenses that error uses against her power. Give her but room, and do not bind her when she sleeps, for then she speaks not true.[53]

Thus does Milton issue his grand proclamation: "Give me the liberty to know, to utter, and to argue freely according to conscience, above all liberties."[54]

Spinoza agreed: "such freedom is absolutely necessary for progress in science and the liberal arts: for no man follows such pursuits to advantage unless his judgment be entirely free and unhampered."[55] John Locke was another who maintained that truth will fare well in the ideological marketplace:

> Truth certainly would do well enough, if she were once made to shift for herself. She seldom has received, and I fear never will receive, much assistance from the power of great men, to whom she is but rarely known, and more rarely welcome. She is not taught by laws, nor has she any need of force to procure her entrance into the minds of men.[56]

Truth and Free Trade

In 1643, Henry Robinson published *Liberty of Conscience*, a remarkable defense of complete toleration. Robinson was among a growing number of English merchants who opposed trade restrictions and government-granted monopolies. Not surprisingly, therefore, Robinson's case for toleration was based on a free-trade analogy—"free trading of truth," as he put it.[57]

This free-trade analogy became increasingly popular among proponents of toleration. They maintained that free trade in ideas, like free trade in commerce, will benefit all concerned.

John Milton used this analogy in presenting his case against the licensing of books.

> There is yet behind of what I purposed to lay open, the incredible loss and detriment that this plot of licensing puts us to; more than if some enemy at sea should stop up all our havens and ports and creeks, it hinders and retards the importation of our richest Merchandise, Truth.[58]

By the early 1800s, British Liberals explicitly defended freedom in religion as one aspect of free trade. We commonly find expressions like "free trade in religion" and "free trade in Christianity" among foes of the Established Church.

One example should illustrate the point. In 1838, a leading dissenting journal reviewed a book by Thomas Chalmers, *Lectures on the Establishment and Extension of National Churches*. Chalmers, a Professor of Theology at the University of Edinburgh, was a noted defender of the Established Church of England.

Free trade arguments for disestablishment had become so popular—and threatening—that Chalmers considered it necessary to launch an all-out attack on those who were "for the system of free trade in Christianity." Chalmers didn't believe that Christianity should depend on the law of supply and demand. The natural demand for religion is insufficient, so it must be supported by contributions—

or "bounties," to use the economic term. Thus, according to Chalmers, the demand for religion does not govern the supply; rather, through preaching and education, ministers must create a demand for religion that would otherwise be missing.

The anonymous dissenter who reviewed Chalmer's book identified the error in his reasoning. Chalmers confuses voluntary contributions with state bounties. Nothing in the free trade principle forbids the former: "nothing more can be meant by the free-trade principle in religion, than that *Government* should not interfere to restrict the supply by a jealous monopoly."

Chalmers said, "we do not sell the Gospel, but give it," and this is a kind of bounty—the very thing denounced by advocates of free trade. The reviewer responds:

> It is no such thing; it is nothing like what is understood by a bounty, which is a premium paid by government to encourage mercantile enterprises for the ostensible benefit, not of the consumer, but of the producer; and, generally speaking, bounties have been granted to uphold monopolies, and to counteract the effects of beneficial competition. . . . What, in the name of common sense, does Dr. Chalmers understand by the principle of free trade? The epithet has no meaning, in this connexion, but as opposed to injurious monopolies and restrictions. [Free trade] only requires that the State should not embarrass by fiscal restrictions the operations of commerce. Its motto is Laissez-faire. Protect trade, but do not force it by injurious patronage. Let it find its own channels. Do not, by a system of bounties, make the many pay for the benefit of the few.[59]

Chalmers argued that the object of trade is profit, but profit should not be the object of religious instruction. The reviewer agrees with this, but asks, "What has this to do with the question, whether the supply should be *free*—whether, so far as the analogy holds good, the principle of free trade, rather than of monopoly, should be adhered to?"[60]

Previously, we examined the belief that competition in the marketplace of ideas will produce truth. Society doesn't need a central planner, such as an Established Church, to impose its vision of truth on others. British Liberals were committed to free trade in ideas, and this allowed them to pursue common goals, despite a broad range of religious differences. Each sect within Liberalism believed that its version of the truth would emerge victorious.

This point can be illustrated with two Liberals whose religious views were strikingly different: Henry Thomas Buckle, author of *History of Civilization in England* (1857-61), ardent rationalist, and a hero to a generation of freethinkers; and Edward Miall, a Congregationalist and editor of *The Nonconformist*—the leading periodical to call for church disestablishment. Let's first consider Buckle.

Religious persecution, according to Buckle, is "a greater evil than any other," even war. With the advance of knowledge and science, however, Buckle saw progress on the horizon, provided that liberty—the foundation of progress—was preserved. Soon, "men will cease to be terrified by phantoms which their own ignorance has reared. . . . The dominion of superstition, already decaying, shall break away, and crumble into dust."[61]

This requires the lessening of state power. "No great political improvement, no great reform, either legislative or executive, has ever been originated in any country by its rulers." On the contrary, "every government has inflicted on its subjects great injuries." Like Voltaire, Buckle asked why the record of toleration was so much better in England than in France. He attributed France's backwardness to its "protective spirit"—the prevalence of state interference in virtually every aspect of life.

> At the slightest difficulty, [the French] call on the government for support. What with us is competition, with them is monopoly. That which we effect by private companies they effect by public boards. They cannot cut a canal, or lay down a railroad, without appealing to the government for aid. With them, the people look to the rulers: with us the rulers look to the people.[62]

According to Buckle, the English people were sharpened by the discipline of freedom, and they were unwilling to relinquish it. This was the source of their liberties in general and of their religious liberty in particular. Liberty promotes virtue, but the state represses and distorts the best in people. Thus, for Buckle, laissez-faire is not just an economic system; it is a principle that enobles the human spirit. Buckle praises Adam Smith as a great benefactor to mankind, for, in *The Wealth of Nations*, he demonstrated the existence of a natural social order that operates independently of conscious planning.

In 1845, Edward Miall published *Views of the Voluntary Principle.* And although Miall's religious views could scarcely differ more from Buckle's strident rationalism, both writers agree in their social and political principles. Religious liberty is seen by Miall as part of the struggle for liberty in all spheres of life. The failures of Christianity were caused by its attempts to coerce, because coercion injects disharmony and division into human interaction. Quoting Miall:

> National churches are necessarily jealous, selfish, and, as far as the spirit of the age will allow them, tyrannical. Interwoven with the interests of the civil empire, they become to the state additional sources of, and incitements to, hostile collision.[63]

According to Miall, liberty furthers spiritual values, whereas state coercion reduces religion to the mundane level of a struggle for power. Religion "is a matter which should be left to something higher than law to regulate—should represent, not the efficiency of a command from without, but the power of a principle within—should grow out of living motives, rather than stand as the lifeless result of legal authority. . . ."[64]

As an advocate of laissez-faire, Miall believed in a natural spontaneous order—an order that emerges from human action, but is not the result of human design. And, like many of his contemporaries, Miall applies this notion of spontaneous order to the realm of ideas.

> No sooner does truth come in contact with the mind of man, than instantly it diffuses itself so widely, works in individual cases in such a variety of ways, sets in motion so many wheels, that it ceases to be under the management of man. . . . No eye can follow its track—no intelligence can mark its course. . . . It depends upon the will of no mortal, or assemblage of mortals, whether it shall stay on earth, when once it has been introduced hither. It asks no man's leave to stay and live here. Stay and live it will, whoever may say nay.[65]

Miall reaches a radical conclusion: "Though all the machinery of government should be swept away tomorrow, nothing which exists of real Christianity would die."[66]

Thus, Buckle and Miall—a skeptic and a Christian—could both extol the virtues of laissez-faire (economic *and* ideological), thanks to their belief in the value of pluralism.

Much of Classical Liberalism doctrine grew from the struggle for liberty of conscience. Much of it was developed with an eye to man's inner selves—our need for spiritual values and moral autonomy. It is true that economic theory came to play an important role in Liberalism, but this should not be viewed as its sum and substance. Economic laissez-faire, for many Liberals, was simply an application of a broader kind of laissez-faire—the freedom of individuals to think, speak, and act as they see fit, so long as they respect the equal rights of others. This was the lesson to be learned from the struggle for religious toleration.

Notes

1. *To Scapula*, trans. Rev. S. Thelwall, *The Ante-Nicene Fathers* (New York: Charles Scribner's Sons, 1905), vol. III, p. 105.
2. *The Divine Institutes*, trans. William Fletcher, *The Works of Lactantius*, (Edinburgh: T.and T. Clark, n.d.), p. 340.
3. Ibid. pp. 339-40.
4. Ibid., p. 340.
5. Ibid., p. 343.

6. Ibid.

7. *The Political Writings of St. Augustine*, ed. Henry Paolucci (Chicago: Henry Regnery, 1962), pp. 197-8. For an excellent discussion of Augustine's theory of persecution, see Herbert A. Deane, *The Political and Social Ideas of St. Augustine* (New York: Columbia University Press, 1963), pp. 172-220.

8. *The Political Writings*, p. 203.

9. Ibid., p. 214.

10. Ibid., p. 228.

11. Ibid., p. 229.

12. Ibid.

13. William Edward Hartpole Lecky, *History of the Rise and Influence of the Spirit of Rationalism in Europe* (London: Watts and Co., 1946), vol. II, p. 8.

14. Ibid., p. 1.

15. Quoted in G. G. Coulton, *Inquisition and Liberty* (Boston: Beacon Press, 1959), p. 16.

16. Quoted in Christopher Hollis, "Religious Persecution," in *European Civilization: Its Origin and Development* (London: Oxford University Press, 1936), vol. IV, p. 672.

17. Quoted in Friedrich Herr, *The Medieval World*, trans. Janet Sondheimer (Cleveland: The World Publishing Co., 1962), p. 112.

18. Quoted in Zoe' Oldenbourg, *Massacre at Montségur*, trans. Peter Green (New York: Pantheon Books, 1968), p. 84.

19. Quoted in Coulton, *Inquisition and Liberty*, p. 103-4.

20. Quoted in ibid., p. 99.

21. Lecky, *History of the Rise and Influence*, vol. II, p. 12.

22. *Summa Theologica*, in *Great Books of the Western World* (Chicago: Encyclopedia Britannica, 1952), vol. II, p. 438.

23. Ibid., p. 432.

24. Ibid., p. 440.

25. *Martin Luther: Selections from his Writings*, ed. John Dillenberger (Garden City, N.Y.: Anchor Books, 1961), p. 385.

26. Ibid., p. 389.

27. Ibid., p. 385.

28. Ibid.

29. Quoted in John Acton, "The Protestant Theory of Persecution," in *The History of Freedom and Other Essays* (London: Macmillan, 1922), p. 164.

30. Quoted in Roland H. Bainton, *Studies on the Reformation* (Boston:

Beacon Press, 1966), p. 30.

31. Quoted in Roland H. Bainton, *Hunted Heretic: The Life and Death of Michael Servetus, 1511-1553* (Boston: Beacon Press, 1960), pp. 170-1.

32. Quoted in ibid., p. 152-3.

33. See the discussion of Basel in Henry Kamen, *The Iron Century* (New York: Praeger, 1972), pp. 257-263.

34. Quoted in Earl M. Wilbur, *A History of Unitarianism: Socinianism and its Antecedents* (Boston: Beacon Press, 1954), p. 203.

35. Ibid.

36. Quoted in J. H. Elliott, *Europe Divided, 1559-1598* (Ithaca: Cornell University Press, 1968), p. 240.

37. Quoted in Keith Thomas, *Religion and the Decline of Magic* (New York: Charles Scribner's Sons, 1971), p. 170. Cf. John Redwood, *Reason, Ridicule, and Religion: The Age of Enlightenment in England, 1660-1750* (London: Thames and Hudson, 1976).

38. *The Levellers in the English Revolution*, ed. G. E. Aylmer (Ithaca: Cornell University Press, 1975), pp. 90-1.

39. *The Compassionate Samaritane* in *The Writings of William Walwyn*, ed. J. McMichael and B. Taft (Athens, Ga.: The University of Georgia Press, 1989), p. 103. I have modernized spelling and punctuation.

40. *The Works of John Locke*, 12th ed. (London, 1824), vol. 5, pp. 39-40.

41. Aylmer, *Levellers in the English Revolution*, p. 68.

42. Ibid., p. 69.

43. *The Works of John Locke*, pp. 23-4.

44. Ibid., p. 36.

45. Thomas Paine, *Rights of Man* (Harmondsworth: Penguin Books, 1969), p. 107.

46. Benedict de Spinoza, *A Theologico-Political Treatise* in *The Chief Works of Benedict de Spinoza*, trans. R. H. M. Elwes (New York: Dover, 1951), vol. I, p. 263.

47. Ibid, p. 264.

48. Voltaire, *Letters on England*, trans. Leonard Tancock (Harmondsworth: Penguin Books, 1980), p. 41.

49. John Milton, *Aereopagitica* in *Milton's Prose Writings* (London: J. M. Dent, 1958), p. 172.

50. Ibid., p. 176.

51. Ibid., p. 177.

52. Ibid., p. 181.

53. Ibid.

54. Ibid., p. 180.

55. Spinoza, A *Theologico-Political Treatise*, p. 26.

56. *The Works of John Locke*, p. 40.

57. See W. K. Jordan, *The Development of Religious Toleration in England* (Gloucester, Mass.: Peter Smith, 1965), vol. 4, pp. 140ff.

58. Milton, *Aereopagitica*, p. 174.

59. *The Eclectic Review* (July 1838), p. 16.

60. Ibid., p. 17.

61. Henry Thomas Buckle, *History of Civilization in England*, ed. John M. Robertson (London: George Routledge & Sons, n.d.).

62. Ibid., p. 358.

63. Edward Miall, *Views of the Voluntary Principle* (London: Aylott and Jones, 1845), p. 170.

64. Ibid., p. 10.

65. Ibid., p. 18.

66. Ibid., p. 20.

7
Deism and the Assault on Revealed Religion

In 1730, the Anglican Bishop of London, Edmund Gibson, warned the people of his diocese to be on guard against some dangerous ideas:

> The Arguments that have been used to support the Cause of Infidelity, may be reduced to two general Heads; one, That there is not *sufficient Evidence* of the Truth and Authority of the Gospel-Revelation; the other, That Reason being a sufficient Guide in Matters of Religion, there was not Need of such a Revelation. The Tendency of the first is to persuade Men to *reject* the Gospel; and the tendency of the second, to satisfy them that they may without danger or inconvenience *lay aside* and *neglect it*; and wherever *either* of these Arguments prevails, the Work of Infidelity is effectually carried on.[1]

This passage refers to the arguments of the English Deists and their allies. Deism, as many scholars have pointed out, eludes a precise definition. Basically, it refers to the belief in a god of nature—a noninterventionist creator who lets the universe run itself according to natural laws. These natural laws can be known through reason, and knowledge of them (including knowledge of the nature of human beings) is necessary *and* sufficient to guide our conduct. The derivation and elaboration of a proper moral code is the essence of a natural and rational religion—the "religion of nature."

Knowledge of nature, for Deists, is the means by which God reveals himself to man, so they often referred to it as *natural* revelation. This contrasts with *special* revelation—divine knowledge supposedly communicated to a particular person or group of persons. Special revelation was often said to be "above" (though not contrary to) reason, so it collided with the Deistic agenda to subject all knowledge claims to rational examination. Reason should render the final verdict in all spheres of knowledge.

Deistic reactions to special revelation ranged from grudging tolerance to skepticism to outright rejection (most typically the latter). Therefore, the Deists undertook critical examinations of the Bible, miracles, prophecy, religious experience, and faith. This aspect of Deistic thought—*critical* Deism, as Leslie Stephen called it[2]—is the focus of this essay.

The Deistic controversy dominated the theological scene in England for the first several decades of the eighteenth century. Many Deists belonged to a political tradition known as Radical Whiggism (a tradition sometimes associated with John Locke, although it had earlier exponents), and this put them in the front line of the battle for religious and civil liberties.

Deistic tracts and books elicited hundreds of replies, which assailed the religious and political tenets of this troublesome movement. The orthodox were alarmed because the Deists carried their fight to the public arena, and some specifically addressed the "lower classes." In a country with an Established Church, this threatened to undermine the religious *and* political status quo.

Modern freethinkers own an incalculable debt to their Deistic forefathers, but many freethinkers know little if anything about them. Thomas Paine's *Age of Reason* is a familiar book, but that justly esteemed classic was written decades after the peak of the Deistic movement in England. And although Paine was more radical—or at least more forthright—than some of his predecessors, virtually all of the critical material in *Age of Reason* can be found in earlier Deistic works.

I have chosen to discuss those Deists who best illustrate the assault on revealed religion. Two of the persons discussed here—Spinoza and Locke—were not Deists, but I have included them because of their influence. I have not included Thomas Hobbes, another influential non-Deist (he was closer to agnosticism), because his critical analyis of the Bible overlaps so much with that of Spinoza. In addition, Hobbes entered the arena of religious controversy with unclean hands, so to speak. He wished to endow the political sovereign (the "supreme pastor") with absolute control over religious practices—a notion wholly alien to the Deistic spirit. If the Deists borrowed from Hobbes, they did so selectively.

Edward Herbert

Edward Herbert (Lord Cherbury) is often called the father of English Deism (a somewhat misleading title, as we shall see). In 1624, while serving as the English ambassador to France, Herbert published *De Veritate* (*On Truth*). This book laments the disunion and disarray of Christianity, which had splintered into a "multitude of sects, divisions, sub-divisions, and cross-divisions." Herbert proposes a solution: five "common notions," which, he argues, are universally accepted and comprise the essence of all true religions. Without these common notions, "it is impossible to establish any standard of discrimination in revelation or even in religion." These notions allow us to pare down religion to essentials, thereby eliminating some needless and divisive dogmas: "Some doctrines due to revelation may be, some of them ought to be, abandoned."

Herbert's attempt to isolate the core precepts of a true religion, and his disdain for superfluous doctrines based on special revelation, anticipate the later Deistic defense of a natural and rational religion.

Herbert spurns some common precepts about faith—e.g., reason must be discarded to make room for faith, the Church is infallible, one should not trust one's private judgment in religious matters, and so forth. Such precepts, Herbert warns, will support the false as easily as the true.

> Now these arguments and many other similar ones . . . may be equally used to establish a false religion as to support a true one. Anything that springs from the productive, not to say seductive seed of Faith will yield a plentiful crop. What pompous charlatan can fail to impress his ragged flock with such ideas? Is there any fantastic cult which may not be proclaimed under such auspices?[3]

Clergymen who "base their beliefs upon the disordered and licentious codes of superstition" are like "people who with the purpose of blinding the eyes of the wayfarer with least trouble to themselves offer with singular courtesy to act as guides on the journey." In religion as elsewhere, we should follow our own judgments, not the judgments of others. Indeed, God "requires every individual to render an account of his actions in the light, not of another's belief, but of his own." This call for independent judgment was destined to become the hallmark of Deism and of freethought generally.

Herbert's common notions function as standards to judge alleged revelations as true or spurious, so that "the genuine dictates of Faith may rest on that foundation as a roof supported by a house." These notions are as follows:

(1) "There is a Supreme God." (Even in polytheism, Herbert contends, a supreme god is recognized. He is blessed, the cause of all things good, just, and wise.) (2) "This Sovereign Deity Ought to be Worshipped." (3) The essential features of religion are virtue and piety. (4) Sins must be expiated by repentance (and, by implication, predestination is incompatible with the justice of God—a slap at Calvinism). (5) "There is Reward or Punishment after this life."[4]

According to Herbert, if a religion doesn't conform to these five notions, then, viewed comprehensively, it is not good, nor does it provide a means to salvation. The key to salvation is good conduct, not belief in various dogmas. "For how could anyone who believes more than is necessary, but who does less than he ought, be saved?"

What is the epistemological status of Herbert's five notions? He regards them as innate ideas implanted by God in the mind from birth.[5] Herbert is aware of the problems generated by a theory of innate ideas, and he tries (rather feebly) to dispose of them. If the existence of a supreme god is an innate idea, then how can we explain the existence of atheists? Herbert replies: "I am not deterred by the fact that irreligious men exist, and even some who appear to be atheists." In fact, such people are not really atheists, because they merely reject a god who has been endowed by some with unworthy attributes. If these "atheists" were presented with a correct portrait of God, "they would pray that such a God might exist, if there were no such Being."[6]

If we still insist on the existence of real atheists, then Herbert bids us to remember that there are always a few "madmen and fools" around—those "men so stubborn and unreasonable that they were incapable of distinguishing truth from probability, possibility and falsity." Herbert is concerned only with "what all men of normal mind believe."[7]

Thus, having posited innate ideas, Herbert dismisses counter-examples as products of abnormal minds. This won't wash, and John Locke, writing decades after Herbert, knew it. In *An Essay Concerning Human Understanding*, Locke launched a devastating attack on innate ideas generally and on Herbert's doctrine specifically. Locke's empiricism rather than Herbert's innate ideas became the foundation of English Deism. Indeed, among the major Deists, only Charles Blount—who wrote his tracts before the appearance of Locke's *Essay* in 1690—adopted Herbert's common notions, subdividing them into seven. This is why it is misleading (in a sense) to call Herbert the father of English Deism. Locke, though not a Deist, had a greater impact on Deistic thought than did Herbert.

Spinoza

In 1656, Baruch Spinoza, a twenty-two-year-old Jewish scholar who displayed brilliance and great promise, was excommunicated and anathematized by the elders of the Amsterdam Synagogue. Spinoza changed his name to Benedict (the Latin equivalent of Baruch), and in 1670 he published—anonymously and with the imprint of a fictitious printer—the *Theologico-Political Treatise*. The *Treatise*, as Richard Popkin notes, "is a devastating critique of revealed knowledge claims, which has had an amazing effect over the last three centuries in secularizing modern man."[8]

Spinoza's infuence on Deists is difficult to establish from their writings. Spinoza was not a Deist; he was a pantheist who flirted with atheism—"Nature herself is the power of God under another name. . . ."[9] Spinoza's reputation as an atheist made him, along with Thomas Hobbes, a dangerous precedent to cite, especially for those Deists who sought to distance themselves from that odious label. We may surmise, however, that most Deists knew of Spinoza, for many of their arguments resembled his. (At least one prominent Deist, John Toland, abandoned Deism for Spinoza's brand of pantheism.)

In his unparalleled effort to establish the sovereignty of reason, Spinoza criticized the Bible with a boldness that had rarely been seen before. He proclaimed the Bible to be "faulty, mutilated, tampered with, and inconsistent." We don't know the authors, circumstances, or dates of many biblical books. Moreover, "we cannot say into what hands they fell, nor how the numerous varying versions originated; nor, lastly, whether there were not other versions, now lost."[10]

Spinoza drew on various sources for his critique of the Bible. He credits Abraham ibn Ezra, a twelfth-century Rabbi, with discovering that Moses did not write all of the Pentateuch (the first five books of the Bible). According to Spinoza, Ezra "confined himself to dark hints which I shall not scruple to elucidate, thus throwing full light on the subject." Spinoza's "light" consists of denying the Mosaic authorship altogether: "it is thus clearer than the sun at noonday that the Pentateuch was not written by Moses, but by someone who lived long after Moses."[11]

Spinoza was not the first writer of his century to make this claim. In *Leviathan* (1651), Thomas Hobbes, while conceding that Moses may have written much of the Pentateuch, argued that he "did not compile those books entirely, and in the form that we have them. . . ." The modern pioneer of biblical criticism, however, was Issac La Peyrère, a renegade Calvinist who espoused his own peculiar brand of mysticism and Messianism. Writing a decade before Hobbes, La Peyrère denied the Mosaic authorship of the Pentateuch altogether, he identified many inaccuracies and contradictions in the Bible, he proclaimed the existence of mankind before Adam, he denied the universality of the flood, and he embraced many other heretical views. (La Peyrère later abjured—insincerely, under threat of force—over one hundred such heresies.) Spinoza was familiar with La Peyrère's theories, and he incorporated many of them in the Treatise.[12]

Authorship of the Pentateuch may strike the modern reader as arcane—a topic scarcely important enough to become excited or upset about. Yet the veracity of the Bible as a divinely inspired document revolves around such issues, as Christians and their critics well knew. The authenticity of a purported revelation depends on the credentials of its human messenger. A miracle, if reported by a divinely inspired prophet, degenerates into a tall yarn, if reported by an unknown and uninspired storyteller. As the Deist Thomas Paine put it in *Age of Reason:*

> Take away from Genesis the belief that Moses was the author, on which only the strange belief that it is the word of God has stood, and there remains nothing of *Genesis,* but an anonymous book of stories, fables, and traditionary or invented absurdities, or downright lies.[13]

In the *Treatise,* Spinoza renders the Bible virtually useless as a source of knowledge—at least for those who are able to reason philosophically. Biblical narratives, he argues, may sometimes illustrate moral precepts, such as justice and charity, but unaided reason can discover these virtues as well, without recourse to revelation (and with more certainty). So of what use is the Bible? Spinoza replies that most people lack the inclination or ability to follow a long chain of philosophical arguments, so they must learn their morality from easily digested stories and examples. This is where the Bible plays a role. It does not provide definitions and proof, so it cannot provide the philosophical knowledge available through reason, but the Bible's "sayings and reasonings are adapted to the understanding of the masses." Belief in the Bible (or certain parts of it) "is particularly necessary to the masses whose intellect is not capable of perceiving things clearly and distinctly." Moreover, ordinary people are likely to read the biblical stories without grasping their moral import, so the masses "are always in need of pastors or church ministers to explain them to their feeble intelligence."[14]

For Spinoza (as for many Deists), the essence of a good religion is its ability to improve moral conduct. A person may believe every word of the Bible, but if this doesn't make him more virtuous, "he might employ himself just as profitably in reading the Koran or the poetic drama, or ordinary chronicles. . . ." On the other hand, a person may be wholly ignorant of the Bible, but if he is a good person and leads a good life, "he is absolutely blessed and truly possesses in himself the spirit of Christ." The natural light of reason, for those skilled in its use, is sufficient to show us "the true way of salvation."[15] (Spinoza did not believe in personal immortality, so the meaning he gives to "salvation" is obscure.)

With this background, we can understand why the *Theologico-Political Treatise* created a maelstrom among Spinoza's contemporaries. Although some theologians—Catholic, Protestant, and Jewish—invested reason with an important and independent role, they still insisted that revelation provides knowledge inaccessible and superior to reason, knowledge essential to salvation. Spinoza wants none of this. Reason, he insists, is supreme and sufficient. If people "hawk about something superior to reason, it is a mere figment, and far below reason. . . ."[16] Spinoza was "thoroughly convinced, that the Bible leaves reason absolutely free, that it has nothing in common with philosophy, in fact, that Revelation and Philosophy stand on totally different footings. . . . [E]ach has its separate province, neither can be called the handmaid of the other."[17]

This sounds like an important concession to revelation, but, as we have seen, the "province" that Spinoza assigns to revelation is rather mundane. Obedience, not knowledge, is the "sole object" of revelation, and even here revelation is needed only when dealing with the dull-witted masses. The Bible does not presume to teach philosophy "but only very simple matters, such as could be understood by the slowest intelligence."[18]

Do reason and revelation conflict? Early in the *Treatise*, Spinoza remarks that he found nothing "taught expressly by Scripture, which does not agree with our understanding, or which is repugnant thereto. . . ."[19] This apparent concession proves to be deceptive, however. Later in the *Treatise*, Spinoza states: "I insist that [the Bible] expressly affirms and teaches that God is jealous . . . and I assert that such a doctrine is repugnant to reason." After mentioning additional irrational teachings, Spinoza pushes his case even further. He argues that the Bible contains many contradictions, thereby exposing the "absurdities" of accepting the Bible as a source of knowlege.[20]

How are we to reconcile Spinoza's claim that the Bible and reason are consistent with his laundry list of biblical absurdities and contradictions? Quite simply: reason gives us knowledge, whereas revelation does not. Reason conflicts with revelation only if we take the Bible to be more than a collection of handy moral lessons directed to those persons who cannot "acquire the habit of virtue under the unaided guide of reason." The Bible is useful but not necessarily true. Reason reigns supreme in matters of knowledge; it is "the light of the mind, and without her all things are dreams and phantoms."[21]

In defending the supremacy of reason, Spinoza disposes of a possible competitor—prophecy, or "sure knowledge revealed by God to man." Technically, even ordinary knowledge comes from God, because all knowledge depends on God and his laws (i.e., nature). But prophets claim to possess a superior wisdom—a knowledge transcending reason and therefore inaccessible to the uninspired.

We must keep in mind that Spinoza uses the word "prophecy" to mean more than predicting the future; it refers generally to all claims of special revelation, and a "prophet" is a person who claims to have received this knowledge. Spinoza's critique of "prophecy," therefore, is nothing less than a critique of special revelation—in contradistinction to the general revelation available to everyone through the study of nature and natural laws.

How, according to the Bible, did God speak to prophets? Spinoza finds only one occasion (transmission of the Ten Commandments to Moses) when God is said to have spoken in a real voice. But there are two conflicting reports of the Commandments in Exodus and Deuteronomy, so we cannot accept them literally. The Commandments "were not intended to convey the actual words of the Lord, but only his meaning."[22] Moreover, the entire account of the Ten Commandments is questionable, because it implies that God has a form (as when Moses saw the "hinder parts" of God). The Bible, "in concession to popular ignorance," frequently saddles God with human characteristics and so should not be taken literally.

In reporting other cases of divine revelation, the Bible often refers to visions and dreams. Imagination clearly played a key role in these cases, so Spinoza suggests that prophecy requires "a peculiarly vivid imagination" rather than a keen mind. The prophets "perceived nearly everything in parables and allegories, and clothed spiritual truths in bodily forms, for such is the usual method of imagination."[23]

Perhaps the prophets were inspired by the "the spirit of God." Spinoza points out that this phrase is given different meanings throughout the Old Testament. If "the spirit of God" refers to a communion with the mind of God, then Spinoza does not object. But this is not a privilege enjoyed solely by prophets; the "eternal thoughts" of God are impressed on the mind of every human being. The Hebrew prophets were wrong to claim a special status for their revelations. Indeed, if "the Jews were at a loss to understand any phenomena, or were ignorant of its cause, they referred it to God."[24] This "explanation," however, explains nothing:

> Everything takes place by the power of God. Nature herself is the power of god under another name, and our ignorance of the power of God is co-extensive with our ignorance of Nature. It is absolutely folly, therefore, to ascribe an event to the power of God when we know not its natural cause, which is the power of God.[25]

Since the prophets relied on imagination, it is hardly surprising that they claimed to possess knowledge that transcends reason; for the imagination, when unrestrained by the principles of reasoned knowledge, often inspires fantastic claims. In truth, "prophecy never rendered the prophet wiser than he was before." To accept the prophetic reports as a source of knowledge, natural or spiritual, is "an utter mistake"—mere superstition. And, as Spinoza repeatedly reminds his readers, "I care not for the girdings of superstition, for superstition is the bitter enemy of all true knowledge and true morality."[26]

If prophecy suffered at Spinoza's hand, miracles fared even worse. Spinoza unequivocally rejects the possibility of miracles.

A miracle is said to be an event that contravenes the laws of nature. These natural laws, however, are themselves manifestations of the divine nature, so to say that God contravened natural law is to say that God "acted against his own nature—an evident absurdity."[27] Indeed, since God is perceived through the "immutable order of nature," our knowledge of God increases along with our understanding of nature. A miracle, however, cannot be understood, so it actually diminishes our knowledge of God.

In addition, a miracle insults the divine nature, because it implies that "God has created nature so weak, and has ordained for her laws so barren," that he must repeatedly tinker with his flawed creation through miracles.[28] (Deists would later have a field day with this observation.)

A miracle is also said to be an event that cannot be explained through natural reason. But this is ignorance masquerading as explanation: "Plainly, they are but triflers who, when they cannot explain a thing, run back to the will of god; this is, truly, a ridiculous way of expressing ignorance."[29]

Spinoza refuses to distinguish an event that is *against* natural law from an event that is *beyond* natural law. "A miracle, whether in contravention to, or beyond, nature, is a mere absurdity. . . ." Spinoza concludes:

> We may, then, be absolutely certain that every event which is truly described in Scripture necessarily happened, like everything else, according to natural laws; and if anything is there set down which can be proved in set terms to contravene the order of nature, or not to be deducible therefrom, we must believe it to have been foisted into the sacred writings by irreligious hands; for whatsover is contrary to reason is absurd, and, *ipso facto*, to be rejected.[30]

In attacking special revelation and miracles, Spinoza sought to purge Christianity and Judaism of all supernatural elements—or "mysteries," as they were often called. In 1696, when the Deist John Toland published *Christianity Not Mysterious*, he was following in the footsteps of Benedict Spinoza. Spinoza and the Deists agreed: if the tenets of a religion cannot meet the test of reason, they should be rejected by reasonable people.

Charles Blount

Charles Blount (1654–1693) was one of the most radical and influential Deists of the seventeenth century. He, along with John Toland, sparked the great Deistic controversy that would dominate English theology well into the next century.

The scion of a good family (his father, Sir Henry Blount, was a successful author), Charles Blount was a radical Whig and a stout defender of civil liberties, especially liberty of the press. (Blount's pamphlet on this subject was taken—some would say plagiarized—from John Milton.) Blount was also heavily influenced by Edward Herbert; indeed, Blount's *Religio Laici* (1683) is little more than a translation of Herbert's *De Religione Laici*.

In criticizing some of Christianity's most cherished beliefs, Blount often uses an indirect method that would prove to be a favorite among later Deists and freethinkers. He points to parallels between Christianity and pagan religions, thereby suggesting that Christianity was not unique. This technique is most apparent in his translation of the first two books of *Apollonius of Tyana*—an ancient Greek work by Philostratus that chronicles the miraculous deeds of Apollonius, a Pythagorean wonder-worker.

Blount annotated his translation with so many notes that they occupy more space than the text itself. These notes express Blount's Deism, and they suggest a thesis fatal to Christianity: Jesus was but one among many wonder-workers of his era, and his cult survived because of historical circumstances, not because of instrinsic merit or divine favor. If Christians of his day frowned on the superstitious antics of Apollonius, Blount (paraphrasing Thomas Hobbes) reminds them that a fine line separates Christianity from superstition: "For to believe any stories that are not approved by the public authority of our church, is superstition; whereas to believe them that are, is religion." (Blount does not hesitate to cite Hobbes and Spinoza, the two most despised "atheists" of the seventeenth century. This fact alone ranks Blount as one of the most radical Deists. Many Deists, wishing to avoid the stigma of "atheism"—a common refrain of critics—chose more respectable company.)

Throughout his writings, Blount questions traditional Christian beliefs, including the Virgin Birth (many ancient heroes, he points out, were said to be born of virgins), the stories of paradise, the fall, Noah's ark, and the miraculous manna supplied to the Jews during their desert sojourn. Blount even questions the biblical account of creation, and he uses the findings of Copernican astronomy to criticize biblical cosmology.

One of the most interesting of Blount's works is *Great Is Diana of the Ephesians* (1680), a thinly veiled attack on Christian rituals, dogmas, and clergy. Blount ostensibly criticizes ancient heathen religions, which, under the auspices of self-serving and ignorant priests, had become encrusted with absurd dogmas and rituals. Blount proposes to examine these religions critically:

> Now most religions (excepting ours), being tainted with the Interest of the Clergy, [we] must examine and consider them accordingly: For if a Porter should come and tell me, he had brought me such a Letter from my Father, and the first part of the Letter should teach Obedience to Parents, but the latter part of it should command me to give the said Porter half my Estate; in this case I should (notwithstanding the Testimony of his Brother Porters), without some further demonstration, believe the Letter a Counterfeit; as also that the first part of it, which taught Obedience, was only to make way for the second and principal clause, viz. the giving the Porter Money. Now most of the Heathen Priests were such Porters. . . .[31]

To debunk the "mysteries" of heathen religions may seem unnecessary when addressing a Christian audience, but Blount's subtext was clear enough to his readers, despite disclaimers like this: "what I have here written concerns [Heathenish Religions] only. . . ." Again, while commenting on heathen sacrifices, Blount notes that his criticisms might seem to apply to Moses as well, but he reassures his audience in a not-too-convincing fashion:

> Now if any Hypocrite to glorifie his own zeal, should pretend that a discourse of this nature does through the Heathen Sacrifices, reproach those of *Moses*, which resembled them but in outward appearance, he must retrieve himself from that error, if he rightly apprehends the difference. . . .[32]

Just what is the difference between heathen sacrifices and those advocated by Moses? It is this: heathen priests invented sacrifices to hoodwink and bilk their followers, whereas Moses was directed by the "true God." This is all that Blount says on the matter. Little wonder, then, that pious readers rightly suspected Blount of duplicity. Christianity, not heathenism, was his target.

Blount, following in the footsteps of Edward Herbert, sees true religion as natural and rational; its primary purpose is to "teach Virtue and Piety." This pure religion, however, was corrupted by self-serving "heathen" priests to serve their own agenda. Instead of teaching virtue and piety, priests "introduced Fables and Fictions of their own coining," thereby persuading the masses to distrust their own judgments and to rely instead on priests, those self-proclaimed repositories of divine knowledge. The priests, by teaching impertinent, absurd, and impious tenets about God and religion, sought to confine religious knowledge to "what they themselves taught." This "Sacerdotal villany" assured them a livelihood without honest labor.

To propagate superstition is one thing, to establish it institutionally is another. Here, according to Blount, the priest worked hand-in-hand with the prince, or civil power: "the one made the Idol, and the other ordain'd the worship of it." With the power of government behind them, priests were able to enrich themselves and persecute dissenters. This (of course) is true only of the heathen clergy: "They not being like the Pastors of the Christian Church, who (according to Christ's rule) ought to be like Sheep amongst Wolves; whereas the others were rather like Wolves among Sheep."[33]

What did the prince gain from his alliance with the priest? Whenever the people became agitated with some political matter, they consulted the priest, who then consulted the gods. Not surprisingly, the priest usually conveyed a divine message that was perfectly agreeable to the political status quo.

Charles Blount had the effrontery to posit self-interest (or "self-love," as he calls it) as an explanatory motive of religious behavior and institutions. Nearly a century later, a Scotsman named Adam Smith used the same kind of explanatory method for economic behavior and institutions. Smith is proclaimed a genius for his efforts, whereas Blount, if he is remembered at all, is usually dismissed as a simplistic crank. This intriguing and tragic scholar (he committed suicide when his dead wife's sister refused marriage) deserves better.

John Locke

It would be inaccurate to label John Locke (1632–1704) a Deist, but the course of Deism was heavily influenced by his theory of knowledge, his discussion of faith and reason, his critique of immediate revelation, and his stress on the "reasonableness" of Christianity. Far more than Edward Herbert, John Locke was a revered, if unwilling, "father" of English Deism.

In *An Essay Concerning Human Understanding* (1690), Locke sets out "to lay down *the measures and boundaries between faith and reason.*" And the role that Locke assigns to faith is more restrictive than many Christians would like.

> *Faith* . . . is the assent to any proposition, not thus made out by the deductions of reason, but upon the credit of the proposer, as coming from God, in some extraordinary way of communication. This way of discovering truths to men, we call *revelation.*[34]

This is fairly conventional, but the plot thickens when Locke discusses the epistemological status of revelation. All knowledge, Locke believes, is ultimately derived from experience, so language—the means by which knowledge is transmitted—has meaning only within the context of our experience. This causes problems when language is used to communicate divine revelation.

Suppose God were to endow one man with a unique sixth sense. That man "could no more, by words, produce in the minds of other men those ideas imprinted by that sixth sense" than we can convey, by words, the idea of color to a blind man. Of course, God can reveal a unique kind of knowledge if he so chooses, but the receiver of that knowledge will be unable to communicate it to others. All he can say is that there are such things "as eye hath not seen, nor ear heard, nor hath it entered into the heart of man to conceive."[35]

Suppose God reveals knowledge that is also "discoverable to us by reason." Here, according to Locke, "there is little need or use of revelation," for reason, unlike faith, can give us certain knowledge. Indeed, in responding to a critic who argued that faith produces a greater certainty than reason, Locke says that faith is unable to produce certainty at all: "Bring it to certainty, and it ceases to be faith."[36] We *believe* something to be true through faith, but we *know* something to be true through reason.

The same principle applies to knowledge gained immediately through sense experience. Why, for example, do Christians believe that Moses wrote the story of the flood? They accept it on faith because they believe the Bible. But their conviction would be stronger if they had actually seen Moses write the account, so "the assurance of its being a revelation is less still than the assurance of [the] senses."[37]

For Locke, the central issue is not the veracity of revelation per se (because God neither errs nor deceives). Rather, the issue is this: how, in any given instance, do we know that we are dealing with an authentic revelation? The problem is with the credentials of the messenger, so to speak, not with the message itself.

Locke insists that a supposed revelation should not be believed if it contradicts "our clear intuitive knowledge."

> Because this would be to subvert the principles and foundations of all knowledge, evidence, and assent whatsoever: and there would be left no difference between truth and falsehood, no measures of credible and incredible in the world, if doubtful propositions shall take place before self-evident.[38]

Although reason and faith are independent, reason must still determine what qualifies as a genuine revelation.

> Whatever God hath revealed is certainly true: no doubt can be made of it. This is the proper object of faith: but whether it be a *divine* revelation or no, reason must judge.[39]

Since reason must pass judgment on the authenticity of revelation, to accept an irrational belief as revelation "must overturn all the principles and foundations of knowledge." Revelation cannot invalidate the decrees of reason, "nor can we be obliged, where we have the clear and evident sentence of reason, to quit it for the contrary opinion, under a pretence that it is a matter of faith. . . ."[40]

Locke does invest faith with some legitimate functions, especially when reason can arrive at only probable conjectures. But even here reason must assess the authenticity of revelation "and of the signification of the words wherein it is delivered."[41]

Having, in effect, demoted faith to a handmaid of reason, Locke proceeds to demolish another claim to revealed knowledge—immediate revelation, or what we call today a religious experience. Though rarely given its due, even by freethinkers, Locke's critique of the argument from religious experience is one of the most devastating ever penned.

In the fourth edition of *An Essay Concerning Human Understanding*, Locke added a chapter called "Of Enthusiasm." During the seventeenth century, enthusiasm ("being possessed by a god") referred to a direct experience with God—an "immediate revelation." According to some commentators, Locke was simply attacking an overly emotional kind of religious experience, but, in fact, his strictures apply to *all* cases where the strength of one's inner assurance is accepted as proof of divine inspiration. Locke begins his analysis with an insightful observation:

> He that would seriously set upon the search of truth, ought the first place to prepare his mind with a love of it. . . . There is nobody in the commonwealth of learning who does not profess himself a lover of truth: and there is not a rational creature that would not take it amiss to be thought otherwise of. And yet, for all this, one may truly say, that there are very few lovers of truth, for truth's sake, even amongst those who persuade themselves that they are so.[42]

Since nearly everyone professes to be a seeker of truth, how can we distinguish the sincere from the insincere? Locke suggests "one unerring mark" of the earnest truthseeker:

> The not entertaining any proposition with greater assurance than the proofs it is built upon will warrant. Whoever goes beyond this measure of assent, it is plain receives not the truth in the love of it; loves not truth for truth's sake, but for some other bye-end.[43]

For Locke, the strength of our beliefs should not exceed the evidence, arguments, and proofs that support them. If we exceed those limits, then we betray the search for truth and succumb to our "passions and interests" instead. The person who claims to have received knowledge directly from God, but who has no evidence to support this claim, cannot be regarded as a lover of truth, however much he may protest to the contrary. He has adopted passion and interest, not reason, as his guides to knowledge. He simply believes what he wants to believe, rather than pursuing "the tedious and not always successful labour of strict reasoning."

Locke proposes to "examine a little soberly this internal light" of enthusiasm. Consider the person who claims to have been inspired by God. We need not dispute whether this person really saw or felt *something,* but we do need to inquire as to *what* he saw or felt. A person, through a flash of insight, may suddenly "see" the truth of a proposition, but this doesn't establish where the knowledge came from, much less that it came from God. Likewise, a person may suddenly feel an inclination to do something, but this doesn't mean that God caused the feeling.

According to Locke, knowledge derives either from self-evident truths or from reasoning. Revelation and faith play no role here. But sometimes, using faith, we believe a proposition on the testimony of someone else. This is not irrational, provided that we can verify the source. In the case of divine testimony, "I must see that it is God that reveals this to me, or else I see nothing."[11] This generates an essential question: "How do I know that God is the revealer of this to me . . . ?" Pretenders to immediate revelation, Locke insists, fail to answer this question satisfactorily.

> If they say, by the light it brings with it, which shines bright in their minds, and they cannot resist: I beseech them to consider whether this be any more than what we have taken notice of already, viz. that it is a revelation, because they strongly believe it to be true. For all the light they speak of is but a strong, though ungrounded, persuasion of their own minds, that it is a truth.[45]

The argument from enthusiasm boils down to this: "*It is a revelation, because they firmly believe it; and they firmly believe it, because it is a revelation.*" This, Locke argues, "is a very unsafe ground to proceed on, either in our tenets or actions." It overthrows reason and establishes "fancy for our supreme and sole guide." Disastrous consequences are sure to follow, because if inner assurance is accepted as proof, then "contrary opinions have the same title to be inspirations" and contradictory propositions will be accepted as divine truths. Moreover, "if strength of persuasion be the light which must guide us; I ask how shall any one distinguish between the delusions of Satan, and the inspirations of the Holy Ghost?"[46]

For Locke, an immediate revelation must be accompanied by an external sign, such as a miracle, before we can accept it. Deists would later destroy the credibility of such signs and leave special revelation without a leg to stand on.

John Toland

The Irishman John Toland (1670–1722) journeyed from Catholicism to Presbyterianism to latitudinarianism (an extremely liberal form of Protestantism) to Deism to pantheism. Having studied at the universities of Glasgow, Edinburgh, and Leyden, Toland set out to earn his way as a writer and as a publicist for Radical Whig causes. Nearly two hundred works are attributed to Toland; and, as the historian David Berman remarks, he "is perhaps the first professional freethinker."[47]

Toland is best known for *Christianity Not Mysterious* (1696), a book that Leslie Stephen called "the signal-gun" of the Deistic controversy. The purpose of this book is clearly stated in its subtitle: *A Treatise Shewing, That there is nothing in the Gospel Contrary to Reason, Nor Above it: And that no Christian Doctrine can be properly call'd A Mystery*. The title page also bears a quotation from Archbishop Tillotson, a liberal Anglican who was admired by Deists:

> We need not desire a better Evidence that any Man is in the wrong, than to hear him declare against Reason, and thereby acknowledg[e] that Reason is against him.

Toland insists that he is a sincere Christian who wishes only to purge Christianity of its irrational accretions (mysteries) and restore it to a pure, undefiled (rational) condition. Yet critics correctly recognized *Christianity Not Mysterious* to be an attack on Christianity, not a defense. (The Irish Parliament ordered the first edition, published anonymously, to be burned.)

Toland himself may have let the cat out of the bag. In the preface, he notes "the deplorable Condition of our Age, that a Man dares not openly and directly own what he thinks of Divine Matters. . . ." One is forced to remain silent "or to propose his Sentiments to the World by way of Paradox under a borrow'd or fictitious Name." Those who have the courage to state what they really think risk numerous penalties, legal and social.

As this passage suggests, Toland's profession of Christianity may have been a ruse to protect himself. If so, he was neither the first nor last skeptic to employ it.

Toland is firm in his commitment to reason: "I hold nothing as an Article of my Religion, but what the highest Evidence forc'd me to embrace." He refuses to captivate his understanding (a Hobbesian phrase) "to any Man or Society whatsoever." Religion, as Toland sees it, should be reasonable, and he provides this classic statement of the freethinking Deistic ideal:

> Since Religion is calculated for reasonable Creatures, 'tis Conviction and not Authority that should bear Weight with them. A wise and good Man will judg[e] of the Merits of a Cause consider'd only in itself, without any regard to Times, Places, or Persons.[48]

Toland is unimpressed with religious scholars who flaunt their knowledge of ancient languages and declare themselves authorities. The "vulgar," Toland maintains, are able to assess the Bible critically and make up their own minds, even though they must rely on translations:

> Truth is always and every where the same; And an unintelligible or absurd Proposition is never the more respected for being ancient or strange, for being originally written in Latin, Greek or Hebrew.[49]

The great freethought scholar, J. M. Robertson, makes a similar point in *The Dynamics of Religion:*

> It is one of the stock theorems of modern Christian scholarship that no one is entitled to reject the New Testament without a good knowledge of Greek, though all are entitled to believe it without knowing one Greek letter from another, and though all Christians are free to reject the Koran without having so much as seen a letter of Arabic.[50]

Contrary to some theologians, who "gravely tell us *we must adore what we do not comprehend,*" Toland insists that everything, even revelation, must pass the test of reason or be rejected. Why? Because humans are fallible and easily deceived. Reason enables us to distinguish between fact and fancy, certainty and probability. If we abandon or ignore the dictates of reason, then we are cast adrift in a sea of conflicting beliefs with no rudder to steer our course. Questionable propositions will be accepted as axioms, old wive's fables will be mistaken for moral certainty, and human impostures will be seen as divine revelations.[51]

Essential to Toland's case is his conception of reason, which he defines as "that Faculty of the soul which discovers the Certainty of any thing dubious or obscure, by comparing it with something evidently known."[52] Following Locke, Toland argues that sense perception provides us with simple and distinct ideas, which we then compound into complex ideas. Reason is the faculty by which we perceive the agreement or disagreement of our ideas.

Like Locke, Toland says that some knowledge is self-evidently true, such as axioms. Strictly speaking, reason is not used in these cases, since we perceive the truth of self-evident propositions immediately and without the aid of intervening ideas. But when the agreement between ideas cannot be immediately perceived, then intermediate ideas—connecting links, so to speak—are required, and this is where reason steps in. Reason compares a new, untested idea with an idea that is already known, thereby determining whether the new idea is consistent with our store of knowledge.

Toland pushes this conception of reason further than Locke was willing to go. If, in order to attain knowledge, we must compare ideas for their compatibility, then those ideas themselves must be clear and distinct. Otherwise, no comparison is possible, because "when we have no Notions or Ideas of a thing, we cannot reason about it at all. . . ."[53]

This notion of reason threatens to undermine venerable Christian "mysteries," such as the Trinity, because it is intrinsically hostile to truths that supposedly transcend reason. Thus, by using Locke's theory of knowledge, Toland dragged an unwilling Locke into the Deistic controversy.

Edward Stillingfleet, Bishop of Worcester, published A *Discourse in Vindication of the Trinity* (1696), wherein he argues that Locke's epistemology, as used by Toland, promotes infidelity and skepticism, especially in regard to the Trinity. Locke, however, maintains that Toland misunderstood his theory. Toland "made, or supposed, clear and distinct ideas necessary to certainty; but that is not my notion. . . ." Locke, it should be noted, nowhere affirms his belief in the Trinity; he simply maintains that his theory of knowledge is irrevelant to that controversy one way or the other—a remarkably dubious claim. Quoting Locke:

> My notion of certainty by ideas is, that certainty consists in the perception of the agreement or disagreement of ideas such as we have, whether they be in all their parts perfectly clear or no: nor have I any notions of certainty more than this one.[54]

As Toland saw the matter, he was simply extending Locke's theory of reason to its logical conclusion. Toland had a point, for it is difficult to understand how reason can compare ideas unless those ideas are clear to begin with. Indeed, as Toland says, the nature of the human mind is such that we cannot truly assent to a proposition unless we clearly understand its meaning.

> A man may give his verbal Assent to he knows not what, out of Fear, Superstition, Indifference, Interest, and the like feeble and unfair Motives: but as long as he conceives not what he believes, he cannot sincerely acquiesce in it, and remains depriv'd of all solid Satisfaction.[55]

This problem cannot be solved by faith, for we must at least understand a proposition before we can accept it on faith. The Christian may claim to believe in the unintelligible, but this is meaningless verbal assent—"rash presumption and an obstinate prejudice." The Christian may just as well claim to believe in a "Blictri" (a traditional nonsense word):

> Could that Person justly value himself upon being wiser than his Neighbors, who having infallible Assurance that something call'd *Blictri* had a Being in Nature, in the mean time knew not what this *Blictri* was?[56]

Toland was perhaps the first to argue that many traditional Christian doctrines are literally meaningless. "Mystery" is a mere euphemism for "unintelligible," and reason rebels at both.

Where does revelation fit into this scheme? Revelation, Toland says, is a "means of information," not a "motive of assent."[57] We should carefully distinguish the *method* by which we acquire information from the *justification* we have to believe it. If a person reveals information to us and expects us to believe it, that testimony must be intelligible or it signifies nothing. Suppose this person claims to have seen a cane without two ends. We cannot believe this absurd statement, even if we want to, because we don't know what it means. What if the person, claiming divine inspiration, calls the peculiar cane a "mystery"? This is no help, Toland argues; we still don't know what he is talking about, and neither does he.

> Whoever reveals any thing, that is, whoever tells us something we did not know before, *his Words must be intelligible, and the Matter possible.* This Rule holds good, let God or Man be the Revealer.[58]

According to Toland, if we are to rescue the Bible from the depths of absurdity, we must interpret much of it figuratively; otherwise, "the highest Follies and Blasphemies may be deduc'd from the Letter of *Scripture.*" What of those theologians who claim that a literal reading only *seems* to conflict with reason? This won't do, says Toland: "A seeming contradiction is to us as good as a real one." We cannot make sense of a contradiction, real or apparent, so it is "certainly but lost labour for us to trouble ourselves about it."[59]

Indeed, it is impious to suggest that God, after endowing humans with the the faculty of reason, would require belief in the irrational as a condition of salvation. This supposition also breeds skepticism, for if reason demands one thing while God demands another, we can never be certain which to follow. Toland concludes with a spirited statement of the Deistic credo: "I acknowledge no ORTHODOXY but the TRUTH; and, I'm sure, where-ever the TRUTH is there must also [be] the CHURCH, of God. . . ."[60]

Anthony Collins

In 1703, shortly before his death, John Locke wrote to a young friend, Anthony Collins:

> Believe it, my good friend, to love truth, for truth's sake, is the principal part of human perfection in this world, and the seed-plot of all other virtues; and if I mistake not, you have as much of it as ever I met with in any body. What then is there wanting to make you equal to the best; a friend for any one to be proud of?[61]

Anthony Collins (1676–1729), a likeable man with considerable philosophic gifts, was a materialist, determinist, and freethinker. He was possibly the best Deistic writer of his time (although there is some evidence that he was really an atheist).[62] In his influential book, A *Discourse of Free-Thinking* (1713), Collins writes:

> By free-thinking I mean the use of the understanding in endeavoring to find out the meaning of any proposition whatsoever, in considering the nature of the evidence for or against it, and in judging of it according to the seeming force or weakness of the evidence.[63]

Richard Bentley, a renowned classical scholar, ridiculed this notion of freethinking; no one, he said, would dispute it, so Collins appears silly when he parades "freethinking" as a mark of intellectual independence.

Bentley's criticism misses the point. "Freethinking," as Collins uses the word, conveys moral implications that many theologians of his day found unacceptable. States Collins: "[W]e have a right to know or may lawfully know any truth. And a right to know any truth whatsoever implies a right to think freely."[64]

This assertion of a *moral* "right to think freely" is significant, and it resembles Spinoza's earlier call for "free philosophizing." Obviously, Collins opposes any legal meddling in religious matters, but he means more. He contrasts freethinking with the moral restraints imposed by religious creeds—tenets that it is *sinful* to disbelieve.

If we shackle the reason of others through law, or if we shackle our own reason through moral prohibitions, then we "must run into the grossest absurdities imaginable both in principle and practice." To illustrate his case, Collins draws a parallel between religious faith and "eye-sight faith."

Suppose a group of men decide that some great purpose requires everyone to believe alike in matters of sight, so they compose a list of articles to which everyone must subscribe. These articles of eye-sight faith state that "a ball can go through a table; that a knot can be undone with words; that one face may be a hundred or a thousand," and so forth. No one is allowed publicly to contradict these articles;

moreover, if a philosopher questions them, he will be told that these propositions are "above, but not contrary to, eye-sight."

> Instances will be given of ten thousand mistakes in using our eyes. It will be esteemed dangerous trusting to carnal eye-sight, and be said that we ought to rely on the authority of those men who have pensions and salaries on purpose to study those things, and would not deserve what they receive should men use their own eye-sight. And as for those few men who should dare to use their own eyes, the least evil they could expect would be to be rendered odious to the multitude under the reproachful ideas of "skeptics," "Latitudinarians," "free-seers," men tied by no authority.[65]

Collins points out that our knowledge of astronomy, originally "rude and imperfect," improved over time "by gradual progress in thinking." This is the way of all knowledge, including religious knowledge. But opponents of freethinking proclaim some opinions to be literally "damnable"; so, rather than champion freethinking, they insist that everyone must hold the same opinions, if those opinions are deemed necessary for salvation.

Collins protests. If holding a correct opinion is so important, then freethinking—"the surest and best method of arriving at truth"—is absolutely essential. He who adopts freethinking as a guide does his best to find the truth—and this, surely, is all that a reasonable God can require of him. "And should he prove mistaken in many opinions, he must be as acceptable to God as if he received none but right opinions."[66]

This was part and parcel of the Deistic worldview. If God created man in his own image, then God must be a rational being. And no rational being could possibly punish another rational being for an honest error of judgment. Moreover, if God will punish us for the diligent use of our reason, then why did he endow us with this ability in the first place? The Deists viewed God as a reasonable and tolerant being—a kind of freethinker writ large. Such a being, if he cares at all, would admire reasonable, inquisitive individuals more than slavish conformists.

The main contribution of Anthony Collins to the critical side of the Deistic debate is *A Discourse of the Grounds and Reasons of the Christian Religion* (1724). This is a clever and thorough dissection of Old Testament prophecies, which, according to Christians, were fulfilled by Jesus and therefore prove his messiahship. If Jesus did not fulfill these prophecies, Collins argues, then belief in Jesus as the messiah, the bedrock of Christianity, cannot be defended.

> [I]f the Proofs for Christianity from the Old Testament be not valid; if the Arguments founded on those Books be not conclusive; and the *Prophecies* cited from thence be not fulfill'd; then has Christianity no just Foundation; for the Foundation, on which Jesus and his Apostles built it, is then invalid and false.[67]

In his examination of the prophecies, Collins employs a ruse that was popular among Deists. He argues that if the prophecies are to stand, they must be interpreted allegorically, not literally. The prophecies fail if viewed literally—as Collins is happy to demonstrate—so Collins, proposing the allegorical method instead, steps forward as a champion who will save an imperiled Christianity. Orthodox Christians replied, in effect: With friends like this, who needs enemies?

Collins considers the messianic prophecies one by one and demolishes them one by one. The *Discourse* was a convenient handbook for future generations of freethinkers; when Thomas Paine wrote a similar critique of the prophecies, he clearly drew from Collins. Unlike Collins, however, Paine did not cloak his disdain for Christianity; he attacked it openly, forcefully, mercilessly. Thus did the tree planted by Collins and other Deists bear fruit in America.

Thomas Woolston

Thomas Woolston (1669–1733), a Cambridge graduate admired by Voltaire, was the most villified of the Deists. Critics did more than respond to Woolston's attacks on the Bible; they accused him of insanity—"poor mad Woolston, most scandalous of the deists," as Leslie Stephen put it.

According to Stephen, Woolston attacked the Gospel narratives as "preposterous," and this "would have been sufficient of itself to raise doubts of its author's sanity." He was "a mere buffoon jingling his cap and bells in a sacred shrine." Even Stephen admits, however, that there are "queer gleams of distorted sense, and even of literary power, in the midst of his buffoonery."[68]

Woolston believed that "hireling preachers" were conspiring against him—another mark of paranoid insanity, Stephen assures us. Yet Woolston's fear of persecution proved to be well founded. In 1729, he was convicted of blasphemy and fined; then, unable to pay a large bond to insure his future good conduct, Woolston is reported to have spent four years in prison until his death in 1733. (Voltaire, in England at the time, denied that Woolston had died in prison: "Several of my friends have seen him in his house: he died there, at liberty.")[69]

A contemporary critic charged Woolston with "scurrilous buffoonery and gross raillery," and this charge has been echoed by modern historians. G. R. Cragg, for example, has called Woolston's attack on the Bible "hysterically abusive."[70]

Few historians mention the reason for Woolston's "abusive" tactics. Ridicule and humor, he contends, will often succeed where a serious approach might fail. In his words:

> I am resolved to give the Letter of the Scripture no Rest, so long as God gives me Life and Abilities to attack it. . . . And how then is such a Work to be performed to best Advantage? Is it to be done in a grave, sedate, and serious Manner? No, I think Ridicule should here take the Place of sober Reasoning, as the more proper and effectual means to cure Men of their foolish Faith and absurd Notions. As no wise Man hardly ever reprehends a Blunderbuss for his Bull, any other way, than by laughing at him; so the Asserters of nonsensical Notions in Theology should, if possible, be satirised and jested upon, or they'll never . . . desert their absurd Doctrines.[71]

Woolston, following the example of some early Christian apologists, calls for an allegorical interpretation of the Bible. In *Six Discourses on the Miracles of Our Savior* (1727–1729), his most scandalous work, Woolston applies his freewheeling wit and sarcasm to the task of demolishing the literal belief in the miracles of Jesus. Rather than accept the "absurdities, improbabilities, and incredibilities" of those reported miracles, we should view them "as prophetical and parabolical narratives"—mystical symbols, in effect, that convey spiritual messages.

Scarcely any New Testament miracle escapes Woolston's withering touch. For example, Woolston comments on the report that Jesus cured a blind man "by the means of eye-salve made of dirt and spittle." If divine power healed this man, what was the point of the homemade "ointment and wash"? This treatment makes Jesus look like "a juggling imposter." Elsewhere, Woolston calls Jesus "a strolling fortune-teller." As for the story that Jesus cast demons into a herd of swine: if he had done the same thing in England to a herd of cattle, "our laws, and judges, too, of the last age would have made him swing for it."

By the time he wrote the *Sixth Discourse,* Woolston had hit his stride. There, speaking through a fictitious Rabbi, Woolston argues that a literal reading of the New Testament makes Jesus a "deceiver, imposter, and malefactor" for whom "no punishment could be too great."[72] Then, as if anticipating *The Passover Plot,* Woolston presents the resurrection as a fraud perpetrated by the disciples—"the most bare-fac'd Imposture that ever was put upon the World."

Jesus, according to Woolston's "Rabbi," used fraudulent tricks to agitate the masses, and this threatened to bring the wrath of the Roman State upon the Jewish people. Fortunately, he was "cut off" before he could inflict more damage, but, before being executed, he predicted his resurrection in three days. The chief priests wished to prevent his followers from stealing his body—thereby faking a resurrection—so they persuaded Pilate to seal the corpse in a guarded tomb.

Despite these precautions, the disciples managed to steal the body. This was done on Sunday morning, probably by bribing the guards. Hence, with an empty tomb as evidence, the disciples proclaimed that Jesus had risen from the dead.

Woolston points out that Jesus was executed on Friday, so, for his three-day prophecy to be accurate, he should have arisen on Monday, not Sunday. If Jesus had wished to convince the world of his resurrection and eliminate the possibility of fraud, he should have waited for the priests to return to the tomb on Monday, break the seal, and see him alive. But they never got the chance. The body was clandestinely moved a day early, the disciples lied about having seen Jesus alive, and the resurrection myth was off and running.

Woolston, let us remember, does not believe this account; he rejects any literal rendering of the resurrection and calls instead for an allegorical interpretation, wherein the story is seen "as emblematical of [Jesus'] spiritual Resurrection."[73]

Woolston's basic point is sound. If we accept the resurrection story as reported, then we need to find the most reasonable explanation. And an explanation based on fraud and trickery, however unlikely, is more plausible than the revival of a corpse. After all, we have never witnessed the dead come to life, but we have witnessed a good many frauds.

> Who knows not, that many Errors in Philosophy, and as many Frauds in Religion have been sometimes accidentally, sometimes designedly espous'd and palm'd upon Mankind, who in Process of Time become so wedded to them thro' Prejudice and Interest, that they will not give themselves Leave to enquire into the Rise and Foundation of them. False Miracles have been common Things among Christians; and as the Resurrection of Jesus is their grand and fundamental one, so it is not at all difficult to account for the Rise, Propagation and Continuance of the Belief of it.[74]

David Hume would later propose a similar argument against the historicity of miracles, and no one, so far as I know, ever accused him of insanity. But "poor mad Woolston" was packed off to jail, having offended the pious and humorless sensibilites of respectable society.

Notes

1. *The Bishop of London's Second Pastoral Letter to the People of His Diocese* (London, 1730), pp. 1-2.

2. Leslie Stephen, *History of English Thought in the Eighteenth Century*, 2nd ed. (London: Smith, Elder and Co., 1881), vol. I, pp. 186ff.

3. Edward, Lord Herbert of Cherbury, *De Veritate*, trans. Meyrick H. Carre' (Bristol: printed for the University of Bristol by J. W. Arrowsmith), p. 289.

4. Ibid., pp. 293ff.

5. This traditional interpretation has been challenged by E. Graham Waring in his article on Herbert in *The Encyclopedia of Unbelief*, ed. Gordon Stein (Buffalo: Prometheus Books, 1985).

6. Herbert, *De Veritate*, pp. 295-6.

7. Ibid., p. 301.

8. Benedict de Spinoza, A *Theologico-Political Treatise*, trans. R. H. M. Elwes (NY: Dover Publications, 1951), p. 229.

9. Ibid., p. 25.

10. Ibid., p. 111.

11. Ibid., pp. 121, 124.

12. See Richard H. Popkin, *The History of Scepticism from Erasmus to Spinoza*, rev. ed. (Berkeley: University of California Press, 1979), pp. 214-28.

13. Quoted in ibid., p. 221.

14. Spinoza, A *Theologico-Political Treatise*, pp. 78-9.

15. Ibid., p. 80.

16. Ibid.

17. Ibid., pp. 9-10.

18. Ibid., p. 175.

19. Ibid., p. 9.

20. Ibid., p. 193.

21. Ibid, p. 195.

22. Ibid., p. 16.

23. Ibid., p. 25.

24. Ibid., p. 21.

25. Ibid., p. 25.

26. Ibid., p. 27.

27. Ibid., p. 83.

28. Ibid., p. 84.

29. Ibid., p. 86.

30. Ibid., p. 92.

31. [Charles Blount], *Great is Diana of the Ephesians: or, The Original of Idolatry, Together with the Politick Institution of the Gentiles Sacrifices* (London, 1695), p. 4.

32. Ibid., p. 2.

33. Ibid., pp. 7-9.

34. John Locke, *An Essay Concerning Human Understanding*, ed. Alexander Campbell Fraser (Oxford: Clarendon Press, 1894), vol II, p. 416.

35. Ibid., p. 417.

36. Quoted in Maurice Cranston, *John Locke: A Biography* (London: Longmans, Green, and Co., 1957), p. 414.

37. Locke, *Essay Concerning Human Understanding*, p. 419.

38. Ibid., pp. 420-1.

39. Ibid., p. 425.

40. Ibid., pp. 421, 423.

41. Ibid., p. 424.

42. Ibid., p. 429.

43. Ibid.

44. Ibid., p. 435.

45. Ibid., p. 436.

46. Ibid., p. 438.

47. David Berman, article on John Toland in *The Encyclopedia of Unbelief*.

48. [John Toland], *Christianity Not Mysterious* (London, 1696), p. xv.

49. Ibid., p. xx.

50. J. M. Robertson, *The Dynamics of Religion*, 2nd ed. (London: Watts and Co., 1926), p. 139. This book, a sympathetic treatment of the Deists, is still one of the best accounts.

51. Toland, *Christianity Not Mysterious*, p. 16.

52. Ibid., pp. 12-13.

53. Ibid., p. 13.

54. John Locke, *To the Right Reverend the Lord Bishop of Worcester's Answer to his Letter. . . .* , in *The Works of John Locke*, 12th ed. (London, 1824), vol. III, p. 123.

55. Toland, *Christianity Not Mysterious*, p. 35.

56. Ibid., p. 133.

57. Ibid., p. 38.

58. Ibid., pp. 41-2.

59. Ibid., pp. 28, 34.

60. Ibid., p. 175.

61. *The Works of John Locke*, vol. IX, p. 271.

62. The case for Collins as a closet-atheist is presented in David Berman, *A History of Atheism in Britain: From Hobbes to Russell* (London: Crom Helm, 1988), pp. 70-92.

63. Anthony Collins, *A Discourse of Free-Thinking*, in *Deism and Natural Religion: A Sourcebook*, ed. E. Graham Waring (NY: Frederick Ungar, 1967), p. 56.

64. Ibid.

65. Ibid., pp. 58-9.

66. Ibid., p. 59.

67. [Anthony Collins], *A Discourse of the Grounds and Reasons of the Christian Religion* (London, 1737), p. 62.

68. Stephen, *History of English Thought*, pp. 229, 231.

69. J. M. Robertson, *A History of Freethought*, 4th ed. (London: Watts and Co., 1936), vol. II, p. 730.

70. Gerald R. Cragg, *Reason and Authority in the Eighteenth Century* (Cambridge: Cambridge University Press, 1964), p. 76.

71. Thomas Woolston, *A Sixth Discourse on the Miracles of Our Savior* (London, 1729), p. 50.

72. Ibid., p. 5.

73. Ibid., p. 68.

74. Ibid., p. 69.

8
The Literature of Freethought

"By free-thinking," wrote Anthony Collins in 1713, "I mean the use of the understanding in endeavoring to find out the meaning of any proposition whatsoever, in considering the nature of the evidence for or against it, and in judging of it according to the seeming force or weakness of the evidence." Freethought, argued Collins, is opposed to any religion that condemns doubt as sinful, or that demands the acceptance of doctrines on authority or faith.

Freethinkers thus include atheists, agnostics, deists, secularists, rationalists, and others who appeal to reason in order to challenge religious orthodoxy. The literature of freethought is enormous, running into thousands of books and countless pamphlets and periodicals. It is obviously futile, therefore, to attempt anything near a comprehensive bibliography in one essay. I have focused on eighteenth- and nineteenth-century freethought, primarily in England, with a final note on "Jesus revisionism."

A major problem with freethought literature is that it is difficult

---

Reprinted from *The Libertarian Review* (Jan./Feb. 1977).

to find, even in university libraries. Most of the choice items have been out of print for many years, so only the dedicated used-book fanatic stands a chance of obtaining the better works. The "Atheist Viewpoint" reprint series (Arno, 1972) has some good items, but the overall selection is poor. Hence many freethought classics remain buried in obscurity.

I am indebted to my friend, Dr. Gordon Stein—an inveterate freethought scholar and bibliophile—for making me aware of the extent of freethought literature. Aside from the historical works I mention, my selections have been somewhat arbitrary; I have simply selected books with which I am personally familiar or which I personally like. If readers consult the major freethought references, they will be guided through the thousands of works omitted here. Particularly recommended are two bibliographies by Gordon Stein: *Freethought in the United States*, coauthored with Marshall G. Brown (Greenwood, 1978); and *Freethought in the United Kingdom and the Commonwealth* (Greenwood, 1981).

Indispensable for the history of freethought is the work of the great rationalist scholar J. M. Robertson. His *History of Freethought, Ancient and Modern, to the Period of the French Revolution* (2 vols., 4th ed., rev., Watts, 1936) remains the definitive work in its time period, as does *A History of Freethought in the Nineteenth Century* (2 vols., Watts, 1929). Also valuable is Robertson's *A Short History of Christianity* (Watts, 1902).

For those who desire a briefer overview of freethought, James Thrower's *Short History of Western Atheism* (Pemberton, 1971) is informative in some areas but strangely oblivious to the American and British freethought movements. Somewhat better in this regard is J. B. Bury's *History of Freedom of Thought* (1913; rev. by H. J. Blackman, Oxford, 1952).

There are several good reference works pertaining to freethought, including two biographical dictionaries. J. M. Wheeler's *Biographical Dictionary of Freethinkers* (Pioneer Press, 1889) is a mine of useful information, as is Joseph McCabe's *A Biographical Dictionary of Modern Rationalists* (Watts, 1920). Another useful book by McCabe is

A *Rationalist Encyclopedia* (Watts, 1950). The two works by McCabe, however, should be read with caution for errors of dates and details. By far the best reference work is *The Encyclopedia of Unbelief*, edited by Gordon Stein (2 vols., Prometheus Books, 1985). These volumes are indispensable to any serious student of freethought.

Many books, although not confined to freethought, deal sympathetically with what may be termed the rationalistic spirit in the development of philosophy, religion, and science. A superb reference of this kind is Harry Elmer Barnes, *An Intellectual and Cultural History of the Western World* (3 vols., 3rd ed., rev., Dover, 1952). Though first published in 1865, F. A. Lange's *The History of Materialism* (one volume trans., Humanities Press, 1950) may still be profitably consulted. A problem with Lange's treatment, prevalent among many commentators on "materialism," is an intolerably vague conception of what the term "materialism" purportedly signifies.

A. D. White's *History of the Warfare of Science with Theology in Christendom* (2 vols., 1896; Dover, 1960) is deservedly a classic in its field. Although it has been convicted of some errors of detail—which is almost inevitable in any pathbreaking work—its major theses have withstood the test of time. A precursor to White, though less satisfactory in its overall treatment, is John Draper's *History of the Conflict Between Religion and Science* (Appleton, 1875). Rejoinders to White and Draper—which delight in pointing out that many great scientists were and are devout Christians—are remarkably adept at missing the point.

A superb study of philosophic thought from the late Middle Ages to the mid-nineteenth century is found in John H. Randall, Jr., *The Career of Philosophy* (2 vols., Columbia Univ. Press, 1962). Also outstanding is Preserved Smith, *A History of Modern Culture* (2 vols., Henry Holt, 1930, 1934). Both Randall and Smith give sympathetic accounts of the influence of freethought and secularism.

More specifically focused on religious skepticism during the same general period are, George T. Buckley, *Atheism in the English Renaissance* (1932; Russell and Russell, 1965); Don Cameron Allen, *Doubt's Boundless Sea* (John Hopkins, 1964); and Richard Popkin, *The History of Skepticism from Erasmus to Descartes* (rev., Harper and Row, 1968). Allen's book is bulging with information about the many antiatheist treatises during a period when there were few, if any, real atheists. Popkin's work is a seminal study of the revival of Pyrrhonic skepticism in the sixteenth century and its effect on theological and philosophical controversies.

One of the most significant precedents to modern freethought was the British deistic movement of the eighteenth century. Some deists sought to "reform" Christianity, while others were openly antagonistic, but they shared belief in a god of "nature," who, after creating the universe, left it to its own devices. Deists were usually hostile to revealed religion, whether in the form of alleged miracles or sacred scripture, and they became notorious for their attacks on traditional Christian doctrines.

A famous but unfairly negative account of British deism is Leslie Stephen, *History of English Thought in the Eighteenth Century* (2 vols., 3rd ed., 1902; Harcourt, Brace & World, 1962). Stephen was an agnostic, but he was hard on such deists as Anthony Collins and Thomas Woolston. His excesses are counteracted by the more judicious treatment of J. M. Robertson in *The Dynamics of Religion* (1897; 2nd ed., rev., Watts, 1926).

A balanced view of deism is presented in Ernest C. Mossner's *Bishop Butler and the Age of Reason* (Macmillan, 1936), and an exhaustive summary of the deists and their works is found in John Orr's *English Deism: Its Roots and Its Fruits* (Eerdmans, 1934). S. G. Hefelbower, *The Relation of John Locke to English Deism* (Univ. of Chicago, 1918) explores this sticky issue, while Norman Torrey, *Voltaire and the English Deists* (1930; Archon, 1967) gives a reliable summary of the French skeptic's reliance upon his English predecessors. For those who wish to sample the deists first hand, an excellent selection of deistic works is found in E. Graham Waring, *Deism and Natural Religion: A Sourcebook* (Ungar, 1967).

Important preludes to the deistic movement include *De Veritate* (1624) by Lord Herbert of Cherbury, who is often referred to as the "Father of English Deism"; *Leviathan* (1651), by Thomas Hobbes, who scandalized the intellectual community with his broadside attacks on established religious doctrines; and *Theological-Political Treatise* (1670), by Spinoza, who subjected the Bible to the court of reason with consumate skill.

The writings of the British deists are too numerous to be catalogued here, but we can survey a few of the significant items.

Charles Blount, although he professed loyalty to Christianity, produced three works that laid the foundation for later deistic works. These were *Anima Mundi* (1679), *Great is Diana of the Ephesians* (1680), and *Oracles of Reason* (1693). Influenced by Hobbes and Spinoza, Blount upheld reason over revelation and launched a critical analysis of the Bible.

Another professed Christian reformer, John Toland, wrote *Christianity not Mysterious* in 1696, which proved to be one of the most influential deistic books ever written. Building upon Locke's theory of knowledge, Toland sought to remove from Christianity anything that claimed to transcend reason. He received a cold reception from Locke, but this was preferable to the warmer reception of the Irish Parliament, which saw fit to burn the first edition of his work.

Another follower of Locke was Anthony Collins, author of the classic *Discourse of Freethinking* (1713), which was largely a plea for toleration. Collins also wrote *Discourse of the Grounds and Reasons of the Christian Religion* (1724), a pathbreaking analysis of Old Testament prophecies allegedly fulfilled by Jesus. Showing the absurdity of taking the prophecies literally, Collins called for an allegorical interpretation—but in the appeal to allegory, common among deists at the time, it is difficult to separate sincerity from a ruse to escape legal penalties for blasphemy.

Then there was Thomas Woolston, called by one critic "poor mad Woolston, most scandalous of the deists," and charged by another with "scurrilous buffoonery and gross raillery." This learned Cambridge graduate was thought quite sane until he attacked the reported miracles of the New Testament with uncompromising vigor in a series of six *Discourses on the Miracles of Our Savior* (1727–29).

Woolston, like Collins, sought refuge in allegorical interpretation, but unlike Collins, he signed his name to his books. This led to his conviction on a charge of blasphemy in 1729, for which he was fined and imprisoned.

In his charges that Jesus was an imposter and magician, Woolston instigated a ribald, popular form of freethought that influenced such figures as Voltaire. A more dispassionate form of deism with a more constructive emphasis appeared in Matthew Tindal's *Christianity as Old as Creation* (1730). Often called the Deistic Bible, this work marked the apex of British deism, eliciting over 150 replies. Here were compiled the most cogent arguments for a "Natural Religion." The slant of this book may be gleaned from some of its chapter titles: "That the Perfection, and Happiness of all rational Beings, Supreme, as well as Subordinate, consists in living up to the Dictates of their Nature"; "That the Religion of Nature is an absolutely perfect Religion; and that external Revelation can neither add to, nor take from its Perfection . . . ."

Deism was carried to the "working class" mostly through the writings of Peter Annet. His *History and Character of Saint Paul* (1750) portrayed Paul as lazy, greedy, and dishonest, and *The Resurrection of Jesus Considered* (1744) appealed to the unreliable and contradictory nature of the resurrection accounts as a basis for discounting their credibility. "If it not be fit to examine into Truth," declared Annet in a passionate appeal common among freethinkers, "Truth is not fit to be known." Apparently the British government disagreed. For attempting to "diffuse and propagate irreligious and diabolical opinions in the minds of His Majesty's subjects, and to shake the foundations of the Christian religion," Annet, at the advanced age of seventy, was pilloried (with a paper on his forehead inscribed "blasphemy") and sentenced to a year of hard labor in prison.

(An interesting sidelight to Annet is his book, *Social Bliss Considered: In Marriage and Divorce; Cohabitating Unmarried, and Public Whoring*, published under the pseudonym of "Gideon Archer" in 1749. This work calls for the legalization of divorce, unmarried cohabitation, and prostitution.)

Among other important deistic works of the same period, we should mention the following: *The True Gospel of Jesus Christ Asserted* (1739) by Thomas Chubb; the posthumous *Philosophical Works* of Lord Bolingbroke (1754); *Free Inquiry into the Miraculous Powers, which are Supposed to have Subsisted in the Christian Church* (1749) by Conyers Middleton; and *The Religion of Nature Delineated* (1722) by William Wollaston (which, incidentally, contains a little-known but superb defense of property rights from a libertarian perspective).

Finally, there was David Hume, the philosophic genius who, although he did not enter the fray of religious controversy to the extent of other deists, contributed the most sophisticated and influential arguments against Christianity and revealed religion—the most famous being his celebrated attack on miracles in *An Inquiry Concerning Human Understanding* (1748). His other works pertaining to religion were *The Natural History of Religion* (1757) and *Dialogues Concerning Natural Religion* (apparently written around 1757 but not published until 1779, after his death). For a good exposition of Hume, see Antony Flew's *Hume's Philosophy of Belief* (Routledge & Kegan Paul, 1961).

Freethought reached its highpoint in nineteenth-century Britain, where it became militantly anti-Christian and often atheistic. This period is discussed in detail in J. M. Robertson, *A History of Freethought in the Nineteenth Century (supra)*; a readable survey of the intellectual climate, with a different emphasis than Robertson, is A. W. Benn's *The History of English Rationalism in the Nineteenth Century* (2 vols., 1906; Russell & Russell, 1962). Edward Royle's superb *Victorian Infidels* (Univ. of Manchester, 1974) concentrates on the secularist movement initiated by G. J. Holyoake. Several other works fill out the century: W. S. Smith's *The London Heretics, 1870–1914* (Dodd, Mead, 1968) is excellent, as is David Tribe's *100 Years of Freethought* (Elek, 1967). A. H. Nethercot *The First Five Lives of Annie Besant* (Univ. of Chicago, 1960) explores the dynamic but unstable life of this enigmatic woman during her association with Charles Bradlaugh and the freethought movement, prior to her conversion to Theosophy under the spell of Mme. Blavatsky.

Of the many significant figures in British freethought, only a few will be mentioned here. George Jacob Holyoake (1817–1906) was a disciple of Robert Owen and a major exponent of "co-operation"—a kind of voluntary socialism. (See his *History of Co-operation*, rev., T. Fisher Unwin, 1908.) Holyoake coined the term "secularism," which he believed preferable to "atheism," and as the founder and editor of about ten magazines he exerted a great deal of influence. For his suggestion that the deity be put on "half-pay," he served a six-month prison sentence—the details of which are recounted in his *History of the Last Trial by Jury for Atheism* (1851; Arno, 1972). Among Holyoake's better works are *The Trial of Theism* (rev., Trubner & Co., 1877), an excellent defense of atheism, and *English Secularism* (Open Court, 1896). Like many freethinkers of his day, Holyoake actively engaged in debates with the clergy. One of his better known was with Rev. Brewin Grant on *Christianity and Secularism* (Ward & Co., 1854), which occupied six evenings. A rambling autobiography of Holyoake is found in his *Sixty Years of an Agitator's Life* (2 vols., T. Fisher Unwin, 1900), and additional details are provided in Joseph McCabe, *Life and Letters of George Jacob Holyoake* (2 vols., Watts, 1908).

Charles Bradlaugh (1833–1891) was the most important atheist ever produced by Britain. A superb orator, writer, and organizer, Bradlaugh replaced Holyoake as the militant force in British freethought. He edited the *National Reformer*, a freethought weekly, and in 1866 he founded the National Secular Society. In 1876 he and Annie Besant were prosecuted for publishing C. Knowlton's *Fruits of Philosophy* (a pamphlet on birth control), but Bradlaugh, an excellent lawyer, succeeded in quashing the indictment. (For an account of the trial, see *The Queen v. Charles Bradlaugh and Annie Besant*, Freethought Publishing Co., n.d.) Although elected to Parliament in 1880, Bradlaugh's atheism prevented him from being seated until 1886.

Some of Bradlaugh's better essays—including his magnificent "Plea for Atheism"—are contained in *Humanity's Gain From Unbelief* (Watts, 1929), and articles by and about Bradlaugh are found in J. P. Gilmour, ed., *Champion of Liberty: Charles Bradlaugh* (Watts, 1933; Arno, 1972). An outstanding biography of Bradlaugh is David Tribe's *President*

Charles Bradlaugh, M. P. (Archon, 1971), which contains an extensive list of his writings. Still useful is the older biography by Bradlaugh's daughter, H. B. Bonner, *Charles Bradlaugh: A Record of His Life and Work* (with J. M. Robertson, 2 vols., T. Fisher Unwin, 1898).

One of the great contributions of nineteenth-century freethinkers was their dogged persistence in fighting for freedom of speech and press. Many well-known freethinkers—such as Holyoake, Robert Taylor, and G. W. Foote in Britain, and D. M. Bennett in the United States—were routinely trotted off to jail, sometime for long sentences, not to mention heavy fines. The highest price paid was by the publisher Richard Carlile, who, between 1817 and 1835, served over nine years in prison for publishing, among other items, Paine's *Age of Reason*. In addition, Carlile's wife, sister, and over twenty of his workers served time, sometimes for two years or more. But the freethinkers had a knack for making adversity work for them, and Carlile was no exception. As a result of the publicity surrounding one of his trials, sales of the *Age of Reason* skyrocketed to over 2,000 within two months. Moreover, Carlile read the entire text of the *Age of Reason* during his defense, which was then allowed to circulate as part of the verbatim trial transcript. In this inexpensive form it sold over 10,000 copies. For details on Carlile, see Guy A. Aldred, *Richard Carlile, Agitator* (Pioneer Press, 1923). A summary account of blasphemy prosecutions is contained in H. B. Bonner, *Penalties Upon Opinion* (Watts, 1913).

Freethought in eighteenth-century America, as in England, took the form of deistic belief in a god of nature and vigorous attacks on Christian revelation. An excellent treatment of American deism is Adolf Koch, *Republican Religion* (1933), reprinted as *Religion of the American Enlightenment* (Thomas Crowell, 1968). The first overt American attack on Christianity was Ethan Allen's *Reason the Only Oracle of Man* (1784), a rambling and poorly written collection of essays compiled by Allen since his youth. In stark contrast is Thomas Paine's classic masterpiece, *Age of Reason* (Pt. I, 1794; Pt. II, 1796). Although it appeared after the peak of the deistic movement and contains little that is original,

Age of Reason is perhaps the finest deistic piece ever penned, thanks to Paine's literary genius.

Concerning Paine's religious views, see M. D. Conway, *The Life of Thomas Paine* (1892; G. P. Putnam's Sons, 1909); and Ira M. Thompson, Jr., *The Religious Beliefs of Thomas Paine* (Vantage, 1965). Recent biographies of Paine include Audrey Williamson, *Thomas Paine* (Allen & Unwin, 1973); and David F. Hawke, *Paine* (Harper & Row, 1974).

Early nineteenth-century American freethought is surveyed in A. Post, *Popular Freethought, 1820–1850* (Columbia Univ. Press, 1943). This survey is continued in Sidney Warren, *American Freethought, 1860–1914* (Columbia Univ. Press, 1943). A sprawling and rare work that contains much first-hand information about nineteenth-century American freethinkers, is S. P. Putnam, *400 Years of Freethought* (Truth Seeker, 1894). Another informative account of American freethought, centering around the history of *The Truth Seeker* (a freethought paper started by D. M. Bennett in 1873), is George MacDonald's *Fifty Years of Freethought* (2 vols., Truth Seeker, 1929, 1931).

The giant of American freethought was Robert G. Ingersoll (1833–1899). One of America's greatest orator's, he was immensely successful in popularizing the ideas of freethought. Many different editions of his speeches were published (some of them pirated), but the authorized editions are contained in the "Dresden Edition" of *The Works of Robert G. Ingersoll* (12 vols., C. P. Farrell, 1900). A meticulous bibliography of works by and about Ingersoll is found in Gordon Stein, *Robert G. Ingersoll: A Checklist* (Kent State Univ. Press, 1969). The best biography of Ingersoll to date is Orvin Larson's *American Infidel: Robert G. Ingersoll* (Citadel Press, 1962).

Although this essay deals primarily with freethought in England and America, it would border on criminal negligence not to mention the tremendously important contributions of eighteenth-century French freethinkers, commonly referred to as philosophes.

J. S. Spink's *French Free-Thought from Gassendi to Voltaire* (Univ. of London, 1960) is a reliable, scholarly treatment. The formative period of the Enlightenment, 1680–1715, is treated by Paul Hazard in *The European Mind* (1935; World, 1963). A sympathetic account of the philosophes is contained in Peter Gay, *The Enlightenment: An Interpretation* (Vol. I, Knopf, 1967). Also recommended is George R. Havens, *The Age of Ideas* (1955; Collier, 1962). An excellent selection of Enlightenment writing is found in Peter Gay, ed., *The Enlightenment: A Comprehensive Anthology* (Simon & Schuster, 1973).

One of the important influences on the French Enlightenment was Pierre Bayle's *Historical and Critical Dictionary,* first published in 1697 and revised on several subsequent occasions. An abridged translation of this voluminous work is in the Library of Liberal Arts series (Richard Popkin, ed., Bobbs-Merrill, 1965). Although Bayle professed Calvinism, his sincerity has been questioned due to his many scandalous remarks about Christianity and the Bible. It is widely believed that Bayle, like other unorthodox thinkers of his time, professed to be more religious than he really was in an effort to avoid potentially severe legal penalties. This is the general view, for instance, of Howard Robinson's *Bayle the Sceptic* (Columbia Univ. Press, 1931). More recently, however, scholars have granted more credibility to Bayle's fideism (attacking reason to make room for faith), as is demonstrated in Karl C. Sandberg, *At the Crossroads of Faith and Reason: An Essay on Pierre Bayle* (Univ. of Arizona, 1966).

The best known figure of the French Enlightenment was François-Marie Arouet, better known as Voltaire. His writing is extensive and is available in many easily located editions. A representative selection of his work is contained in Peter Gay's edited translation of the *Philosophical Dictionary* (Basic Books, 1962). Of the numerous biographies of Voltaire, one of the best is Theodore Besterman, *Voltaire* (Harcourt, Brace, and World, 1969).

As a deist, Voltaire was at loggerheads with the more radical atheists of his time, such as Diderot and d'Holbach. Diderot, known primarily as the editor of the monumental *Encyclopedia* (which he worked on from 1751–65), paid his dues with three years of imprisonment. Arthur M. Wilson's *Diderot* (Oxford, 1972) is a brilliant biography of this amazing and versatile mind. Some of Diderot's opinions on religion—e.g., "The Christian religion teaches us to imitate a God that is cruel, insidious, jealous, and implacable in his wrath"—are contained in "Thoughts on Religion," an essay reprinted by Richard Carlile in 1819. For an anthology of Diderot's philosophical writing, see J. Kemp, ed., *Diderot: Interpreter of Nature* (International Pub., 1963).

Baron d'Holbach, an import from Germany and a patron of the philosophes, is justly famous for his *System of Nature*, published in 1770 under the name of "Mirabaud" (a French writer who died in 1760)—a device to conceal and protect the true author. D'Holbach was probably assisted by Diderot and other Paris intellectuals, and the result was a magnificent, if somewhat prolix, defense of atheism and naturalism—the first explicit atheistic treatise of Western civilization (or at least the first one to survive). "Let us then conclude," wrote d'Holbach, "that the word *God* . . ., not presenting to the mind any true idea, ought to be banished [from] the language of all those who are desirous to speak so as to be understood" (H. D. Robinson, trans., J. P. Mendum, 1889). This is typical of the vigorous, uncompromising tone of *The System of Nature*, the best and most influential defense of atheism ever written.

A greatly condensed version of d'Holbach's masterpiece is available under the title *Superstition in all Ages* (Peter Eckler, 1889; reprinted many times by various freethought publishers), which is mistakenly attributed to Jean Meslier, a priest who declared himself a heretic posthumously in his *Testament*. (This mistaken authorship remains uncorrected even in the 1972 Arno Press edition.)

I shall conclude this survey of freethought works with an important but neglected body of literature that denies any basis for belief in a historical Jesus, even the watered-down Jesus of Protestant liberalism. The first mention of this "Jesus revisionism" is by Voltaire, who reported that he was visited in 1769 by "some disciples of Bolingbroke, more ingenious than learned," who argued that Jesus never existed. Voltaire was unconvinced, but the mythicist theory was given shape by two Frenchmen: Count Volney in *Ruins of Empires* (1791) and Charles Francois Dupuis in *Origins of all Religions* (5 vols., 1795).

Dupuis contended that Christianity is a variation of the ancient Solar Myth and that Jesus is merely another guise of ancient mythical deities. "The hero of the legends known by the name of gospels," he wrote, "is the same hero who has been celebrated with far more genius in the poems written in honor of Bacchus, Osiris, Hercules, Adonis, and others."

Another staunch defender of the mythicist thesis was the renegade British clergyman, Robert Taylor. During his first imprisonment for blasphemy, he wrote *Syntagma of the Evidences of the Christian Religion* (1828; J. P. Mendum, 1876) and *The Diegesis, Being a Discovery of the Origin, Evidences, and Early History of Christianity* (1829; J. P. Mendum, 1853). Taylor was a learned and original—if sometimes unreliable—scholar. This last is understandable considering the difficult conditions under which he worked.

Better known than Taylor was German theologian Bruno Bauer, who, in a series of books appearing after 1840, denied the historicity of Jesus. Bauer regarded Jesus as a fictitious character invented by the author of Mark as an expression of faith. (For an account of Bauer and other radical theologicans during the same period, see Albert Schweitzer, *The Quest of the Historical Jesus*, 1906; Macmillan, 1968.)

Another interesting presentation of the mythicist case is *Revelations of Antichrist*, published anonymously but written by W. H. Burr (1879; Arno, 1972).

The most scholarly and formidable presentation of the mythicist thesis was penned by John M. Robertson. His major works on this subject were *Christianity and Mythology* (Watts, 1900; rev., 1910) and *Pagan Christs* (Watts, 1903; rev., 1911). These were followed by three volumes in which he expanded his case and replied to his critics: *The Historical Jesus* (Watts, 1916), *The Jesus Problem* (Watts, 1917), and *Jesus and Judas* (Watts, 1927).

Among the other books defending Jesus revisionism, the following are noteworthy: *The Christ Myth* (Open Court, 1911) and *The Witness to the Historicity of Jesus* (Watts, 1912; Arno, 1972), both by Arthur Drews; *Ecce Deus* (Watts, 1912) by W. B. Smith; *The Origins of Christianity* (4th ed., Watts, 1933) by Thomas Whittaker;

The Creation of Christ (2 vols., Watts, 1939) by P. L. Couchoud; and *Ancient History of the God Jesus* (Watts, 1938) by Edouard Dujardin.

An excellent overview of the mythicist controversy, written by a rationalist scholar who believed in the historical reality of Jesus, is A. Robertson, *Jesus: Myth or History,* (2nd ed., Watts, 1949). More recently, an excellent defense of the mythicist thesis is found in Herbert Cutner's *Jesus: God, Man, or Myth?* (Truth Seeker, 1950). And the mythicist gauntlet has been skillfully wielded by G. A. Wells in two books: *The Jesus of the Early Christians* (Pemberton, 1971) and *Did Jesus Exist?* (Elek, 1975). Both of these detailed works are highly recommended.

Part 2

Ayn Rand

9
Atheism and Objectivism

The atheism of Ayn Rand is regarded by many people, especially political conservatives, as the most pernicious aspect of Objectivism. Yet, though vehemently opposed to faith and mysticism, Rand has never placed much emphasis on atheism per se. The Objectivist position on atheism was summarized by Nathaniel Branden in *The Objectivist Newsletter*.

> As uncompromising advocates of reason, Objectivists are, of course, atheists. We are intransigent atheists, not militant ones. We are for reason; therefore, as a consequence, we are opposed to any form of mysticism; therefore, we do not grant any validity to the notion of a supernatural being. But atheism is scarcely the center of our philosophical position. To be known as crusaders for atheism would be acutely embarrassing to us; the adversary is too unworthy.

The significance of Ayn Rand's atheism lies in its philosophical underpinnings, especially in her theory of knowledge. Rand's epistemology distinguishes her from many atheists as well from religionists. It is for this reason that the charges of epistemological skepticism, nihilism, and pessimism leveled at some atheists (sometimes legitimately) do not apply to Rand.

Atheism has been defended from a number of different philosophical perspectives, and the fact that a person is an atheist does not necessarily mean that he has something significantly in common with other atheists. Philosophers who differ from Rand in crucially important areas have, nonetheless, defended atheism. Existentialists, Marxists, logical positivists, linguistic analysts—all of these, to name but a few, have defended atheism. But some of these approaches offer weak or invalid defenses of atheism, or they defend atheism at an enormously high cost, such as rejecting theism as a corollary of rejecting metaphysical inquiry altogether. Thus, in the course of examining Objectivist atheism, I shall outline other approaches to atheism, pointing out their strengths and weaknesses, and I shall contrast these approaches with that of Objectivism.

Before proceeding, it is necessary to specify briefly what I mean by the terms *theism* and *atheism*. *Theism* is the belief in a god or in any number of gods. But what is a god? This can be a rather complex question. For the purpose of this discussion, I shall consider a god to be any supernatural being—any being, in other words, that is "above" or "beyond" natural law. A god is exempt from some or all of the natural laws that characterize entities existing within the framework of the natural universe.

It is important to note that in order for a being to qualify as a god in this sense, it is not enough that it be superior to man in terms of its attributes and capacities. It is possible, for example, that we may eventually discover some kind of superior life on another planet, but these creatures, since they would be subject to natural law, would not qualify as gods. Nor does the fact that one man is extraordinarily strong make him a god in relation to weaker men. If the dispute between theism and atheism is to have any *philosophical* significance, a god must differ from natural beings in kind, not merely in degree.

A *theist*, therefore, is a person who believes in the existence of a supernatural being, and, because the supernatural lies beyond our comprehension, a theist also believes in the existence of the unknowable.

What is atheism? The prefix "a" means "without," so *atheism* literally means "without theism," or "without belief in a god or gods." One who does not believe in the existence of a god or supernatural being is properly designated as an atheist.

Atheism is sometimes defined as the belief that there is no god of any kind, or the claim that a god cannot exist. While these are catagories of atheism, they do not exhaust the meaning of atheism, and they are somewhat misleading with respect to the basic nature of atheism. Atheism, in its basic form, is not a belief; it is the absence of belief. An atheist is not primarily a person who believes that a god does not exist; rather, he does not believe in the existence of a god.

The first kind of atheism I shall call ethical atheism, by which I mean the rejection of theistic belief for ethical reasons. This approach is found in existentialist atheism, as promulgated by Sartre and Camus, whose position may be unsympathetically summarized as follows: If God existed, life would not be absurd and meaningless. Life is absurd and meaningless, therefore God does not exist. In the name of misery, anxiety, and helplessness, existentialists have espoused atheism.

A major theme in existentialism is human freedom, and the existence of a god, it is claimed, would jeopardize this freedom. At first glance, this position appears to have merit, but this merit soon disappears upon closer examination. By freedom, existentialists do not mean simply the freedom to choose one's own values; they mean, in effect, the freedom to choose one's own nature. Man, according to existentialism, is born into an absurd, meaningless world, without purpose and without values. Man exists, but he is without an essence. His existence precedes his essence. This, understandably, fills him with dread and despair; and to escape the inherent meaninglessness of life, man must, through freely chosen commitment, shape his own essence.

Where Objectivism says that man should freely select his values according to a rational standard of value—a standard determined by man's nature—existentialism says that each man must choose his own standard of value. Each man must decide for himself, through some unspecified and presumably arbitrary means, what is good and what is evil, what is right and what is wrong. Good and evil depend solely on individual choice; existentialists defend ethical subjectivism, and they reject God in the name of this subjectivism.

To introduce God into the universe would be to introduce a kind of objectivism into ethics, because the good would become synonymous with God's decrees. With this universal standard of goodness, man would no longer be free to choose his own good. In more blunt terms, existentialists reject theism because the existence of God would eliminate ethical caprice, and caprice is essential to the ethics of existentialism. There is a very important sense in which "freedom," for existentialists, means freedom from the facts of reality, and it is in behalf of this kind of freedom that they defend atheism.

With ethical atheism of the existentialist variety, we see a paradigm of what is the most disastrous move that an atheist can make: to defend atheism in the name of subjectivism. Ethical subjectivism, or the denial of objective ethical standards, is only a step removed from ethical nihilism, or the obliteration of ethics altogether. To defend atheism in the name of subjectivism is to grant theism an honor that it does not deserve; it is to imply that theism is on the side of reason in ethics, whereas this kind of atheism is basically antireason. This is not an atheism which is in any sense desirable.

Of course, some forms of ethical atheism do not defend subjectivism. Some atheists, such as Erich Fromm, have criticized religion because it promotes moral authoritarianism, and this Fromm regards, rightly, as antithetical to human happiness and autonomy. But any variety of ethical atheism is on weak theoretical ground, because the ethical consequence of theism is a secondary issue beside the issue of truth and falsehood. Can the belief in a god be justified rationally? If so, one should be a theist. If not, one should be an atheist. The existence of a god would indeed have unfortunate consequences for morality—especially if this god were the God of Christianity—but these unfortunate consequences do not, in themselves, refute theism. The issue of morality should arise only after the rationality of theistic belief has been determined.

Another kind of atheism is psychological atheism, which means the rejection of theistic belief through an explanation of its psychological origins. A little-known philosopher who took this approach was Ludwig Feuerbach, a nineteenth-century German philosopher who greatly influenced such men as Nietzsche, Marx, and Freud. In *The Essence of Christianity,* Feuerbach argued that the belief in a god represents man's highest aspirations in an otherworldly form. Man dehumanizes his ideals, such as love, strength and wisdom, and places them in a supernatural realm under the name of God. But this alienates man from these ideals, making them seem appropriate only to God and unattainable to man. Thus, according to Feuerbach, we should reject God, but not the divine attributes themselves. These should be returned to the natural world, within the grasp of man, where they properly belong. (Freud used a variant of this approach, postulating the desire for a father image as the origin of religious belief. "God," wrote Freud, "is at bottom nothing but an exalted father.")

Without considering the validity of these psychological pronouncements, it is important to recognize that they constitute invalid grounds for atheism. They commit what is known as the *genetic fallacy*, which means the attempt to refute a belief through an examination of its psychological origins. How we acquired our beliefs does not affect their present cognitive value, as long as we are willing to argue for them. Psychologizing is not the business of a philosopher, and to explain the psychological origins of religious belief does not constitute a philosophical refutation. Any variant of psychological atheism, even if its psychological analysis is correct, simply misses the point. It is an altogether incorrect approach to atheism.

Next we come to what may be called, for lack of a better name, sociological atheism. This is the doctrine, prominent among many nineteenth-century socialists and anarchists, that says religion has served as a repressive force throughout history, justifying the ruling class and its atrocities. According to Engels, God represents "the alien domination of the capitalist mode of production." "Slaves of God," wrote the anarchist Bakunin in *God and the State*, "men must also be slaves of Church and State, in so far as the State is consecrated by the Church."

Although it is true that churches have often exerted influence through the power of the state, this is an issue of political theory, not of atheism. The fact that Christians have practiced torture and repression does not refute theistic belief any more than comparable behavior by Communists refutes atheism. Like ethical and psychological atheism, sociological atheism is based on irrelevant reasons.

Another general approach to atheism may be described as pragmatic atheism. This is the belief that, although theism may have fulfilled man's needs in the past, it is no longer sufficient for that task. In other words, belief in a god is deemed no longer "useful" and is therefore rejected on pragmatic grounds.

This approach is so nebulous and philosophically inept that it is rarely defended explicitly. There are strains of it, however, in that modern, absurd spectacle known as "Death of God" theology, whose advocates claim that a transcendent god is no longer relevant to the requirements of contemporary society. The God of traditional theology, therefore, is pronounced dead.

Pragmatic atheism is also defended by the would-be philosopher who wants to offer an apparently sophisticated reason for atheism, and so tells us that theistic belief is not useful or relevant—without specifying, of course, the criteria of usefulness and relevance and without specifying what all this has to do with the rational basis for theistic belief.

There is no need to comment on this approach in detail. Pragmatic atheism evades completely the issue of truth and falsehood, not to mention its suggestion that theistic belief was at one time "useful," which extends to theism undeserved credit.

Another variety of atheism is metaphysical atheism, or the rejection of theism on metaphysical grounds. This approach is most often found in strict materialists, such as Baron d'Holbach (1723–1789) and Karl Marx. According to materialistic atheism, only matter exists. But God is allegedly immaterial; therefore, God does not exist.

Within certain limits, this approach may have some merit—at

least more than the approaches discussed thus far—but, as used by most materialists, it has unfortunate implications. When reductive materialists say that only matter exists, they rule out, not only God, but consciousness and conceptual thought as well. Consciousness, according to strict materialists, is reducible to physical movements in the brain. Other materialists take a moderate position, claiming that consciousness is not synonymous with physical events, but is a byproduct of matter. In any case, metaphysical atheism, whatever form it may take, tends to be a weak defense, primarily for the reason that it shifts the burden of proof from the theist to the atheist. The metaphysical atheist must now demonstrate that only matter exists, and his atheism depends on the effectiveness of this demonstration. In a proper defense of atheism, however, the onus of proof resides entirely with the theist; the metaphysical atheist, by shifting this responsibility, places himself in a precarious position.

Finally, we come to the most significant variety of atheism, the variety of which Objectivism is a subcategory. This is epistemological atheism, or the rejection of theism on epistemological grounds. It is epistemological atheism that delves into such issues as the meaning of theistic terms and the evidence in their favor.

Most contemporary atheists are epistemological atheists, and there are many subcategories of this approach. First, there is skeptical atheism, which derives from a skepticism about all knowledge (or at least *certain* knowledge), whether of God or anything else. Of course, if one can't know anything, then one can't know of God's existence, and atheism follows inevitably—but this is a disastrously high price to pay in defense of atheism, not to mention that it is an absurd positon to maintain.

Although not an atheist himself, the eighteenth-century philosopher David Hume laid the foundation for skeptical atheism in some respects. Hume did not deny the possibility of all knowledge, but he did uphold certain epistemological positions, which, if carried to their logical extremes, lead inevitably to epistemological nihilism. This is not to deny Hume's contributions to the critique of theism—his *Dialogues Concerning Natural Religion*, for example, is a masterful work—but many of Hume's criticisms of religion are based on a more basic critique of human knowledge in general. For instance, one of Hume's most famous doctrines is his denial that the principle of necessary causation has any metaphysical basis. Belief in causality, for Hume, results from psychological conditioning. There is nothing logically impossible, Hume believed, involved in a cat giving birth to baby elephants. We don't see such things happening, so we assume that they are impossible; but we must recognize, argued Hume, that this is mere psychological prejudice on our part with no metaphysical foundation.

Many alleged proofs for the existence of a god rest on causal inferences, such as the supposed inference we must make to a first cause of the universe. But if causal inference in general is invalid, as Hume maintained, then none of these theistic arguments are valid. Such theistic demonstrations, therefore, are doomed to failure. In the process of this attack, however, every other argument that rests on causal inference—whether theistic or naturalistic—is doomed as well. Here we have an example of excluding theism as a byproduct of excluding a crucial element of knowledge.

It should be stressed that epistemological skepticism, while providing a superficial defense of atheism, works more in favor of theism than atheism. If it is impossible to justify our knowledge claims, then one belief becomes as good as any other. The theist cannot justify his beliefs, but, according to skepticism, neither can the atheist. Skepticism invites people to play deuces-wild with their knowledge claims; the belief in a god becomes as defensible—or, more accurately, as indefensible—as any other.

Consider the fact that most forms of theistic belief rely heavily on the concept of faith. Consider also that skepticism is the precursor of faith; it opens the door that makes faith possible. People who defend skepticism set the stage for faith.

Suppose that one maintains that every claim to knowledge must meet the minimum requirements of rational demonstration or be rejected as irrational. This, which is the position of the antiskeptic, excludes the possiblity of faith; there is no room for faith in such a scheme. Suppose, however, that one maintains that many claims to knowledge can never, in principle, be justified. This, which is the position of the skeptic, leaves an opening for faith. Since we cannot justify our beliefs rationally, argues the theist, we must rely on faith. Christians will frequently defend faith in God by claiming that the atheist also has faith, but the atheist places faith in reason rather than in God. Christians will thus claim that the position of the atheist is no stronger than their own.

If atheists rely on skepticism, it will inevitably turn against them and be used as major defensive ploy by the theist. It is the theist, not the atheist, who must align with skepticism.

Another prominent variety of epistemological atheism stems from the school of philosophy known as logical positivism. Logical positivism is now out of style among philosophers, but its influence is still felt. Its most famous doctrine was the principle of verification, which stated that any proposition that cannot be verified by sense experience is literally meaningless.

In *Language, Truth, and Logic*, the bible of logical positivism published in 1936, A. J. Ayer argued that "to say that 'God exists' is to make a metaphysical utterance which cannot be either true or false. And no sentence which purports to describe the nature of a transcendent god can possess any literal significance." As indicated by this passage, theism was rejected by positivists as a corollary of their rejection of metaphysical inquiry altogether. God was discarded, but so were such topics as causality, natural law, and ethics. In fact, most logical positivists held that ethical judgments were cognitively meaningless; this later evolved into the theory known as emotivism, the doctrine that ethical judgments are nothing more than expressions of emotion. The atheism of logical positivism was another instance of throwing out the baby with the bathwater.

Next we come to the atheism of that school of thought known as linguistic analysis, or "ordinary-language philosophy." Analysts are united primarily by their common conception of the nature and scope of philosophy. According to linguistic philosophy, the primary function of philosophy, and perhaps the only function, should be the analysis and clarification of language. The endless and confusing problems of past philosophers, claim the analysts, can be resolved through linguistic exploration—exploration that will reveal widespread misuse of language. A person who pays close attention to language will not become embroiled in the many pseudo-problems that have perplexed traditional philosophers. Analytic philosophy has its good points and its bad points, which may be summarized as follows.

On its positive side, analytic philosophy has stressed that the meaning of theistic terms, such as "god," must precede any judgment of truth or falsehood regarding theistic claims. Before we can determine the truth or falsehood of the proposition, "God exists," we must understand the meaning of "god." If no intelligible description or definition is forthcoming, the case for theism collapses. Some analysts have also attacked the pompous and verbose terminology that is so typical of theology, and this is another respect in which analytic philosophy has performed a valuable task in defense of atheism.

On the negative side, however, some analysts have severely restricted the scope and, consequently, the importance of philosophy. Whereas medieval theologians made philosophy into the handmaiden of theology, analysts have transformed philosophy into the handmaiden of language. Language, not reality as a whole, is made the subject matter of philosophy, and philosophy is reduced to a kind of linguistic therapy.

An unfortunate consequence of this reliance on language is that analytic philosophy sometimes functions as a defense of the status quo, linguistically speaking. Starting from the manner in which language is ordinarily used, it becomes extremely difficult for analysts to discard certain words that have been used for thousands of years, such as the term "god." This has been recognized by some theists, who have subsequently enlisted the aid of linguistic analysis. Religious propositions, these theists argue, have been used by millions of persons for thousands of years, so they must serve some legitimate function. It is not within the province of philosophy to discard them as ridiculous or nonsensical, rather, we must accept these religious propositions as given and proceed to analyze what people have meant by them. It is in this way that ordinary language philosophy opened another door for theism.

Our last variety of epistemological atheism is Objectivist atheism. As mentioned previously, there are some similarities between Objectivist atheism and a few of the approaches discussed thus far. For example, Objectivist atheism stresses, but did not originate, the idea that the term "god" must be defined before any attempt is made to establish its existence. It also stresses the "onus of proof principle," or the idea that the burden of proof falls entirely on the theist to establish his case rationally, and that the atheist is obliged to do nothing more than answer theistic arguments. There is no "positive case" for atheism. If theistic arguments fail, theism fails, and atheism emerges as the only rational alternative.

Despite this common ground, Objectivism differs radically from most other forms of atheism. The most important difference is that, unlike most atheists, Rand is an Aristotelian. Although much of Objectivism (especially its metaphysics) differs significantly from Aristotelian philosophy, Rand falls generally within the Aristotelian tradition, particularly in her view of philosophy, the nature of human cognition, and the role of ethics in our lives.

The emergence of an Aristotelian atheist on today's scene appears somewhat paradoxical, because the staunchest contemporary defenders of Aristotle are the Thomists—the Catholic followers of Thomas Aquinas, the great medieval theologian who was largely responsible for the reintroduction of Aristotle into Western Civilization. With Objectivism and Thomism we have two philosophical movements claiming Aristotle as their intellectual ancestor, but that are on opposite sides of the religious spectrum.

It is owing to her Aristotelianism that Rand is unusual in her atheism. For one thing, she opposes the general trends of positivism and analytic philosophy, opting instead for a much wider conception of philosophy as the discipline that provides man with a systematic and fundamental knowledge of reality. And, unlike many atheists, Rand is a declared foe of epistemological skepticism. Her rejection of God does not stem from the limitation or distrust of reason, rather, it is in the name of reason that she rejects faith, mysticism, and belief in the supernatural.

Rand's advocacy of reason extends into the sphere of ethics. Unlike many atheists, Rand rejects the supposed dichotomy between values and facts, arguing that the values required by man derive from the facts of his nature—a notion that has strong Aristotelian overtones. In virtually every area of philosophy, Rand is what may be called a philosophical optimist; she projects strong confidence in the ability of the human mind to acquire knowledge of reality. Nowhere in Rand will one find the pessimism so typical of existentialist atheism, or the skepticism inherent in Humeian and positivistic atheism, or the philosophical myopia of analytic atheism.

In short, the atheism of Ayn Rand is not destructive in the least. In rejecting God, Rand does not reject metaphysics, ethics, certainty, or the possibility of happiness. On the contrary, it is because Rand has so much positive value to offer that she considers atheism to be a comparatively minor issue.

The Thomistic philosopher Etienne Gilson once remarked, "God will really be dead when no one will still think of denying his existence." By emphasizing her constructive philosophy to the extent that the issue of theism fades into the background, Ayn Rand may be said to have written God's epitaph. And this time there will be no resurrection.

10
Ayn Rand: Philosophy and Controversy

Ayn Rand was one of the most intriguing and dynamic figures in twentieth-century thought. She had enormous power to inspire or to frustrate, to engage one's sympathies or to enrage them. While primarily a novelist, Ayn Rand constructed a philosophic system, which, although sketchy at times, is integrated, coherent, and compelling.

Many modern libertarians came to their present views by reading Ayn Rand. Whether they now favor limited government or some form of anarchism, it was Rand who first fired their imaginations and impressed upon them the crucial role of principles in thought and action.

Possibly because of the fierce emotions, pro and con, that Rand evokes, there has appeared relatively little in the way of competent reflection on Ayn Rand as philosopher. Accounts of Objectivism written by Rand's admirers are frequently eulogistic and uncritical, whereas accounts written by her antagonists are often hostile and, what is worse, embarrassingly inaccurate.

Evaluations of Rand in the academic community vary widely. On one extreme, the head of a philosophy department at a major university once called Rand "the worst philosopher in the history of Western Civilization." On the other extreme, the late Hiram Hadyn, an accomplished scholar who disagreed with Rand, remarked that Rand had constructed the most impressive philosophic edifice since Thomas Aquinas in the thirteenth century.

How, then, are we to evaluate the work of Ayn Rand as philosopher? How are we to judge the work of this astonishing woman who wrote with such intellectual passion?

I shall not attempt to analyze or criticize Rand's theories; this complex task would require far more than a single essay. Nor shall I assess Rand's influence on the climate of opinion, for this requires a perspective that can come only with the passage of time.

Another approach to Rand's ideas, and the one I shall adopt here, is to examine Objectivism for points of similarity to other philosophies. As I shall demonstrate, many features of Objectivism can be found elsewhere. In epistemology and ethics, some of Rand's arguments are strikingly similar to the arguments of Aristotelians, especially to those modern followers of Thomas Aquinas known as Thomists. In political philosophy, Rand's approach to natural rights and limited government falls squarely in the tradition known as Classical Liberalism.

Although Rand is often represented as a philosophic maverick, she actually represents a throwback to philosophy in the classical sense. The true mavericks are found in logical positivism, ordinary language philosophy, existentialism, and other schools that (until recently, perhaps) dominated much of modern philosophy. Unlike many of her contemporaries, Rand addressed the same basic questions that have vexed philosophers for centuries: What is the nature of existence? How do we acquire knowledge? What are concepts? What is ethics, and why do we need this discipline? What is the proper role of government?

Uncovering precedents and parallels to Rand's philosophy is not a popular enterprise among her more ardent disciples. For these true believers, it is not enough for Rand to be totally right; she must also be totally *original*. The problem here, of course, is what we mean when we call a philosopher "original."

Ayn Rand was not especially well-read in philosophy, and this fueled some of her originality. If previous philosophers anticipated some of her arguments or if some of her contemporaries made similar points, Rand seemed largely oblivious to those facts. Thus, in citing precedents and parallels, I don't wish to suggest that Rand borrowed from other philosophers without acknowledgment (although this does seem likely in a few instances). Rather, I believe that Rand originated most of her ideas; that is, she worked them out for herself, unaware that they had been previously worked out by others. She reinvented a number of wheels, so to speak. Whether this kind of originality is especially praiseworthy is an open question, but it at least demonstrates a remarkable ingenuity.

I do think that Rand was original in a more fundamental sense. A philosophy is (or should be) more than unconnected theories and arguments bundled together by a common name. A philosophy is an integrated and organized system of theories and arguments. Therefore, even if many elements of Objectivism can be found in other philosophers, this does not mean that Objectivism, considered as a philosophical system, is unoriginal.

In the final analysis, originality may or may not be admirable. A new method of torture may be original, but this does not recommend it. Conversely, to say that torture is wrong may be unoriginal but important nonetheless. It is always better to reaffirm old truths than to originate new falsehoods.

Another problem haunts Ayn Rand's philosophy. Rand was a sharp polemicist who gave no quarter to her adversaries. Many philosophers have retaliated by exiling her beyond the pale of respectable discussion. This is a mistake. Whether you like the woman or not, her brilliance and influence cannot be gainsaid. If Rand is to be excluded from serious consideration because of her polemicism, then why not exclude other polemical philosophers as well?

Nietzsche was an ardent polemicist, as was Marx, but both are taken seriously. The same is true of Arthur Shopenhauer, whose caustic attack on Hegel (the most respected philosopher of his day) was more vindictive than anything ever written by Rand. Consider these remarks by Shopenhauer:

> If I were to say that the so called philosophy of this fellow Hegel is a colossal piece of mystification which will yet provide posterity with an inexhaustible theme for laughter at our times, that it is a pseudo-philosophy paralyzing all mental powers, stifling all real thinking, and, by the most outrageous misuse of language, putting in its place the hollowest, most senseless, thoughtless, and, as is confirmed by its success, most stupefying verbiage, I should be quite right.
>
> Further, if I were to say that this *summus philosophus* . . . scribbled nonsense quite unlike any mortal before him, so that whoever could read his most eulogized work, the so-called *Phenomenology of the Mind*, without feeling as if he were in a madhouse, would qualify as an inmate for Bedlam, I should be no less right.[1]

There is another reason why some philosophers snub Ayn Rand: she was not an academic. She addressed a popular audience, not other philosophers. Here again, Rand was a throwback to an earlier conception of philosophy. Rand sincerely believed that philosophy *matters*, that it influences not just other philosophers, but the general culture as well. Quoting Rand:

> The professional intellectual is the field agent of the army whose commander-in-chief is the *philosopher*. The intellectual carries the application of philosophical principles to every field of human endeavor. He sets a society's course by transmitting ideas from the "ivory tower" of the philosopher to the university professor—to the writer—to the artist—to the newspaperman—to the politician—to the movie maker—to the night-club singer—to the man in the street.[2]

Rand was at once a philosopher and a professional intellectual who wished to transmit ideas to a broad audience. Furthermore, she was a *market* intellectual. Like the Sophists of ancient Greece, she sold her ideas in the intellectual marketplace; and, like those unjustly maligned teachers, she has incurred the wrath of the establishment.

As a market intellectual, Rand addressed the nonacademic masses, using vigorous and lively prose. She believed in the ability of the average person to deal with basic philosophical issues. This should count in Rand's favor, but more often it is used against her. She is dismissed as a "popularizer"—rather like Plato's attack on the Sophists. Plato distrusted the average person's ability to discern philosophic truth, so he assailed the Sophists—itinerent teachers of wisdom—who sold their wares to all comers. Perhaps modern philosophers agree with Plato's assessment; if so, such elitism is their problem, not Rand's.

Lastly, some of the disdain for Rand has been caused by her more dogmatic and abrasive disciples. Ironically, some of these disciples, having praised Rand as the savior of western civilization, later turn against her with a vengeance—thereby exhibiting a kind of true-believer/heretic syndrome. As true believers, these persons praised Rand as the greatest philosopher in history; then, as heretics, they assail Objectivism as worthless and even harmful. Ayn Rand is transformed from the Pope to the Antichrist—two sides of the same dogmatist coin. The true believer turned heretic has accomplished nothing more than to reverse direction in a sea of ignorance.

William James once observed that a new philosophy often passes through three stages during its reception: First, it "is attacked as absurd; then it is admitted to be true, but obvious and insignificant; finally it is seen to be so important that its adversaries claim that they themselves discovered it."[3] This, perhaps, is the fate of Objectivism.

Rand's view of philosophy is grand and delightfully old-fashioned. In the style of Aristotelian philosophers, who call philosophy "the queen of the sciences," Rand writes:

> Philosophy studies the fundamental nature of existence, of man, and of man's relationship to existence. As against the special sciences, which deal only with particular aspects, philosophy deals with those aspects of the universe which pertain to everything that exists. In the realm of cognition, the special sciences are the trees, but philosophy is the soil which makes the forest possible.[4]

Similarly, Cardinal Mercier, a major figure in the revival of Thomism in the late nineteenth century, maintains that philosophy "does not profess to be a particularized science." Instead, philosophy "comes *after* the particular sciences and ranks *above* them, dealing in an ultimate fashion with their respective objects, inquiring into their connexions and the relations of these connexions. . . ." Philosophy, Mercier concludes, "deserves above all to be called the *most general science. . . .*"[5]

A key element in Rand's philosophy is what she calls the "primacy of existence." For Rand, any attempt to prove the existence of a world external to consciousness is absurd on its face. We cannot begin, as Descartes did, with the certainty of consciousness while doubting the existence of an external world. Why? Because consciousness presupposes the existence of something external to consciousness, something to be conscious *of*. In Rand's words:

> If nothing exists, there can be no consciousness: a consciousness with nothing to be conscious of is a contradiction in terms. A consciousness conscious of nothing but itself is a contradiction in terms: before it could identify itself as consciousness, it had to be conscious of something. If that which you claim to perceive does not exist, what you possess is not consciousness.[6]

Rand's argument is sound, but it is scarcely new. On the contrary, it has a long and distinguished history. We find essentially the same argument, for example, in Thomas Aquinas:

> No one perceives that he understands except from this, that he understands *something*: because he must first know *something* before he knows that he knows; and the consequence is that the mind comes to actually know itself through that which it understands or senses.[7]

Thomistic philosophers sometimes refer to this as the reflexive nature of consciousness. We first become aware of something external to consciousness, and then (and only then) we become aware of our awareness by reflecting on the process by which we became aware. The distinguished Catholic philosopher Jacques Maritain put it this way:

> One cannot think about a "thought thing" until after one has thought about a "thinkable thing"—a thing good for existing, i.e., at least a possible real. The first thing thought about is being independent of the mind. . . . We do not eat what has been eaten; we eat bread. To separate object from thing . . . is to violate the nature of the intellect.[8]

Celestine N. Bittle, an author of Thomistic textbooks, has described the reflexive nature of consciousness in words that are almost identical to Rand's: "Consciousness has a content. In order to be conscious, we must be conscious of something." Bittle also agrees that consciousness, as Rand puts it, is an axiomatic concept—an irreducible primary that cannot "be reduced to other facts or broken into component parts." Consciousness, according to Bittle, is "an ultimate datum of experience" that "lies at the very root of all mental activity." Bittle, like Rand, argues that consciousness "*admits of no strict definition*" and can only be defined ostensively, i.e., "pointed out and described."[9]

A venerable epistemological debate concerns the reliability of sense perception. Do our senses somehow deceive us or transmit inaccurate data about the external world? Rand defends the reliability of sense perception as follows:

> [T]he day when [man] grasps that his senses cannot deceive him, that physical objects cannot act without causes, that his organs of perception are physical and have no volition, no power to invent or to distort, that the evidence they give him is an absolute, but his mind must learn to understand it, his mind must disover the nature, the causes, the full context of his sensory material, his mind must identify the things that he perceives—that is the day of his birth as a thinker and scientist.[10]

Many philosophers have argued this way, but, again, Rand's formulation most closely resembles the arguments of Thomists. Consider this passage from Peter Coffey's *Epistemology*, published in 1917:

> [T]he *senses themselves neither err nor deceive.* They do not err because they do not judge or interpret, but merely present, register, report a "something," a "datum," an "object" to the conscious perceiver. They do not *themselves* deceive because they always present or register or report that precisely which under the circumstances they must: they simply could not present a datum other or otherwise than they actually do; according to the organic condition in which they are, and according to the condition in which the external influence impresses them, so much the presented datum be, nor can it be otherwise: nor can the perceiver be deceived in judging that he has this datum consciously present to him.[11]

Another problem addressed by Rand is causation. In opposition to David Hume, who denied any necessary connection between cause and effect, Rand links causality to the law of identity and locates necessity in the natures of the entities involved in the causal process. Quoting Rand:

> The law of causality is the law of identity applied to action. All actions are caused by entities. The nature of an action is caused and determined by the nature of the entities that act; a thing cannot act in contradiction to its nature.[12]

This argument may be found in H. W. B. Joseph's book on logic, published in 1916:

> [T]o say that the same thing acting on the same thing under the same conditions may yet produce a different effect, is to say that a thing need not be what it is. But this is in flat conflict with the Law of Identity. A thing, to be at all, must be something, and can only be what it is. To assert a causal connection between *a* and *x* implies that *a* acts as it does because it is what it is; because, in fact, it is *a*. So long therefore as it is *a*, it must act thus; and to assert that it may act otherwise on a subsequent occasion is to assert that what is *a* is something else than the *a* which it is declared to be.[13]

The philosopher Brand Blanshard, writing in 1939, also links causation to the law of identity: "To say that *a* produces *x* in virtue of being *a* and yet that, given *a*, *x* might not follow, is inconsistent with the laws of identity and contradiction."[14]

Although Rand defends necessary causation, she also defends free will, or volition, in humans. Working from an agency theory of causation, where the human agent is said to be the cause of his actions, Rand locates free will in the choice to think or not to think. Man, says Rand, is "a being of volitional consciousness."

A few Thomistic philosophers have presented arguments similar to Rand's. For instance, Michael Maher, in a Thomistic work on psychology, refers to "the active power of selective attention" and to the "power of the mind to modify through selective attention." Maher elaborates:

> If I study by introspection any process of voluntary attention, such as that involved in recalling a forgotten incident, or in guessing a riddle, I observe that *I myself* deliberately *guide* the course of my thoughts. I am conscious that I do this by fostering the strength of some ideas, and starving others. . . . I determine not only what representations, but what *aspect of those representations* shall occupy my consciousness. In such cases I am conscious of exerting *free volition*. Further, throughout this process I apprehend myself as *causing* my mental activity—I am immediately conscious of my attention as the exercise of *free causal energy* put forth by me.[15]

Arthur Koestler, himself a philosophic maverick, has offered a similar view of volition. Koestler discusses activities that can be performed automatically until something unexpected happens.

> At that moment a strategic choice has to be made, which is beyond the competence of automatized routine, and must be referred to "higher quarters." *This shift of control* of an ongoing activity from one level to a higher level of the hierarchy—from "mechanical" to "mindful" behaviour—seems to be of the essence of conscious decision-making and of the subjective experience of free will.[16]

According to Rand, morality (or ethics)—"a code of values to guide man's choices and actions"[17]—is necessary for human survival, well-being, and happiness. The "law of existence"—the need to achieve particular values in order to sustain and promote life—applies to all living beings, including man. Quoting Rand:

> They, who pose as scientists and claim that man is only an animal, do not grant him inclusion in the law of existence they have granted to the lowest of insects. They recognize that every living species has a way of survival demanded by its nature, they do not claim that a fish can live out of water or that a dog can live without its sense of smell—but man, they claim, the most complex of beings, man can survive in any way whatever, man has no identity, no nature, and there's no practical reason why he cannot live with his means of survival destroyed, with his mind throttled and placed at the disposal of any orders they might care to issue.[18]

As this passage illustrates, Rand's theory of ethics is based on natural law, an approach that was exceedingly popular for many centuries (we find it in the ancient Stoics, for instance). As natural-law ethics fell into disfavor, Rand was one among a minority of philosophers (mainly Aristotelians) who attempted to resurrect this tradition—although, here as elsewhere, Rand labored under the misapprehension that she was giving birth to a new approach rather than breathing new life into an old one. In *Moral Values*, an introductory text published in 1918, Walter Everett expressed views very similar to Rand's:

> Moral law is just as real as human nature, within which it has its existence. Strange, indeed, if man alone of all living beings could realize his highest welfare in disregard of the principles of his own nature! And this nature, we must remember, is what it is—is always concrete and definite. Indeed the sceptic nowhere else assumes the absence of principles through obedience to which the highest form of life can be attained. He does not assume that a lily, which requires abundant moisture and rich soil, could grow on an arid rock, nor that a polar bear could flourish in a tropical jungle. No less certain

> than would be the failure of such attempts, must be the failure of man to realize, in disregard of the laws of his being, the values of which he is capable. The structure of man's nature, as conscious and spiritual, grounds laws just as real as those of his physical life, and just as truly objective.[19]

An important feature of Rand's meta-ethics—one cited frequently by Objectivist writers—is her contention that the concept of "value" is conceptually dependent upon the concept of "life." "It is only the concept of 'Life'," she writes, "that makes the concept of 'Value' possible. It is only to a living entity that things can be good or evil."[20] Similar statements have been made by other philosophers (although, in fairness to Rand, it should be mentioned that she develops this insight in more detail than most other philosophers).

According to Friedrich Nietzsche, "When we speak of values we do so under the inspiration and from the perspective of life. . . ."[21] The modern theorist G. H. von Wright has argued in a similar vein: "The attributes, which go along with meaningful use of the phrase the good of 'x', may be called *biological* in a broad sense. . . . [T]hey are used as attributes of beings, of whom it is meaningful to say that they have a *life*."[22] Richard Taylor stands in basic agreement: "[T]he things that nourish and give warmth and enhance life are deemed good, and those that frustrate and threaten are deemed bad."[23]

It is in her ethics that Rand most closely follows in the footsteps of Aristotle. (Ironically, though she acknowledged the importance of Aristotle's epistemology, she badly misinterpreted his ethical theory and so failed to understand its significance.)[24] Rather than deal with Aristotle directly, I shall call on Henry Veatch, whose book *Rational Man* provides an excellent summary of an Aristotelian ethics. The similarities between *Rational Man* and Rand's essay "The Objectivist Ethics" are more than superficial.

Rand and Veatch agree in their rejection of the modern dichotomy between facts and values. According to Rand, "the validation of value judgments is to be achieved by reference to the facts of reality."[25] And, in a similar vein, Veatch contends that "values are simply facts of nature."[26]

Rand and Veatch agree in other areas as well. Ethics, Veatch contends, "can be based on evidence and . . . is a matter of knowledge."[27] Rand concurs: "Ethics is an *objective, metaphysical necessity of man's survival*" and falls within "the province of reason."[28]

Both philosophers maintain that happiness is properly the purpose of ethics. Following Aristotle, who held that "whatever creates or increases happiness or some part of happiness, we ought to do," Veatch maintains that "moral rules are more in the nature of counsels of perfection or instructions as to what one ought or ought not to do in order to attain happiness."[29] Or, as Rand puts it: "The task of ethics is to define man's proper code of values and thus to give him the means of achieving happiness."[30]

Both writers view happiness objectively, within the total context of one's life, and not merely as momentary satisfaction or pleasure. "Happiness," Rand contends, "is possible only to a rational man."[31] Similarly, Veatch argues that any so-called happiness that comes from something other than "living intelligently" has "somehow become perverted and corrupted."[32]

In other words, both Rand and Veatch see happiness as a concomitant of the good life, which consists of pursuing rational goals in a rational manner. Writes Veatch: "[M]an's true good, his natural end or goal, and his living intelligently, may, in turn, be equated with happiness."[33] Rand stands in basic agreement: "The maintenance of life and the pursuit of happiness are not two separate issues. To hold one's own life as one's ultimate value, and one's own happiness as one's highest purpose are two aspects of the same achievement."[34]

Although Veatch does not call himself an egoist, he makes it clear that "learning how to live," which is what ethics teaches us, "is no more than [learning] what is in one's best interests."[35] As for the view that the goal of ethics is self-sacrifice, Veatch writes:

> [A]ny such identification of ethics with altruism is radically at variance with the sort of ethics of the rational man that we have been trying to defend in this book. In Aristotle's eyes ethics does not begin

> with thinking of others, it begins with oneself. The reason is that every human being faces the task of learning how to live, how to be a human being, just as he has to learn how to walk or to talk.[36]

Although the terminology differs, this passage is clearly in accord with the following statement by Rand:

> A being who does not know automatically what is true or false, cannot know automatically what is right or wrong, what is good for him or evil. Yet he needs that knowledge in order to live. . . . And *this* . . . is why man needs a code of ethics.[37]

The least original part of Rand's philosophy is her political theory. Indeed, she says little that was not said many times over by Classical Liberals—advocates of natural rights, free markets, and limited government—during the eighteenth and nineteenth centuries. Here, more than elsewhere, many parallel quotations could be placed alongside passages from Rand. I shall confine myself, however, to a few representative passages.

Let's begin with Rand's defense of natural rights:

> *Rights* are conditions of existence required by man's nature for his proper survival. If man is to live on earth, it is *right* for him to use his mind, it is *right* to act on his own free judgment, it is *right* to work for his values and to keep the product of his work. If life on earth is his purpose, he has a *right* to live as a rational being: nature forbids him the irrational.[38]

Compare this to the argument of Herbert Spencer, one of the greatest Liberals of the last century:

> Those who hold that life is valuable, hold, by implication, that men ought not to be prevented from carrying on life-sustaining activities. In other words, if it is said to "right" that they should carry them on, then, by permutation, we get the assertion that they "have a right" to carry them on. Clearly the conception of "natural rights" originates in recognition of the truth that if life is justifiable, there

> must be a justification for the performance of acts essential to its preservation; and, therefore, a justification for those liberties and claims which make such acts possible.[39]

Rand condemns the initiation of force or the threat of force in human relationships:

> The precondition of a civilized society is the barring of physical force from social relationships—thus establishing the principle that if men wish to deal with one another, they may do so only by means of *reason:* by discussion, persuasion and voluntary, uncoerced agreement.[40]

Auberon Herbert, like Herbert Spencer and many other nineteenth-century Liberals, made exactly the same point:

> Nobody has the moral right to seek his own advantage by force. That is the one unalterable, inviolable condition of a true society. Whether we are many, or whether we are few, we must learn only to use the weapons of reason, discussion, and persuasion.[41]

Rand points out that the prohibition of force applies only to the *initiation* of force; individuals may use force in self-defense:

> The necessary consequence of man's right to life is his right to self-defense. In a civilized society, force may be used only in retaliation and only against those who initiate its use. All the reasons which make the initiation of physical force an evil, make the retaliatory use of physical force a moral imperative.[42]

Again, Auberon Herbert sounds like an early version of Rand:

> [A]s long as men . . . are willing to make use of [force] for their own ends, or to make use of fraud, which is only force in disguise, wearing a mask, and evading our consent, just as force with violence openly disregards it—so long we must use force to restrain force. That is the one and only one rightful employment of force . . . force

> in the defense of the plain simple rights of property, public or private, in a word, of all the rights of self-ownership—force used defensively against force used aggressively.[43]

For Rand, the proper function of government is to protect individual rights:

> The only proper purpose of a government is to protect man's rights, which means: to protect him from physical violence. A proper government is only a policeman, acting as an agent of man's self-defense, and, as such, may resort to force *only* against those who *start* the use of force.[44]

This is a concise statement of the role of government as defended by Classical Liberals. Wilhelm von Humboldt, writing in 1791, argued that "any State interference in private affairs, where there is no reference to violence done to individual rights, should be absolutely condemned." Humboldt continues:

> [I]n order to provide for the security of its citizens, the state must prohibit or restrict such actions, relating directly to the agents only, as imply in their consequences the infringement of others' rights, or encroach on their freedom or property without their consent or against their will. . . . Beyond this every limitation of personal freedom lies outside the limits of state action.[45]

With Ayn Rand no longer on the scene, it is interesting to speculate on the future of Objectivism. Two distinct trends have already emerged. We have the official school of Objectivism headed by philosopher Leonard Peikoff, a talented thinker and writer—and Rand's self-proclaimed "intellectual heir" (a peculiar label at best). Peikoff has decreed Objectivism to be a "closed system" and has rooted out heretics, thereby assuming the role of a Randian Grand Inquisitor. Such tactics will accomplish nothing more than to plunge Objectivism into a deep intellectual coma. A philosophy will not attract young philosophers with first-rate minds if they must agree with everything Rand has written. Inquisitive, original thinkers are unwilling to confine themselves to exegesis, even if the text to be interpreted is a good one.

Fortunately, the fate of Objectivism does not depend solely on the official Randians. Some capable neo-Randians have emerged during the past two decades; and these philosophers, while willing to credit Rand where credit is due, are also willing to criticize Rand where criticism is due. Most importantly, the neo-Randians are philosophers, not expositors; they wish to expand the frontiers of Objectivism, not build walls around it.

Prominent among the neo-Randians are Tibor Machan, who has argued extensively for a Randian approach to rights in *Human Rights and Human Liberties, Individuals and Their Rights*, and other books; and David Kelly, who has ably defended Rand's epistemology in *The Evidence of the Senses: A Realist Theory of Perception*. Important work has also been undertaken by Douglas Den Uyl, Douglas Rasmussen, Eric Mack, Jack Wheeler, and others. (A sample of their work may be found in the anthology *The Philosophic Thought of Ayn Rand.*)

If Objectivism is to have a future beyond the works of Ayn Rand, the hope lies with the neo-Randians rather than with the official school. Randian clones can mimic her writing style, regurgitate her ideas, and denounce heretics—but that is all. They can never duplicate her genius. As Etienne Gilson has written:

> I wish I could make clear from the very beginning that in criticizing great men, as I shall do, I am very far from forgetting what made them truly great. No man can fall a victim to his own genius unless he has genius; but those who have none are fully justified in refusing to be victimized by the genius of others. . . . There is more than one excuse for being a Descartes, but there is no excuse whatever for being a Cartesian.[46]

Paraphrasing Gilson: There is more than one excuse for being an Ayn Rand, but there is no excuse whatever for being a disciple of Ayn Rand. Her admirers should heed the words of Aristotle: I love Plato, but I love the truth more.

Notes

1. Arthur Shopenhauer, *On the Basis of Morality*, trans. E. F. J. Payne (Indianapolis: Bobbs-Merrill, 1965), pp. 15-16.

2. Ayn Rand, "For the New Intellectual," in *For the New Intellectual* (New York: Signet Books, 1963), p. 26.

3. William James, "Pragmatism's Conception of Truth," in *Essays in Pragmatism*, ed. Alburey Castell (New York: Hafner), p. 159.

4. Ayn Rand, "Philosophy: Who Needs It?" in *Philosophy: Who Needs It?* (Indianapolis: Bobbs-Merrill, 1982), p. 2.

5. Cardinal Mercier, *A Manual of Modern Scholastic Philosophy*, 3rd ed., trans. T. L. Parker and S. A. Parker (London: Routledge and Kegan Paul, 1953), vol. I, pp. 2, 7.

6. Ayn Rand, "This is John Galt Speaking," in *For the New Intellectual*, p. 124.

7. Quoted in John Peifer, *The Mystery of Knowledge* (Albany: Magi Books, 1964), p. 32.

8. Jacques Maritain, *The Degrees of Knowledge*, trans. Bernard Wall (New York: Charles Scribner's Sons, 1938), p. 108.

9. Celestine N. Bittle, *The Whole Man* (Milwaukee: The Bruce Publishing Company, 1945), pp. 406-7. For Rand's comments on consciousness and other axiomatic concepts, see *Introduction to Objectivist Epistemology* (New York: The Objectivist, Inc., 1967), pp. 52ff.

10. Rand, "This is John Galt Speaking," p. 156.

11. P. Coffey, *Epistemology* (Gloucester, Mass.: Peter Smith, 1958), vol. II, p. 93.

12. Rand, "This is John Galt Speaking," p. 151.

13. H. W. B. Joseph, *An Introduction to Logic*, 2nd ed. (Oxford: Clarendon Press, 1916), p. 408.

14. Brand Blanshard, *The Nature of Thought* (London: George Allen and Unwin, 1939), vol. II, p. 513.

15. Michael Maher, S.J., *Pyschology: Empirical and Rational*, 9th ed. (London: Longmans, Green and Co., 1925), p. 406.

16. Arthur Koestler, *The Ghost in the Machine* (New York: Macmillan, 1967), p. 208.

17. Ayn Rand, "The Objectivist Ethics," in *The Virtue of Selfishness* (New York: New American Library, 1964), p. 13.

18. Rand, "This is John Galt Speaking," p. 123.

19. Walter G. Everett, *Moral Values* (New York: Henry Holt, 1918), pp. 332-3.

20. Rand, "This is John Galt Speaking," p. 121. Cf. "The Objectivist Ethics," p. 17.

21. Friedrich Nietzsche, *Twilight of the Idols*, trans. R. J. Hollingdale (Harmondsworth: Penguin Books, 1968), p. 45.

22. Georg Henrik von Wright, *The Varieties of Goodness* (London: Routledge and Kegan Paul, 1963), p. 50.

23. Richard Taylor, *Good and Evil* (New York: Macmillan, 1970), p. 126.

24. In "The Objectivist Ethics" (p. 14), Rand argues that Aristotle "based his ethical system of observations of what the noble and wise men of his time chose to do, leaving unanswered the questions of why they chose to do it and why he evaluated them as noble and wise." On Rand's misunderstanding of Aristotle, and for a comparison of their ethical theories, see Jack Wheeler, "Rand and Aristotle: A Comparison of Objectivist and Aristotelian Ethics," in Douglas J. Den Uyl and Douglas B. Rasmussen, eds., *The Philosophic Thought of Ayn Rand* (Urbana: University of Illinois Press, 1986), pp. 81-99.

25. Rand, "The Objectivist Ethics," p. 17.

26. Henry Veatch, *Rational Man* (Bloomington: Indiana University Press, 1962).

27. Ibid.

28. Rand, "The Objectivist Ethics," p. 23.

29. Veatch, *Rational Man.*

30. Rand, "The Objectivist Ethics," pp. 29-30.

31. Ibid., p. 31.

32. Veatch, *Rational Man.*

33. Ibid.

34. Rand, "The Objectivist Ethics," p. 29.

35. Veatch, *Rational Man.*

36. Ibid.

37. Rand, "The Objectivist Ethics" p. 22.

38. Rand, "This is John Galt Speaking," p. 182. For a more detailed presentation of Rand's theory of rights, see "Man's Rights," in *The Virtue of Selfishness*, pp. 92-100.

39. Herbert Spencer, *The Man Versus the State* (Baltimore: Penguin Books, 1969), p. 171.

40. Ayn Rand, "The Nature of Government," in *The Virtue of Selfishness*, p. 108.

41. Quoted in *Liberty and the Great Libertarians*, ed. Charles Sprading (Los Angeles: Libertarian Pub. Co., 1923), p. 399.

42. Rand, "The Nature of Government," p. 42.

43. *Liberty and the Great Libertarians*, p. 411.

44. Rand, "This is John Galt Speaking, p. 183.

45. Wilhelm von Humboldt, *The Limits of State Action*, ed. and trans. J. W. Burrow (Cambridge: Cambridge University Press, 1969), p. 90.

46. Etienne Gilson, *The Unity of Philosophical Experience* (New York: Charles Scribner's Sons, 1952), p. 7.

11
Objectivism as a Religion

Many philosophers have challenged religion's virtual monopoly on ethics, but few of them have influenced popular culture. Ayn Rand is a striking exception. Her readers number in the millions, making her one of the most influential atheistic philosophers of this century.

Considering that Rand's philosophy of Objectivism is diametrically opposed to religion in letter and spirit, a "religious" adherence to Objectivism itself may appear paradoxical. But the phenomenon of religious Objectivism is fairly common, as anyone familiar with Rand's more ardent followers can attest.

The most extreme form of religious Objectivism occurs in those evangelical, intolerant, true-believing Randians who, through some quirk of fate, missed their true calling as Christian missionaries. This kind of religiosity is easy to detect and explain. Some people find Jesus Christ, others find Karl Marx, and still others find Ayn Rand—but true believers everywhere, whatever the object of their belief, are unwilling to criticize their deity. Thinking for oneself is hard work,

---

This essay is a revised form of one published in *Invictus* (1972).

so true believers recite catechisms and denounce heretics instead.

There also exist more subtle manifestations of Objectivist religiosity, especially in the realm of moral behavior. Although many Objectivists never intend to treat moral standards like religious rules, they use moral concepts, connotations, and psychological cue-words that reek of religion. This is the kind of religious Objectivism that I shall explore in this essay.

Before proceeding, I should clarify some points for those readers who are unfamiliar with Ayn Rand and the subculture she inspired. In criticizing Objectivist religiosity, I do not mean to suggest that this attitude is found in most of Rand's admirers. Nor do I mean to suggest, as did Albert Ellis in *Is Objectivism a Religion?*, that Rand's philosophy is inherently religious or dogmatic. Any such assessment is false and foolish.

Ayn Rand is a passionate writer, and passionate writers tend to attract passionate readers, both rational and irrational. If some of Rand's readers, confusing style with substance, revere her as a secular pope, then she cannot be held accountable. Rand repeatedly stresses the value of independent judgment—the "sovereign consciousness," as she calls it.[1] This passage is typical: "Truth or falsehood must be one's sole concern and sole criterion of judgment—not anyone's approval or disapproval. . . ."[2] The virtue of rationality, the centerpiece of Rand's moral theory, entails "that one must never place any value or consideration whatsoever above one's perception of reality. . . . It means that one must never sacrifice one's convictions to the opinions and wishes of others. . . ."[3]

Intellectual passion is the creative engine of philosophy, indeed, of all abstract disciplines. Every philosopher, while etching ideas on that paper mirror known as the printed page, must make a decision: How much emotion should I inject into my arguments? Conventional academic wisdom dicates: none at all, especially if you wish to be published in a professional journal or by a university press.

Ayn Rand choose another path; she was an academic pariah who cared little for academic etiquette. Acerbic and arrogant, she rarely footnoted or quoted anyone except herself. This attitude sometimes got the better of her, as when she based her critique of *A Theory of Justice* by John Rawls on a review published in *The New York Times Book Review*, rather than on the book itself. "Let me say," she proclaimed, "that I have not read and do not intend to read that book."[4] Having herself been victimized by such tactics, one would have expected better from Ayn Rand.

Despite her fondness for pronouncements from on high, Rand's philosophy is just that—a philosophy, not a religion. She labored hard on her theories; and if they sometimes become entangled in rhetoric and prejudice, then surely the reader can exert a little labor to untangle them. Critics who fail to do this call her dogmatic; admirers who fail to do this succumb to religiosity.

Ethics: Rational and Religious

In an important essay, "Causality Versus Duty," Ayn Rand condemns the notion of duty as one of "the most destructive anti-concepts in this history of moral philosophy"—a "psychological killer" that "negates all the essentials of a rational view of life." According to Rand, the term "duty" means "the moral necessity to perform certain actions for no reason other than obedience to some higher authority without regard to any personal goal, motive, desire or interest."[5]

Rand argues that causality, not duty, is the foundation of a rational ethics. Rational moral principles are standards that guide us in the pursuit of goals, especially long-range goals. In Rand's words:

> Reality confronts man with a great many "musts," but all of them are conditional; the formula of realistic necessity is: "You must, if—" and the "if" stands for man's choice: "—if you want to achieve a certain goal." You must eat, if you want to survive. You must work, if you want to eat. You must think, if you want to work. You must look at reality, if you want to think—if you want to know what to do—if you want to know what goals to choose—if you want to know how to achieve them.[6]

Many philosophers other than Rand have spoken out against a duty-based ethics, whether presented in plain clerical garb as religious commandments or in fashionable evening attire as philosophical arguments (e.g., the deontological ethics of Immanuel Kant). I shall mention just a few examples.

Friedrich Nietzsche describes religious morality as "the denaturalization of morality" where, owing to supernatural rewards and punishments, "a concept of good and evil is created that seems to be altogether divorced from the natural concepts of 'useful,' 'harmful,' 'life-promoting,' 'life-retarding'. . . ."[7] Religions are typically laden with concepts like guilt, grace, redemption, and forgiveness—and these, Nietzsche declares, "were invented to destroy the causal sense of man: they are an outrage on the concept of cause and effect!"[8]

The psychologist Erich Fromm distinguishes an "authoritarian ethics" from a "humanistic ethics." An authoritarian ethics "is based not on reason and knowledge but on awe of the authority and on the subject's feeling of weakness and dependence. . . ."[9] Similarly, the British philosopher P. H. Nowell-Smith, in his discussion of "secular" and "religious" morality, argues that there are "two radically different ways of looking at morality, one which sees it as a set of recipes to be followed for the achievement of ends, the other which sees it as a set of commands to be obeyed. . . ."[10] Another philosopher, G. E. M. Anscombe, has suggested that the "ought" derived from "moral duty"—in contrast to the "if-then" kind of "ought"—should "be jettisoned if this is psychologically possible."[11]

In my book, *Atheism: The Case Against God*, I discussed the difference between "rational morality" and "religious morality." After summarizing that discussion, I shall apply it to the problem of religious Objectivism.

In our quest for happiness, in our pursuit of a good life, we be must able to determine specifically, on a day-to-day basis, which actions will best serve our needs and desires. If we are to pursue goals successfully, we need some way to predict which actions are conducive to those goals. This is the function of standards. A standard is a principle used to predict the consequences of one's actions.

As a predictive principle, a standard directs our choices, thus providing the essential link between action and the acquisition of desired values. Standards—the basic method by which we achieve values—constitute the meta-ethical foundation of a rational ethics. Within this framework, our goals are primary, and our standards should be derived accordingly. Moral principles, in this view, serve human purposes in our pursuit of a good life.

A standard-based ethics carries important implications. It makes little sense to speak of "obeying" or "disobeying" a moral standard. One does not obey a standard; one adopts and follows a standard in a given context, for a given purpose. Whether or not one follows a particular standard depends on the desirability of its goal and one's judgment of the standard's effectiveness in achieving that goal. One's motivation to follow a standard stems from the prior motivation to achieve a particular goal.

This view of ethics stands in stark contrast to the kind of ethics promulgated by most religions (especially revealed religions). Religions typically promote, not standards, but commandments, or moral *rules*. A rule, as I use the term, is a *sanctioned* principle of action. A sanction is a physical or psychological means of coercion or intimidation used for the purpose of motivating obedience to a principle of action. Thus, unlike standards, rules demand *obedience*, and they carry the threat of a sanction—a punishment—for disobedience.

The most obvious kind of sanction involves the threat of physical punishment. This external sanction may be supernatural, as when a god threatens eternal hell for disbelievers, or secular, as when a government enacts a law. If one adopts a principle of action because one fears its sanction, then one is responding to that principle as a *rule*.

Sanctions can also be internal, or psychological, in nature. A psychological sanction is a moral term that is used for the purpose of intimidation, which is intended to motivate compliance with rules. Moral terms, when used in this fashion, function as psychological cue-words—words used to trigger emotions, rather than convey information.

A physical sanction, if successful, causes the emotion of *fear*. A psychological sanction, if successful, causes the emotion of *guilt*. Someone motivated by fear may still retain an element of rebelliousness, of determination to strike back given the opportunity. A guilt-ridden person, however, is someone with a broken spirit who will obey the rules without question.

Religions have long recognized the importance of inculcating a sense of guilt as a motivation to obey divine commandments. And this is where the concept of *sin* enters center-stage.

The notion of sin is perhaps the most effective psychological sanction ever invented. For a Christian, to sin is the worst thing imaginable, and even the thought of committing a sin can cause intense guilt. Anyone who comes from a religious background can appreciate the tremendous psychological force of this concept. Sin represents something metaphysically monstrous, something that severely undercuts a person's self-esteem. Friedrich Nietzsche, in his vitriolic but penetrating attack on Christianity, clearly recognized this function of sin.

> Sin . . . that form *par excellence* of the self-violation of man, was invented to make science, culture, every kind of elevation and nobility of man impossible; the priest *rules* through the invention of sin.[12]

Moral standards, because they rely on the causal link between actions and goals, may be described as statements of *natural necessity*. Moral rules, because they interject sanctions into this causal relationship, may be described as the *denaturalization* of moral values. Rules divorce actions from consequences and rely instead on sanctions, both external and internal, to motivate compliance.

As used by the religious Objectivist, moral terms are transformed into secularized versions of sin. When used in a rule-based ethics, the word "immoral" differs from "sin" in name only; both concepts serve the same purpose and convey the same emotional message. In a rule morality, when people are condemned as immoral, or when they pass this judgment on themselves, they are expected to respond with guilt—and obedience is expected to follow.

The religious Objectivist uses morality as a bludgeon to intimidate, cajole, or shame others into obedience. If this rule-mentality disapproves of a person's actions, he will say, "You are behaving immorally"—meaning, "You ought to behave *differently*." If asked to define what he means by "immoral," the rule-mentality will reply, in effect: "Immoral action consists of breaking the correct rules of behavior."

The content of these moral rules is irrelevant, whether it is the duty to serve one's country, the obligation to promote the welfare of society, or even the obligation to behave rationally. In the context of a rule-morality, the answer to "Why is *x* immoral?" is: "Because the rule forbids it."

The subtext here is obvious. Just as the Christian relies on an emotional reaction to "sin," so the secular religionist relies on an emotional reaction to "immoral." Guilt is the desired response. The goal of life, for the rule-mentality, is to be a moral person; morality is an end in itself, not a means to happiness. This is the trademark of the religious Objectivist.

There is little difference between the Christian who says, "I am doing *x* because it is demanded of me by God," and the Objectivist who says, "I am doing *x* because it is demanded of me by 'man's life qua man,' " or some other Randian standard. In each case, the individual is subservient to moral abstractions.

In Rand's ethics, "man's life qua man" is the *standard* of morality, not its *purpose*. One does not act in order to fulfill the requirements of "man's life" in the abstract; one acts in order to fulfill the requirements of one's own life, using the standard of "man's life" as a guide to achieve that goal. Rand makes this point clearly: "The Objectivist ethics holds man's life as the *standard* of value—and *his own life* as the ethical *purpose* of every individual man."[13]

Until the Objectivist understands that he is a concrete instance of "man's life qua man," that he is the existing particular of an abstraction, and that this abstraction is no more valid than its real-life application—then ethics, for this Objectivist, will remain a code of rules to be obeyed because it is demanded by "man's life." Deviance from the code is a "sin" against "man's life" and, hence, a source of self-condemnation and guilt.

For the religious Objectivist, the surrogate god of "man's life qua man" has become an end in itself. He does not ask, "Will this action make me happy?" Rather, he asks, "Does this action meet the requirements of morality?" Rationally, the first question entails the second, at least implicitly, for one needs moral standards as pointers to a good life; but the absence of the first question as one's primary concern and motivation marks the difference between ethics as a code of standards and ethics as a code of rules.

The Objectivist Pedant

Perhaps the most common type of religious Objectivist is the moral pedant—the Objectivist who passes moral judgment for the purpose of intimidation. This type is easily identified by his incessant use of the terms "moral" and "immoral."

When the pedant is asked, "Why should I do *x*?" he replies, "Because it is the moral thing to do." He is asked, "Why is it moral?" He answers, "Because it is in man's interest qua man." He is asked, "But even if that is true, why should I do it?" He replies, in effect, "Because if you don't, you are sub-human." Or: "Because if you don't, you are morally degenerate." Or: "Because if you don't, you betray your status as a human being."

The pedant rarely concretizes moral abstactions and so fails to forge a link between the standard of "man's life" and real humans. Moral principles, in the hands of the pedant, acquire the characteristics of religious rules.

The pedant observes how Rand argues for certain kinds of action (such as productive work) as conducive to happiness, and he then transforms these actions into rules backed by moral sanctions. He defines an immoral action as one that falls outside the prescribed limits, and he defines an immoral person as one who breaks the rules.

If ever the pedant encounters a person who does not fit his preconceived mold—even if that person appears happy—the pedant will condemn that person as immoral. This judgment is supposed to evoke guilt and shame, which will then motivate the nonconformist to snap into line with prescribed rules. Thus, as used by the pedant, the term "immoral" is nothing more than a secularization of "sin." This can be illustrated with a few examples.

(1) For a Christian, to call a person sinful is a blanket condemnation. This is equally true of the pendant's use of "immoral." When this Objectivist says, "You are immoral"—with that tone of indignation and disgust that only he can muster—he might just as well say, "You are a worthless person." The religious Objectivist seeks to demote the condemned to a sub-human species, and, in so doing, he hopes to instill guilt.

(2) "Sin" does not leave room for moral innocence; neither does "immoral" as used by the pedant. This becomes evident when the religious Objectivist searches for the most vicious motives imaginable to explain what he regards as immoral behavior. It is not uncommon to find such Objectivists gleefully relating tales of the vile motives they have uncovered in other people; seemingly insignificant actions are interpreted as devastating insights into the characters of the condemned.

This is sadly apparent in the denunciations of Nathaniel Branden by some Objectivists after his split with Ayn Rand. Rand has pronounced Branden immoral. What else does the upright Objectivist need to know? Branden, we are told, should be shunned; moral people do not read his books or attend his lectures. Such *ex cathedra* thinking would turn the Pope green with envy.

(3) The idea of sin applies not only to actions, but to thoughts and feelings as well. So does the pedant's use of "immoral." For example, the religious Objectivist observes another Objectivist who responds romantically to someone who doesn't agree with Rand's ideas. Is it necessary to elaborate on the conclusions he will draw?

Examples like this could be multiplied endlessly, but they share a common theme rooted in what Objectivist writers call "psycho-epistemology." One's emotional responses are said to be morally significant because they flow from and reveal one's values. Thus emotions themselves become subject to praise or condemnation. To feel an "irrational" emotion is to display a flawed value premise, which suggests that one may be an immoral person.

(4) Christians may feel guilt because they think that God is always watching them. Surely there can be no comparable fear in the religious Objectivist (who is, after all, an atheist).

Although there is no literal parallel here, there is an important psychological one. Some Objectivists seem to feel that John Galt is hovering overhead, peering at them during every moment of their lives. Would John Galt approve of what I am saying? Would John Galt make the same decision I made? Would John Galt become upset with what I am feeling? In other words, the pedant is afflicted with an acute case of moral perfectionism.

The pedant is always out to prove something, even when alone. He will prove that, however miserable he may be, he is a good Objectivist, that he follows the rules faithfully. What of those non-Objectivists who enjoy their lives? Their "mindless pleasure," as the pedant is apt to call it, is not philosophically pure (as if anyone cares about this except the pedant).

The pedant, wound up like a spring, is a walking caricature of moral rigor—rather like Mencken's puritan who is obsessed with the haunting fear that someone, somewhere is happy. The pedant, like the puritan, is sure that he has the key to happiness, even though it doesn't unlock any doors. So the pedant takes his pleasure from possessing the key itself. He is a pious gatekeeper who is unable to pass through his own gate.

The Objectivist Martyr

The Objectivist martyr spends more time evaluating himself than other people. This is pedantry directed inward—moral self-condemnation. Aware of Rand's emphasis on critical self-evaluation, the martyr scrupulously searches within himself for moral flaws and weakness. After finding these in abundance, his self-esteem plummets, and his guilt skyrockets.

The dynamics here are strikingly similar to the post-conversion experience of some "born-again" Christians. The sinner has been saved;

his life will be immediately transformed, or so he thinks. His actions and emotions are supposed to follow suit with his beliefs and change as well, but many of them don't. Clearly, God has done his part, so any remaining blots must be the Christian's own fault.

Likewise, the religious Objectivist has been "saved." He has read *Atlas Shrugged* and is versed in Randian moral theory. Why, then, does the expected transformation not occur? Why do undesirable behavior patterns and emotions still haunt him? For the martyr, there can be only one answer: the lack of change is owing to a defect of the worst kind—a moral defect in the person himself.

When the martyr does something wrong, he does more than evaluate his action as wrong (which normally causes one to feel regret or remorse). He passes a second judgment on himself; he condemns himself as immoral, thereby evoking guilt.

Thus, the martyr doubles his evaluations, and, in so doing, he doubles his misery. Two major consequences often follow from this.

(1) The Objectivist martyr is usually very passive. He pursues only modest, unchallenging goals. If he were to strive for more difficult goals, he might fail, and such failure would only make him feel worse. Even though passivity will not make him happy, he regards his lethargy as preferable to failure-provoked guilt.

Thus, to escape the dreaded, self-imposed judgment of "immoral" (or "inefficacious" or "unworthy" or some other value-laden term) the martyr drifts through a life without challenge. His emotional highs are barely distinguishable from his emotional lows.

(2) The martyr finds it difficult to isolate his specific problems. He does not say, "These are the goals I want to achieve but cannot"; rather, he feels paralyzed, chronically guilty, unable to act. Whenever possibilities are suggested to him, he rejects them with a characteristic, "What's the use?"

The martyr is not especially productive. This violates Objectivist rules, so he feels guilty. Then his guilt reinforces his negative self-image, so he becomes even more passive, preferring lethargy to the risk of violating yet another rule. The martyr is caught in the vicious cycle of rules and guilt, and the results can be devastating.

The Moral and the Prudential

Many philosophers regard morality as consisting entirely of rules. What I have called "standards," according to these philosophers, offer *prudential*, not moral, reasons for action; and moral principles, rather than promoting one's self-interest, should serve to check self-interested behavior. The following remarks by Marcus Singer are fairly typical of this approach:

> In evaluating the prudence of an action, we must consider its effects on the agent. But its morality depends on its effects on others. The fact that an act would tend to harm oneself is a reason for regarding it as imprudent, but not a reason for regarding it as immoral; the fact that an act would tend to harm others is a reason for regarding it as immoral, but not a reason for regarding it as imprudent.[14]

This dichotomy between the moral and the prudential appears quite often in books on ethics, with the result that egoism is thrown out of court as a nonmoral doctrine. Thus, argues Kurt Baier in his influential *The Moral Point of View*, "those who adopt consistent egoism cannot make moral judgments. Moral talk is impossible for consistent egoists."[15] W. T. Stace expresses a similar sentiment:

> The difficulty of the problem of the basis of moral obligation is precisely the difficulty of seeing why I ought to do something which I do not desire to do. Why should I concern myself about the happiness of any person other than myself? No one would think of asking what is the basis of my obligation to try to make myself happy. Or at least I personally should think such a question pointless. Why I should seek my own happiness is obvious. It is simply because I desire to my own happiness. But why I ought to try to make *you* happy, especially if by so doing I decrease my own happiness, is not at all obvious. And to find an answer to this question is, as I understand it, precisely the point of the problem of the basis of moral obligation.[16]

Stace, like many theorists, regards the issue of moral obligation (which, in this case, is synonymous with "duty") to be a central concern of moral theory—and this necessitates an anti-standard, anti-egoistical approach to ethics.

What this issue comes down to is whether we can successfully divorce psychological sanctions and concepts (such as "duty")—those bulwarks of a rule-based ethics—from the idea of morality itself. If we cannot, if morality is inextricably tied to sanctions and duties, then a standard-based ethics represents, not a kind of morality, but a revolt against morality, i.e., a revolt against rules and the obligation to obey them. Egoism, according to Richard Taylor, "does not evoke that peculiar feeling of approbation or condemnation that is a uniquely moral one, and to which we attach the notions of virtue and vice."[17] This, I suggest, is a tacit recognition that a standard-based egoism does not employ psychological sanctions—and this, for some ethicists, disqualifies it as a moral theory. Standards are therefore seen as nonmoral, or prudential, principles of action.

The long tradition of rule-morality may account for why some Objectivists treat Rand's ethics as a system of rules. This suggests an interesting question: Do the terms "moral" and "immoral" function as anything other than psychological sanctions? If they do not, they do not belong in a standard-based egoism.

Although "moral" and "immoral" have legitimate meanings within egoism, such terms can also mislead. Technically, the term "immoral" applies to a voluntary action that violates a given standard of moral value. Thus, egoism, like all moral theories, has its "immoral" actions, i.e., those that are detrimental to one's long-range interest and happiness.

This is not to suggest that, within Objectivist egoism, the "moral" is synonymous with "that which will make one happy." To pronounce an action "moral" means that the action is consistent with the standard of "man's life qua man" (or some derivative standard), whereas to say that an action will lead to happiness refers to an expected emotional response. These judgments refer to two different aspects of the same action. The first signifies conformity to a standard of value, whereas the second signifies the purpose for which an action was taken. Properly considered, the former is the *means* of attaining the latter; standards are the method one uses to predict which actions are most conducive to one's goals. Therefore, within a consistent egoism (and I am assuming that Rand is a consistent egoist), there can be no breach between that which is moral and that which will enhance one's happiness.

If this is true, if "immoral" actions are the same as self-destructive actions, then why would an Objectivist choose to call an action "immoral" rather than identify the self-destructive characteristics of the action? Why not say, "That action will hurt you in the long run"—which is much more informative, much more to the point—and bypass the judgment of "immoral" altogether?

Many Objectivists, I suspect, prefer "immoral" over "self-destructive" for the same reason that Christians like the term "sin." "Immoral" carries an emotional message that is missing in "self-destructive." The term "immoral" contains a built-in condemnation, and this relieves Objectivists of the often complex task of demonstrating why an action is detrimental. Instead, they proclaim the action to be immoral because it does not fall within their rules, and they consider the subject closed.

Moral judgments, however, should not be used as psychological crowbars. To condemn an action as immoral is not enough. Objectivists should introduce purpose and context and demonstrate why, within this framework, the action in question is self-destructive. But, then, they could accomplish this without introducing the term "immoral" at all.

Within egoism, a person should not refrain from an action *because* it is "immoral." Rather, "immoral" signifies an action that is self-destructive, and this is the reason for not doing it. Likewise, a "moral" action promotes one's welfare, and this is the reason for doing it. This approach shows regard for the purpose and context of the moral agent. Moral principles have not become autonomous rules. The person is primary; morality is secondary, a means to an end.

I believe this approach is consistent with the fundamental features of Rand's ethical theory. Unfortunately, however, some of her pronouncements lend aid and comfort to a rule-based ethics. Let's consider some of these problem areas.

Ayn Rand and Rules

(1) Rand's terminology is sometimes difficult to reconcile with a standard-based ethics. For example, in discussing pride, she writes:

> The virtue of Pride can best be described by the term: "moral ambitiousness." It means that one must earn the right to hold oneself as one's highest value by achieving one's own moral perfection—which one achieves by never accepting any code of irrational virtues impossible to practice and by never failing to practice the virtues one knows to be rational. . . .[18]

According to Rand, one should strive to be consistently rational, and she describes this as "achieving one's own moral perfection." At best, this phrasing is misleading; at worst, it is pernicious. "Moral perfection" suggests a kind of moral pyramid that one should ascend, step by step, until one climbs above imperfection onto the pinnacle of moral purity.

Fortunately, hints of perfection and purity are fairly scarce in Rand's writings, and they cut against the grain of her ethics. For example, consider these remarks about the deontological (duty-centered) ethics of Immanuel Kant:

> [A] Kantian does not focus on his goal, but on his own *moral character*. His automatic reaction is guilt and fear—fear of failing his "duty"; fear of some weakness which "duty" forbids, fear of proving himself morally "unworthy." The value of his goal vanishes from his mind, drowned in a flood of self-doubt.[19]

This passage also describes the religious Objectivist, and it is difficult to renconcile with Rand's own use of "moral perfection."

(2) One article that has influenced religious Objectivists is Rand's essay, "The Cult of Moral Grayness." There, Rand attempts to refute the claim that, in moral issues, "There are no blacks and whites, there are only grays." She concludes that "there may be 'gray' men, but there can be no 'gray' moral principles."[20] Some Objectivists, after

reading these remarks, proceed to equate "white" moral principles with noncontextual rules.

Recall an important distinction between rules and standards. Rule-morality defines the "moral" according to whether actions conform to a prescribed code. One either obeys or disobeys a rule; there are no degrees or middle ground here. Since it is concerned only with *behavior*, a rule ignores the purpose and context of the acting agent. If one breaks a rule, regardless of purpose and context, then one has behaved immorally. This rigid, behavioristic approach injects into a rule-morality a strong either-or, black-or-white flavor.

In this sense, a black-or-white morality is antithetical to standards. Recall that a standard is a predictive principle used to attain a desired goal. These standards can be quite flexible—they may require revision in some circumstances, or they may be inapplicable in others. Moreover, one may achieve a goal in degrees, more or less successfully; and one's actions may promote one's happiness in degrees, more or less successfully. And the principles themselves may be partially faulty owing to lack of knowledge or an error in judgment.

Thus, the notion of black-and-white morality is more compatible with rules than with standards. This doesn't mean that standards are somehow "gray"; it simply means that the vocabulary of "black," "white," and "gray" does not fit easily into a standard-based ethics. Such terms are miserably inexact, and, to the extent they do convey meaning, they suggest a rule conception of morality.

The major problem with "The Cult of Moral Grayness" is that Rand attacks the problem, "There are no blacks and whites, there are only grays," while using the loaded terminology of the problem itself. And although Rand uses such terms in a loose, metaphorical sense, the psychological implications remain—and the religious Objectivist, picking up on these implications, transforms the Randian ethics into a system of rules.

"Moral" and "immoral" are either-or terms; they do not comfortably admit degrees, so they can be highly misleading when used in a standard framework. A man who steals a watch is immoral, and so is a mass murderer. Do we then say that the mass murderer is "more immoral" than the thief? Indeed, what does this assertion mean?

Linguistically, standards are more compatible with value terms, such as "good," "bad," and "evil." It makes linguistic sense to speak of a standard as good or bad, or as better or worse than another standard—just as it makes sense to speak of one person as being more (or less) evil than another person. Most value terms are capable of indicating degrees, which gives them a descriptive force absent in "moral" and "immoral." As Paul Taylor has observed, "something may fulfull or fail to fulfill a standard of evaluation to a certain degree. But an act either complies with or breaks a rule."[21]

Having discussed various aspects of religious Objectivism, let me reinforce a point made at the beginning of this essay. Whatever her errors, Ayn Rand struggled mightily against a religious view of morality, and she sought to place ethics on a rational foundation, free of any appeal to faith or force. Rand was a humanist in the best sense; for her, the happiness of the human being is the *summum bonum* of ethics. Religious Objectivism is an affront to the spirit of Ayn Rand's philosophy.

Notes

1. Ayn Rand, "Who Is the Final Authority in Ethics?" in *The Voice of Reason: Essays in Objectivist Thought*, ed. Leonard Peikoff (New York: Meridian Books, 1990), p. 19.

2. Ayn Rand, "The Argument from Intimidation," in *The Virtue of Selfishness* (New York: New American Library, 1964), p. 143.

3. Ayn Rand, "The Objectivist Ethics," in ibid., p. 26.

4. Ayn Rand, "An Untitled Letter," in *Philosophy: Who Needs It?* (Indianapolis: Bobbs-Merrill, 1982), p. 131. Rand concedes that "one cannot judge a book by its reviews," but she avoids this inconvenience by stating that she will review the reviewer, Marshall Cohen, whose "remarks deserve attention in their own right." Then she proceeds to attack Rawls.

5. Ayn Rand, "Causality Versus Duty," in ibid., p. 115.

6. Ibid. pp. 118-19.

7. Friedrich Nietzsche, *The Will to Power*, trans. W. Kaufmann and R. J. Hollingdale (New York: Vintage Books, 1968), p. 90.

8. Friedrich Nietzsche, *The Anti-Christ*, trans. R. J. Hollingdale (Har-

mondsworth: Penguin Books, 1968), p. 165. Compare Rand's argument that the "notion of 'duty' is instrinsically anti-causal." ("Causality Versus Duty", p. 121.)

9. Erich Fromm, *Man for Himself* (Greenwich: Fawcett Books, 1947), p. 20.

10. P. H. Nowell-Smith, *Humanist Anthology*, ed. Margaret Knight (London: Rationalist Press Association, 1961), p. 182.

11. See G. E. M. Anscombe, "Modern Moral Philosophy," in *The Is-Ought Question*, ed. W. D. Hudson (London: St. Martin's Press, 1969), pp. 175-196.

12. Nietzsche, *The Anti-Christ*, p. 166.

13. Rand, "The Objectivist Ethics," p. 25.

14. Marcus G. Singer, *Generalization in Ethics* (New York: Atheneum, 1961), p. 303.

15. Kurt Baier, *The Moral Point of View* (Ithaca: Cornell University Press, 1958), p. 189.

16. W. T. Stace, *The Concept of Morals* (New York: Macmillan, 1937), p. 123.

17. Richard Taylor, *Good and Evil* (London: Collier-Macmillan, 1970), p. 199.

18. Rand, "The Objectivist Ethics," p. 27.

19. Rand, "Causality Versus Duty," p. 120.

20. Ayn Rand, "The Cult of Moral Grayness," in *The Virtue of Selfishness*, p. 79.

21. Paul W. Taylor, *Normative Discourse* (Englewood Cliffs: Prentice-Hall, 1961), p. 33.

PART 3

Other Heresies

12
The Righteous Persecution of Drug Consumers and Other Heretics

"Righteous persecution"—that is how St. Augustine (354–430) described the punishment of Christian heretics. Augustine, called by a biographer "the first theorist of the Inquisition," was not the first to defend the persecution of dissenting minorities. But previous defenders did not presume to punish dissenters for their own good. It was left to the peculiar genius of Augustine to recommend persecution as fulfillment of the maxim, "Love thy neighbor."

Augustine's doctrine of righteous persecution became a rationale for the medieval Inquisition and, later, the Spanish Inquisition. The American government is currently engaged in its own Inquisition: the "war on drugs"—or, more precisely, the war on *consumers* of *illegal* drugs.

The modern drug inquisitor is another Augustine dressed in secular garb. Whereas Augustine sought to save the religious heretic from a literal hell, the modern inquisitor seeks to "save" the social heretic (the drug consumer) from the metaphorical "hell" of his "addiction." And just as Augustine's theory wreaked havoc in previous centuries—

so the same theory, when secularized and applied to the "war on drugs," has created social turmoil and devastated hundreds of thousands of lives through imprisonment.

For over two decades, while Augustine was a bishop in northern Africa, he campaigned against a large group of Christian schismatics known as Donatists. Initially, Augustine favored voluntary conversion, but he later called for a righteous persecution "inflamed by love"—"a love which seeks to heal" heretics and deliver them from "the darkness of error."

Heretics, Augustine believed, imperil their "spiritual helath"; they are destined to suffer the torments of hell. Thus, those who truly "love their neighbor" will recognize their "duty" to compel these "wandering sheep." Righteous persecutors are like physicians who try to help a "raving madman," for heretics "commit murder on their own persons." When motivated by love, persecutors cannot do evil: "Love and you cannot but do well."

In true Augustinian fashion, the modern drug inquisitor seeks to "heal" wayward drug users who "commit murder on their own persons." Indeed, Augustine's defense of righteous persecution anticipates virtually every argument used by drug inquisitors.

For example, our modern inquisitors claim that drug consumers are slaves to evil habits and so require coercive intervention for their own good. Augustine, too, warned against the "fetters" of sinful habits which have "the strength of iron chains." These evil habits ("a disease of the mind") become a "necessity," forming a "chain," which holds the victim "in the duress of servitude."

Sinful humans, according to Augustine, cannot overcome their evil habits without divine intervention—the grace of God. Drug consumers, according to modern inquisitors, cannot overcome their evil habits without secular intervention—the grace of government.

Can coercion change a person's beliefs and compel him to do good? No, said Augustine, but coercion can provide an incentive to avoid evil: "The fear of punishment . . . keeps the evil desire from escaping beyond the bounds of thought." Persecution can break the bonds of habit and induce the heretic "to change his purpose for the better."

Drug inquisitors offer the same justification for their righteous persecution of drug consumers. But what about those consumers who don't change their habits even after they are punished? Augustine faced the same problem with heretics who had stubbornly refused to embrace Catholicism. His response has been echoed by a long line of drug inquisitors: "Is the art of healing, therefore, to be abandoned, because the malady of some is incurable?"

Drug inquisitors love to trot out former users who, having been saved from an earthly "hell," now give thanks to drug laws and their enforcers. Augustine used the same tactic. Converted heretics—"conquests of the Lord"—told how they had wished to return to the Catholic Church earlier but, enslaved by habit, were unable to do so. "Having recovered their right minds," these reformed heretics expressed thanks that "these most wholesome laws were brought to bear against them, with as much fervency as in their madness they detested them." Converted heretics were grateful to their persecutors—their "truest friends"—for having delivered them "from that fatal and eternal destruction."

(Augustine acknowledged that some heretics refused to submit to their persecutors and committed suicide instead. Modern reporters would probably call these "heresy-related deaths.")

Throughout the Middle Ages, it was often difficult for heretics to spread their poison, because book production was confined to monasteries and universities. This changed in the mid-fifteenth century, however, with the invention of printing. German printers carried their art throughout western Europe—to Italy, France, Spain, the Low Countries, Switzerland, and elsewhere.

During the sixteenth century, more and more people became hooked on literacy. These reading addicts, unable to control their habits, demanded more books, a greater variety of books, and books of better quality. Their insatiable demand created a huge market for heretical books, and unscrupulous book lords capitalized on this opportunity.

For example, Geneva, the center of Calvinism, produced some

300,000 volumes each year. These books, "full of abominable errors," recognized no frontiers, as pushers carried their illicit merchandise along trade routes or smuggled them in ships.

Many rulers tried to win the war on heresy with a policy of zero-tolerance. Emperor Charles V established censorship in Germany, backed by the penalties of burning (for men), live burial (for women), tongue-piercing, and confiscation of property. England's Henry VIII issued a list of banned books, and he forbade the importation of books printed abroad in the English language. Frances I prohibited all printing in France. Phillip II decreed the death penalty for importing books into Spain.

Book lords often faced the death penalty. In 1524, the bookseller Herrgott was beheaded in Leipzig, and, three years later, an Anabaptist printer was burned at Nuremberg.

In 1625, the Englishman George Withers attacked booksellers as "the Devil's seedsmen" and as "pernicious superfluities." Booksellers, Withers charged, are concerned only with profit; in pushing their wares, they have no regard "either to the glory of God or the public advantage." Another Englishman complained of "pamphlet-mongers" who "impoison" their pens "for a little mercenary gain." Even John Milton, a critic of prepublication licensing, warned that books "are as lively, and as vigorously productive, as those fabulous dragon's teeth; and being sown up and down, may chance to spring up armed men."

Despite their best efforts, governments found it difficult to curb the growing number of book addicts and their dealers. Indeed, authorities could not even keep proscribed books out of prisons. While French Calvinists (Huguenots) languished in seventeenth-century prisons, they still managed to satisfy their habits with smuggled reading material.

If large, established printers violated antibook laws, they were easily shut down. This was not true of small printers, however, who could publish in homes, dismantle their equipment, and move to other towns.

For example, in sixteenth-century England, a group of Puritans published the notorious "Marprelate tracts." The first of these irreverent attacks on the Established Church was printed near Kingston in the home of Mrs. Crane. Then, with authorities at their heels, the printers moved their press to the north of England and the home of Richard Knightly. (Meanwhile, a pusher disguised as a cobbler smuggled the illicit tracts to London.)

The renegade printers moved their press several more times, until they were finally apprehended at Warrington. There, while the press was being unloaded from a cart, a piece of type fell to the ground. A conscientious townsman became suspicious and reported the incident to the authorities. This brought an end to the activities of the Marprelate book lords.

The underground book-market had a serious drawback. Small printers, in search of quick profits, often did hasty, careless work. This caused many books to become adulterated with errors. For instance, in 1541 Martin Luther complained that reprints of his books were done by printers who "look only to their own greed." Some of his books had become "so garbled that in many places I have not recognized my own work."

Then, of course, there were the children. In 1562, Paris authorities were asked to prosecute a butcher who had given heretical alphabet books to about two hundred children. Centuries later, during Thomas Paine's trial for sedition in England, the prosecutor claimed that candy had been wrapped in pages from *Rights of Man* and then sold to kids. The government, duly alarmed, prohibited that dangerous book.

Righteous persecutors—whether of heretics, printers, book addicts, or drug addicts—are cut from the same cloth. Modern drug inquisitors are nothing more than updated versions of previous zealots who, inflamed with an intolerant self-righteousness, presumed to tell others how to live.

Today, the United States government has targeted millions of citizens for righteous persecution. Thousands of nonviolent Americans are imprisoned each year, civil and economic liberties are fast disappearing, and foreign wars loom on the horizon. The much-heralded "war on drugs" is a war on individual rights—one of the greatest threats to liberty ever experienced by Americans.

13
Will the Real Herbert Spencer Please Stand Up?

"I have had much experience in controversy," wrote Herbert Spencer, "and . . . my impression is that in three cases out of four the alleged opinions of mine condemned by opponents, are not opinions of mine at all, but are opinions wrongly ascribed by them to me. . . ." If this was true of Spencer's contemporary critics, it is even more true of later commentators. Probably no intellectual has suffered more distortion and abuse than Spencer. He is continually condemned for things he never said—indeed, he is taken to task for things he explicitly denied. The target of academic criticism is usually the mythical Spencer rather than the real Spencer; and although some critics may derive immense satisfaction from their devastating refutations of a Spencer who never existed, these treatments hinder rather than advance the cause of knowledge.

Gertrude Himmelfarb, a leading Victorian scholar with a splenetic hostility to libertarian radicals, regards Spencer's system as "a parody

---

Reprinted from *The Libertarian Review* (Dec. 1978).

of philosophy." Spencer—"the dilettante whose writing was a facile as his thinking"—was "amateurish and self-taught, his "image . . . comic and pathetic." Harry Elmer Barnes, who at least gives Spencer his due in some areas, nevertheless attributes Spencer's antistatism to "the traits of his neurotic constitution." Spencer, writes Barnes, had "an extreme 'antiauthority complex,' " and his "persistent and ever growing resentment against the extension of governmental activity probably was personally motivated by a subconscious neurotic reaction."

This pseudo-psychology is bad enough, but it is mild compared to Richard L. Schoenwald's psychoanalytic rape of Spencer in the Summer 1968 issue of *Victorian Studies*—an event that is surely the low point in the history of that otherwise reputable journal. Spencer, Schoenwald informs us, was "an adult whose development had undergone severe twisting." Specifically, "Spencer's self-esteem had been undermined hopelessly in the oral and anal stages of his development; he could commit himself only to paper, not to a woman." It seems that the infant Herbert reveled in his ability to "create" feces, and he bitterly resented the effort of his parents to curb "the anal freedom in which he had gloried." Spencer interpreted his parents' toilet-training efforts as "a fearful attack from behind," and his "once loving parents [were] now revealed as devilish obstructors of the path of glory." This, we are to believe, was the basis for Spencer's hostility to the state. Note well the marvelous explanatory power of this "theory." Why, for instance, did Spencer oppose governmental sanitation regulations? Because he "saw in sanitary reform an attack on his magical anal producing powers. . . ."

Such assertions would be comical if not for their appearance in a leading academic journal. Spencer's contemporaries at least dealt with him on the intellectual plane, criticizing those ideas they believed him to hold. To some modern academics, however, a person *intellectually* committed to uncompromising liberty and justice is inconceivable, so the psychological ax must be unsheathed.

Although Spencer is grudgingly conceded to be a major intellect of the nineteenth century, whose impact rivaled that of Darwin and Marx, he is usually treated as a historical relic who made a presumptuous and wrong-headed attempt to construct an all-embracing philosophical edifice. Spencer is commonly branded a racist, an enemy of the poor and disadvantaged, an apologist for a ruthless "law of the jungle," a conservative defender of the status quo, and so forth. The myths surrounding Spencer's name are so numerous that they cannot all be discussed in a single article. This essay is but a small step in Spencer revisionism, in which we shall consider four of the most common myths about Spencer.

Myth #1: Spencer was a "Social Darwinist."

The most serious misconception about Spencer's purported "Social Darwinism" concerns the "survival of the fittest" doctrine, which we shall discuss shortly. First, however, we must correct some common errors about Spencer's theory of evolution.

Although Spencer was a pioneer in evolutionary theory, he was not a Darwinist. He originated his theory before Darwin, and Darwin borrowed the famous phrase, "survival of the fittest," from Spencer's writing.

Moreover, Spencer was a Lamarckian rather than Darwinian. He was firmly convinced that acquired characteristics are transmitted to later generations. Although he accepted natural selection, he viewed it as only one aspect of the evolutionary process. It was Spencer's Lamarckianism that led to his belief in the inevitability of human progress. The adaptations of one generation that enabled it to survive are transmitted to the next generation, thus giving it superior capabilities, and so on into future generations, until a perfect equilibrium is achieved between the environment and an organism's ability to survive.

An important point to remember about Spencer's theory of evolution is that it is primarily cosmological, not biological, in nature. For Spencer, the laws of evolution, such as the trend from homogeneity to heterogeneity, pertain to all of existence, not merely to living beings. Biology is but one manifestation of the evolutionary process.

Finally, we must note that Spencer did not believe that society is an "organism," as is often claimed. The many biological parallels affixed to his arguments about social development were intended to *illustrate* his general evolutionary principles. Spencer believed that certain parallels exist between a living entity and a society, but that these similarities pertain to underlying laws of development—laws common to all of existence. By providing biological illustrations in conjunction with his sociology, Spencer hoped to clarify the working of natural law—specifically, the law of causation.

Myth #2: Spencer championed a ruthless "survival of the fittest."

More than any other of his ideas, Spencer's "survival of the fittest" doctrine has been used as a smear against him. The BBC production of John Kenneth Galbraith's *Age of Uncertainty* gave us a pallid Spencer citing a passage about survival of the fittest (suitably ripped from its context to make it appear reprehensible) against a background of a jungle and wild animals. The message, in Galbraith's characteristic style, was crude and grossly inaccurate: Spencer allegedly glorified the "law of the jungle" where the strong prey on the weak.

The "survival of the fittest," as presented by Spencer, and the "survival of the fittest," as presented by Spencer's critics, bear little resemblance to each other. The traditional interpretation of Spencer on this point is so fundamentally wrong—in fact, Spencer *explicitly* repudiated it on many occasions—that one must wonder if any of Spencer's critics bother to read him.

Spencer regards the "survival of the fittest" as a law of existence applied to life. It is a formal statement of a necessary condition for the existence of life. To be "fit" is to be adapted to the conditions of survival in a given environment. This is a *description*, not an evaluation. Spencer does not say that the fit "ought" to survive, or that it is "good" that the fit survive; he says simply that the fit *do* survive, whether one likes it or not.

"Fit," in Spencer's usage, is a formal, value-free term. He emphatically denies that it implies a particular trait, such as strength or intelligence, or any degree of approval or disapproval. This doctrine "is expressible in purely physical terms, which neither imply competition nor imply better and worse." Furthermore, writes Spencer, "survival of the fittest is not always the survival of the best."

"The law is not the survival of the 'better' or the 'stronger'. . . . It is the survival of those which are constitutionally fittest to thrive under the conditions in which they are placed; and very often that which, humanly speaking is inferiority, causes the survival."

One necessary condition of life is the adaptation of a living entity to its external environment. The prospect of continued life for an individual or a species is proportionate to the degree to which an individual or a species can adapt to surrounding conditions. Persistent failure to adapt must ultimately lead to death or to a diseased, unhealthy state of life. To be "fit," according to Spencer, is to be adapted to the requirements of survival, whatever those requirements may be.

In a social context, the "fit" are those persons who adapt to the survival requirements of a given society. If, for instance, a society executed all redheads, then it follows that the persons best fitted for survival in such a society would be non-redheads. And the redheads who would stand the best chance of survival would be those who adapted themselves to the conditions, e.g., those who dyed their hair another color. One can state this "survival of the fittest" principle without condoning the penalty against redheads, and without regarding non-redheads as superior people. It is a simple fact: if a society kills redheads, then (all other things being equal) one has a better chance to survive—one is more "fit"—if one is not a redhead.

Similarly, in a primitive, savage society, the physically strongest or the most ruthless may have the best chance to survive. In an authoritarian society, the meek and submissive may live the longest. In a free, industrial society, honest, innovative, and energetic individuals will fare best.

Of course, one's moral evaluation of a ruthless person will differ tremendously from one's evaluation of an honest person. But the fact remains that some kinds of social organization favor the survival of the ruthless, whereas other kinds favor the survival of the honest. If a society penalizes industry and rewards indolence, then one will see a decline of industrious persons while the indolent thrive. The "fittest" (in this case the indolent) will tend to survive at the expense of others. This is the meaning of Spencer's oft-quoted remark, "The ultimate result of shielding men from the effects of folly, is to fill the world with fools."

Spencer's "survival of the fittest" doctrine, therefore, refers to the need of an organism to adapt to the conditions of existence if it is to live. If this sounds tautological, Spencer would agree. He regards this formal, value-free law as "almost self-evident."

When Spencer applies his "survival of the fittest" principle to a free, industrial society, he reaches a conclusion radically different from the one usually foisted upon him by his opponents. True, the sacrifice of one individual for the benefit of another is the general rule for lower life forms. And it is equally true of the lower forms of human society—militant, authoritarian societies (which Spencer calls regimes of status). But with the evolution of peaceful societies—in which voluntary contract and the division of labor replace coercion and the regime of status—there also develops a harmony of interests, through Adam Smith's famous "invisible hand" process.

In a free society, people are free to pursue their own interests as they see fit, provided they respect the equal liberty of others. Cooperation replaces exploitation, and the "fittest" survive, not by exploiting others, but by assisting others through the mechanism of a market economy. One "survives" here by providing others in society with desired goods and services (unless, of course, one wishes to live as a hermit). By pursuing one's own ends, and by observing the principle of justice, one unintentionally benefits others.

Here as elsewhere the "survival of the fittest" is an iron law, but it is clear that the "law of the jungle" image conjured up by Spencer's opponents is far removed from his actual conception. On the contrary, it is precisely in a free society that the "law of the jungle" does *not* apply, because only in a free society is cooperation rather than exploitation the standard of "fitness."

But what of the poor, disabled, and disadvantaged? Was not the grim Spencer an implacable foe of altruistic aid to others? Did he not prefer to see them die off to make room for the "fit"?

This common distortion of Spencer is perhaps the most vicious and inexcusable. The last one hundred pages of *The Principles of Ethics* are devoted to the subject of "Positive Beneficence," the phenomenon in the highest form of society of "spontaneous efforts to further the welfare of others."

Spencer opposed coercive, state-enforced charity, but he favored charity that is voluntarily bestowed. As a matter of justice, one cannot be forced to help others; but as a matter of ethics, one may be obliged to help others. Spencer viewed his system as "more humane" than those which involve state interference, because under state charity many industrious men are "compelled to pay rates and starve their children, that the idle might not be hungry."

Spencer was amazed that his views brought on him "condemnation as an enemy of the poor." In one essay, for instance, he pointed out that it was becoming more common for the rich to contribute in time and money to the "material and mental progress of the masses." This he commended as "the latest and most hopeful fact in human history"; it was a "new and better chivalry," and it "promised to evolve a higher standard of honor" through the eradication of sundry evils.

This scarcely fits the picture of a Spencer devoid of humanitarian concern who anxiously awaited elimination of the poor. But one must read Spencer's extensive treatment of this subject to appreciate fully the flagrant lies perpetrated by his critics. That he was grievously offended and hurt by such lies is dramatically illustrated by the fact that he broke off a close friendship of some forty years with Thomas Henry Huxley when Huxley wrote that, according to the Spencerian individualist, a poor man should be left to starve because charity interferes "with the survival of the fittest." In reply to Huxley's accusations of "reasoned savagery," Spencer pointed out that "for nearly fifty years I have contended that the pains attendant on the struggle for existence may fitly be qualified by the aid which private sympathy prompts." So inexcusable did Spencer consider Huxley's misrepresentation that, even after Huxley's apology, it took several years for the breach to heal.

Myth #3: Spencer was a conservative apologist for the "capitalist class" and the status quo.

To deal with this myth adequately would require a lengthy essay dealing with many different facets of Spencer's philosophy. Here we can only highlight a few major points.

Spencer, even in later life, was never a conservative defender of the status quo, nor was he so viewed by many of his contemporaries. Consider, for example, the anarchist Kropotkin's remark that Spencer has "profound ideas about the role and importance of the State; here Spencer is a continuator of Godwin, the first advocate of . . . anarchism." One must also remember Spencer's radical legacy, typified in England by Auberon Herbert (a radical individualist who championed "voluntary taxation"), and in America by Victor Yarros, co-editor for two years of Benjamin Tucker's *Liberty*—the great individualist-anarchist periodical. (In fact, Spencer's influence on the American anarchist movement was profound, especially in regard to his "law of equal freedom.")

One simply cannot understand the mind of Herbert Spencer unless one understands that the predominant concern throughout his intellectual life was the principle of *justice*. From his twelve articles on "The Proper Sphere of Government" that appeared in Edward Miall's *The Nonconformist* in 1842 (when Spencer was twenty-two), until his death in 1903, justice and its foundation in natural law were the threads that held together the complex fabric of his philosophy. Although he was inconsistent at times, Spencer applied the principle of justice with remarkable integrity and courage, without regard to whom he might offend or alienate.

Those socialists who see Spencer as a lackey for the capitalists will read with considerable discomfort his essay on "The Morals of Trade." Here Spencer bitterly attacks the corruption of English trade and commerce which, he argues, is permeated with fraud, misrepresentation, and cheating. He calls the commerce of his day "commercial cannibalism," where the law of survival is "cheat or be cheated." What was the basic cause of this corruption? Note well the response of this alleged defender of the "robber-barons": "The great inciter of these trading malpractices is, intense desire for wealth. And if we ask—why this intense desire? The reply is—it results from the indiscriminate respect paid to wealth." The "blind admiration which society gives to mere wealth, and the display of wealth, is the chief source of these multitudinous immoralities."

If he thought "this gigantic system of dishonesty" was bad in England, Spencer had even harsher words about some aspects of commerce in the United States. The Americans are worse than the English in their "worship of the 'almighty dollar,' " and this "vicious sentiment" calls for "vigorous protest against adoration of mere success."

Of course, Spencer had no objection to "wealth rightly acquired"; it was his passion for justice which prompted his ruthless denunciation of the injustices committed by the "capitalist class" of his day. Justice is justice, and it applies with equal force to every individual, regardless of class distinctions.

If justice is no respecter of class, neither is it a respecter of country. Spencer's consistent regard for justice is further illustrated by his intransigent opposition to militarism and British imperialism (with the unfortunate exception of Irish Home Rule). He despaired of the regimentation that "is another aspect of that general retrogression shown in growing imperialism and accompanying re-barbarization," and he opined that the increased militarism "is carrying us back to medievalism."

Spencer was among the few intellectual leaders to condemn Britain's role in the Boer War—a war that was quite popular among the rank and file. In his magnificent article on "Patriotism," Spencer lambastes the motive of patriotism, which he calls a "sentiment . . . of the lowest." "To me the cry—'Our country, right or wrong!'—seems destestable." When Spencer was confronted with the charge that he dishonored the British soldiers who were dying for their country, he gave a reply that rivals in terseness and clarity any argument of modern opponents of the Vietnam War: "When men hire themselves out to shoot other men to order, asking nothing about the justice of their cause, I don't care if they are shot themselves."

Spencer's opposition to war and militarism was in the grand tradition of British libertarian thought, as exemplified by Richard Cobden, Henry Thomas Buckle, and John Bright. Unfortunately, many libertarians of today fail to grasp the profound radicalism of the libertarian principle of nonaggression, but the implications were clear to our predecessors of a century past. Justice, not "national interest," was to be the guiding light in foreign affairs.

Myth #4: In later life Spencer abandoned his defense of pure liberty.

This, properly speaking, is not so much a myth as a bundle of partial truths. Spencer was less consistent in later life, but many aspects of his mature theory are significant improvements on his earlier writing. Spencer's views changed in several ways, some for the worse and some for the better. But it is flatly incorrect to hold that he abandoned a natural rights defense of liberty, and it is equally incorrect, though common, to blame his later weak spots on his sociology.

In his first and most famous political work, *Social Statics*, the young Spencer, coming as he did from a tradition of Protestant dissent, placed his defense of natural rights on an essentially theological foundation. "God wills man's happiness," he wrote, and "God intends he should have that liberty" essential to the pursuit of happiness. But Spencer became dissatisfied with this *deus ex machina*, especially as his agnosticism solidified in his later years, and he set out to provide a solid ethical underpinning for the doctrine of rights and the law of equal freedom. Indeed, to place ethics on a scientific footing was Spencer's "ultimate purpose, lying behind all proximate purposes" in writing his formidable ten-volume *Synthetic Philosophy*. And the defense of rights he presented in *The Principles of Ethics*, with its remarkable integration of cosmology, biology, psychology, sociology, and ethics far surpasses the treatment in *Social Statics*. It is unquestionably the most ambitious defense of liberty and rights ever attempted by a libertarian theorist.

Hence Spencer did not abandon natural rights for sociology; instead, his sociology was one facet of the naturalistic foundation from which he constructed a theory and justification of rights. Contrary to popular opinion, Spencer's sociology did not corrupt his dedication to liberty, but rather strengthened it philosophically. One need only consult his magnificent discussion of the "militant" and "industrial" forms of social organization in *The Principles of Sociology* to verify the truth of this claim.

Nevertheless, Spencer did adopt several antilibertarian positions in his later writing, such as his defense of military conscription if it became necessary to fight a defensive war. And there is the irksome omission of "The Right to Ignore the State" from later editions of *Social Statics*. To what can we attribute these and other curious regressions in Spencer's thought?

Spencer's basic problem was in his ethical theory. He was unable to derive a consistent theory whereby abstract ethical principles could be applied to concrete situations without vitiating those very principles in the process. This conflict was evident in *Social Statics*, and it became progressively severe in his later writing. The ethical code elaborated in *Social Statics* was said by Spencer to apply only to the "perfect" or "straight" man—i.e., to man at the highest stage of evolution, which Spencer believed to be inevitable. But since "perfect" individuals do not yet exist, Spencer was faced with the sticky problem of how imperfect humans were to employ a moral code that did not apply to them. (Admirers of "The Right to Ignore the State" often overlook Spencer's remark at the end of the chapter that the ideas presented there will not apply for a long time to come.)

This dichotomy in Spencer's ethics was later transformed into a full-blown theory of "absolute" versus "relative" ethics. The maxims of absolute ethics—where no coercion whatever was permitted—applied only to a perfectly evolved and permanently peaceful society. During the transition, however, when coercion and barbarism were still present, it was often necessary to forego an absolutely right course of action in favor of an alternative that is "least wrong." Thus does Spencer slip in taxation and conscription—such coercive actions, while not absolutely right, are the least wrong in an imperfect society.

This confusion in Spencer's ethical theory was an unmitigated disaster, but it is important to realize that this confusion was with Spencer from the beginning and that it only worsened with time. It had nothing to do with his sociology. In short, the early Spencer was not as "pure" as some libertarians think, nor was the later Spencer as "impure" as they sometimes claim.

Finally, we should mention Spencer's disillusionment and pessimism in later years. These were partially spawned by a more realistic judgment concerning the mechanism of social change. Spencer attributed his "juvenile radicalism" to the belief that it was necessary only "to establish a form of government theoretically more equitable, to remedy the evils under which society suffered." Later he concluded that a change of government is in itself superficial and will invariably result in "replacing the old class-legislation by a new class-legislation." Political change is thus meaningless without a corresponding social change—i.e., a change in the attitudes and habits of persons in a society. Hence, "governmental arrangements can be of use "only in so far as they express the transformed nature of citizens."

In this respect Spencer became more radical as he aged. He became convinced that those who fight for liberty by political means are essentially wasting their time. He turned down a request to run for Parliament because "far too high an estimate" was made of the influence of politicans, and he "should not gain influence, but rather lose influence" by running for office.

Thus we leave Herbert Spencer, brilliant and cantankerous to the end. If there is any intellectual justice in the world, Spencer deserves a place among the intellectual giants. Libertarians would do well to take a closer look at this phenomenal mind in their midst, and a necessary first step in placing Spencer in critical perspective is to revive his works and to read them firsthand. With a few exceptions, secondary accounts of Spencer should be avoided like the plague.

14
Frantz Fanon and John Locke at Stanford

In 1814, Thomas Jefferson denounced one of the "Great Books of the Western World," Plato's *Republic:*

> While wading through the whimsies, the puerilities and unintelligible jargon of this work, I laid it down often to ask myself how it could have been, that the world should have so long consented to give reputation to such nonsense as this? [F]ashion and authority apart, and bringing Plato to the test of reason, take from him his sophisms, futilities and incomprehensibilities, and what remains?[1]

John Adams agreed with Jefferson's assessment. Recalling the "tedious toil" of reading Plato's works, Adams declared: "My disappointment was very great, my astonishment was greater, and my disgust shocking." Adams believed that Plato's defense of communal property (including a community of wives) was "destructive of human happiness" and was "contrived to transform men and women into brutes, Yahoos, or demons."[2]

Reprinted from the *Cato Policy Report* (Jul./Aug. 1989).

The great books are under fire once again, this time at Stanford University. Stanford has scrapped its required Western culture course and replaced it with a program called "Cultures, Ideas, and Values" (CIV). The pilot course for this program, "Europe and the Americas," retains some great books, but it has also made room for minority, feminist, and Third World writers—including Rigoberta Menchu, Zora Neale Hurston, and Frantz Fanon. These writers, their advocates argue, will offset the racism, sexism, and cultural bias inherent in the traditional great books. (One traditional author, Augustine, was born and reared in Africa, but his culture and race presumably strip him of African credentials.)

The traditionalists, of course, are duly alarmed by Stanford's attack on Western civilization. If the reformers have their way, if Stanford freshmen no longer read the great books, what will become of our treasured Western values? What will become of Plato's communism, Augustine's spiritual masochism, Machiavelli's cynical amoralism, More's critique of private property, Luther's strident irrationalism, Marx's authoritarianism, and more?

How important is this debate? Will the great books read by freshmen profoundly influence their lives? Probably not, especially when students breeze through several books (or selections from books) in a semester or two. The great thinkers of the past were not addressing American college students of today. As Robert Hutchins observed, "To read great books, if we read them at all, in childhood and youth and never read them again is never to understand them."[3]

A great books program, skillfully conceived and executed, can accomplish two things: it can fire students with the love of reading and learning, and it can acquaint students with some perennial problems confronting human existence. If a student does not leave an introductory course with the desire to learn more, then that course was a waste of time.

This is where the instructor's skill comes into play. A great book, when taught by a bore, is boring. A great book, when taught by a professor who doesn't understand its relevance, seems irrelevant. A great book, when taught by a professor with an ax to grind, will be chopped into small, unrecognizable pieces.

Required reading in college may become despised reading in later life. Even today I do not enjoy reading Shakespeare. I want to read Shakespeare, but when I try, I am flooded with horrific school-day memories—flashbacks of barely literate students stumbling aloud through Elizabethan verse in monotone drawls—flashbacks of drudgery, pedantry, and suppressed yawns. Who has not had similar experiences?

If the Stanford faculty does to Fanon what my teachers did to Shakespeare, then traditionalists can take heart: No Stanford student, after leaving that institution, will ever read Fanon again.

Social Justice at Stanford

Stanford's CIV program has been defended by Charles Junkerman, assistant dean of undergraduate studies.[4] "[B]ooks," Junkerman asserts, "are to be read and valued for what they have to say, not for the name recognition of their authors." This is reasonable enough, though it would be difficult to find anyone who advocates reading great books because they bear famous names.

Fanon's *The Wretched of the Earth* is now required reading for Stanford freshmen; John Locke's *Second Treatise of Government* is not. Junkerman defends this peculiar choice as follows:

> 50 years ago John Locke seemed indispensable in answering a question like "What is social justice?" In 1989, with a more interdependent world order, a more heterogeneous domestic population, and mass media and communications systems that complicate our definitions of "society" and "individual," it may be that someone like Frantz Fanon, a black Algerian psychoanalyst, will get us closer to the answer we need.[5]

An interdependent world order, a heterogeneous domestic population, and mass media and communications systems—seldom are so many clichés crowded into one sentence. But what do they mean? England doesn't have an especially heterogeneous population—even today. Should we therefore dismiss all English theorists of social justice? As for mass media and communications, is Locke outdated because he didn't have a television, a phone, or a computer? If Junkerman uses these devices, do they render him a more able philosopher than Locke? And have modern conveniences really complicated our definitions of "society" and the "individual"? (Here's a useful test: If you can touch it, it's definitely not a society.)

Junkerman apparently finds Fanon more to his liking than Locke; that is his prerogative. But to recommend Fanon over Locke in a course on "Europe and the Americas" is intellectually irresponsible. Few writers have exerted more influence on modern Western thought than Locke. Adam Smith and Karl Marx are possible candidates, but, of these, only Marx has found his way into the Stanford program. A course on Western thought without John Locke or Adam Smith is like a course on ancient Greek philosophy without Plato or Aristotle.

Locke vs. Fanon

Junkerman has targeted Frantz Fanon and John Locke for comparison, so let's take a look at these two authors.

First published in French in 1961, *The Wretched of the Earth* emerged from Fanon's experiences during the French-Algerian war. Fanon's angry indictment of colonialism and racism is insightful, sometimes brilliant. The same cannot be said, however, of Fanon's socialist agenda for an independent Algeria.

Fanon writes of "the necessity for a planned economy" and "the outlawing of profiteers." A revolutionary government, if it is to rescue the economy of a newly liberated country, "must first and foremost nationalize the middleman's trading sector." While under French rule, Algerian peasants learned a valuable economic lesson—a lesson that Stanford's wealthy donors should ponder as well:

> The people come to understand that wealth is not the fruit of labor but the result of organized, protected robbery. Rich people are no longer respectable people; they are nothing more than flesh-eating animals, jackals, and vultures which wallow in the people's blood.[6]

The government, Fanon writes, should educate the masses politically; this will "make adults of them." Fanon's elitism becomes even more apparent in this passage: "We ought to uplift the people; we must develop their brains, fill them with ideas, change them and make them into human beings."[7]

Why don't Algerians qualify as adults and human beings until their brains are filled with ideas by Fanon and his ilk? Partially because the "young people of the towns, idle and often illiterate, are a prey to all sorts of disintegrating influences." In other words, Algerian youth may pursue activities of which Fanon disapproves—corrupt "capitalist" values, including "detective novels, penny-in-the-slot machines, sexy photographs, pornographic literature, films banned to those under sixteen, and above all alcohol."[8] (Apparently the idle youth have sufficient money to spend on slot machines and movies, and the illiterate youth are sufficiently literate to read detective novels and pornographic literature.) Even the "capitalistic conception of sport," according to Fanon, poses a serious threat to underdeveloped countries.

To combat such evils, "the government's duty is to act as a filter and stabilizer." Youth commissioners will combat the main evil, idleness, by putting young people to work. "For this reason the youth commissioners ought for practical purposes to be attached to the Ministry of Labor"—and this Ministry of Labor ("a prime necessity in underdeveloped countries") will cooperate with the Ministry of Planning ("another necessary institution in underdeveloped countries").[9]

With his call for a planned economy and its attendant bureaucracy, Fanon appears to favor a highly centralized government. But this is not true, he assures us. Throughout his book, Fanon stresses the need to keep power out of the hands of a ruling elite and in the hands of the people. This requires "decentralization in the extreme."

But how can a socialized economy function (to the extent it can function at all) without a centralized government? Perhaps Stanford freshmen can mull this problem over while they wade through Fanon's book.

Fanon vs. Africa

Fanon's economic program is a prescription for disaster modeled, ironically enough, after Western theories of economic planning. So where is the African perspective that Fanon is supposed to offer Stanford freshmen? Does he call for a revival of African culture? Far from it. Fanon attacks African culture with a vehemence second only to his attack on capitalism.

European colonizers demeaned Africans culturally and racially. Understandably, therefore, many Africans seek to reclaim their African heritage through literature, poetry, music, and art. This love of African culture, Fanon says, is shared by some black Americans who "experience the need to attach themselves to a cultural matrix."

But the quest for an African culture, Fanon warns, leads up a blind alley; "There will never be such a thing as black culture." It is "mystification, signifying nothing."[10]

"[E]very culture," Fanon believes, "is first and foremost national." An Algerian who seeks out a precolonial African culture "feels the need to turn backward toward his unknown roots and to lose himself at whatever cost in his own barbarous people." The native should tear himself away from these roots, "painful and difficult though it may be"; otherwise, "there will be serious psycho-affective injuries."[11] (The psychiatrist Fanon, the enemy of Western culture, revels in Western psychobabble.)

African traditions—"the good old customs of the people"—should be jettisoned. Why? Because Fanon worries that Algerians, freed from the yoke of colonialism, will reject his vision of how they should live; they might choose instead to return to the tribalism and feudalism of precolonial Africa. Presumably, those misguided Algerians who feel they have a right to live as they see fit have been corrupted by that Western value known as freedom of choice.

Instead of adopting old customs, Algerians should develop an authentic (Fanon's favorite word) national culture based on revolutionary realities. Authentic culture "is opposed to custom, for custom is always the deterioration of culture." During a revolutionary struggle, the desire to attach oneself to tradition or to revive old traditions means "opposing one's own people." The African artist who looks to the African past for inspiration turns away from actual events and embraces "the castoffs of thought, its shells and corpses." If the native artist wishes to produce an authentic work of art, he must join the revolutionary struggle.[12]

What does all this mean? Put simply, it means that Fanon regards African culture as a pernicious and reactionary myth; it is "a stock of particularisms," "mummified fragments," and "symbols of negation and outworn contrivances." If these elitist remarks had come from a white writer, he would be excoriated as racist, culturally biased, and unsuitable for the Stanford CIV program. But Fanon was a black revolutionary socialist, so never mind.

Was Fanon included in the Stanford program to represent African culture? If so, the Stanford planners have perpetrated a cruel hoax. Fanon is pushing a revolutionary socialism and its national culture, nothing more.

John Locke's Revolutionary Ideas

While in college, I imbibed my John Locke through a professor who was under the spell of C. B. MacPherson's book, *The Political Theory of Possessive Individualism.* I was told that Locke was a political conservative, a defender of a nascent capitalist class, and a member of the "bourgeoisie" (i.e., "middle class" uttered with a sneer). Even this mangled view, however, is a cut above an interpretation based on Locke's culture, race, sex, and time. We may concede the point: Locke was Western and white and male, and he died a long time ago. If these flaws expel him from Stanford classrooms, so be it.

Whether Locke should be included in the Stanford program narrows to a single point: Should freshmen read one of the most influential philosophers of the modern era—a man whose philosophical, political, and educational writings profoundly influenced leading thinkers in England, Scotland, France, America, Germany, and elsewhere?

Locke's *Essay Concerning Human Understanding* set the stage for modern empiricism, and it was deeply admired by the luminaries of the French Enlightenment, such as Voltaire. The impact of Locke's *Second Treatise of Government* is difficult to exaggerate. Reading that tract is essential if students are to understand the ideological background of the American and French Revolutions—two of the most cataclysmic events of the modern era.

In short, it is virtually impossible to understand the past 250 years of Western civilization without referring to Locke. He upheld natural rights, government by consent, religious tolerance, the right to resist unjust laws, and the right to overthrow tyrannical governments. These principles have become indispensable to our vision of a free and open society.

Nevertheless, in the mind of Junkerman, Fanon may "get us closer to the answer we need" in the search for social justice. Ironically, Fanon occasionally sounds like Locke. "The land belongs to those that till it," Fanon asserts. Locke agrees wholeheartedly:

> The *labor* of man's body, and the *work* of his hands, we may say, are properly his. Whatsoever then he removes out of the state that nature hath provided, and left it in, he hath mixed his *labor* with, and joined to it something that is his own, and thereby makes it his *property*.[13]

Fanon tells how Algerian revolutionaries refused "to tolerate any encroachment of this right of ownership." The Algerians, he boasts, "are men of property."[14] Locke would have been very pleased indeed.

Locke, like Fanon, was a revolutionary. Wanted by the English government for sedition, Locke spent six years hiding out in Holland.

And his *Second Treatise* is one of the most vigorous and compelling defenses of violent revolution ever penned.

Who decides when a revolution is necessary? Locke answers: "The people shall be judge." In a passage later drawn upon by Jefferson for his Declaration of Independence, Locke writes:

> If a long train of abuses, prevarications, and artifices, all tending the same way, make the design [to oppress] visible to the people, and they cannot but feel, what they lie under, and see, whither they are going; 'tis not to be wondered, that they should then rouze themselves, and endeavor to put the rule into such hands, which may secure to them the ends for which government was first erected.[15]

What if a revolution involves considerable bloodshed? In this event, argues Locke, the fault lies with the oppressors, not with the oppressed:

> If any mischief come in such cases, it is not to be charged upon him who *defends* his own right, but on him that *invades* his neighbors. If the innocent honest man must quietly quit all he has for peace sake, to him who will lay violent hands upon it, I desire it may be considered, what a kind of peace there will be in the world, which consists only in violence and rapine; and which is to be maintained only for the benefit of robbers and oppressors. Who would not think it an admirable peace betwixt the mighty and the mean, when the lamb, without resistance, yielded his throat to be torn by the imperious wolf?[16]

Perhaps Junkerman can explain why these and many similar passages no longer apply to the modern quest for social justice. Locke, far more than Fanon, provides a philosophical justification for restoring the rights of life, liberty, and property to oppressed peoples everywhere.

Notes

1. *The Writings of Thomas Jefferson* (Washington, D.C.: The Thomas Jefferson Memorial Association, 1903), XIV, p. 148.

2. Ibid., pp. 156–57.

3. *The Great Conversation: The Substance of a Liberal Education* (Chicago: Encyclopedia Britannica, Inc., 1952), p. 76.

4. Letter to the Editor, *The Wall Street Journal*, January 6, 1989.

5. Ibid.

6. Frantz Fanon, *The Wretched of the Earth*, trans. Constance Farrington (New York: Grove Press, 1968), p. 191.

7. Ibid., p. 197.

8. Ibid., p. 195.

9. Ibid., p. 196.

10. Ibid., pp. 216, 234–35.

11. Ibid., pp. 216–18.

12. Ibid., pp. 224, 226, 233.

13. John Locke, *Two Treatises of Government*, ed. Peter Laslett (New York: New American Library, 1965), p. 329.

14. Fanon, *Wretched of the Earth*, pp. 192–93.

15. Locke, *Two Treatises of Government*, p. 463.

16. Ibid., p. 465.

15
For Reasons of State: Public Education in America

"The total and integral education of the Italian," stated Mussolini, "is the principal function of the State." Many proponents of totalitarianism have made similar remarks. Champions of state power have long recognized the invaluable role of education in molding obedient citizens.

Most Americans frown upon indoctrination masquerading as education. These "bad" systems of state education are typically contrasted with "good" systems of state education, such as that found in the United States, where propaganda is supposedly absent.

Government education in America, it is claimed, concentrates on the needs of the children, such as teaching them skills that they will require in later life. In "bad" systems, on the other hand (such as those found in the Soviet Union, China, or Cuba), thought control and propaganda replace objectivity and the search for truth. In short, a "good" system of education exists to benefit the child, whereas a "bad" system exists to benefit the state.

This distinction is useful, but few people realize that it places the American educational system squarely in the "bad" category. The basic justification for our public schools (i.e., government schools) has always been "for reasons of State." The welfare of the child has placed a distant second at best.

This may surprise many people. Even those who have nothing kind to say about public schools commonly assume that the welfare of children was the primary reason for their establishment. Most Americans believe that government schools, however they may have failed in America, were intended to benefit the child rather than the state, thereby qualifying them for the "good" category.

To see state schooling in the U.S. as altruism gone awry is impossible for anyone with even a cursory knowledge of its history. The major ideological advocates for state schooling have argued repeatedly, with a clarity that cannot be misunderstood, that state schools and compulsory attendance exist first and foremost for the benefit of the government. When seen in this perspective, there is little to distinguish government schools in America from their counterparts in the Soviet Union. There are obvious differences of degree, but the basic rationales are identical.

The ideological history of state schooling in America makes this abundantly clear. America's first compulsory-education law was passed by the Massachusetts Bay Colony in 1642, followed by Connecticut (1650), New Haven (1655), New York (1665), and Pennsylvania (1683). The Puritans who settled Massachusetts Bay established a rigid Calvinistic theocracy, and compulsory education was a part of this authoritarian system. The 1642 statute required that children be able "to read and understand the principles of religion and the capital laws of this country," and it enacted fines against negligent parents. This statute mandated education, but it did not provide schools for that purpose. This oversight was remedied in 1647 with the "old deluder, Satan" law, which established grammar schools in towns of one hundred households or more, to be financed by taxes.

In addition to their religious convictions, the Puritans brought with them to the New World a cluster of social and economic doctrines that are commonly called "mercantilism." Mercantilism enjoyed a heyday in sixteenth-century Elizabethan England, which saw a dramatic trend toward the centralization of state power.

The mercantilist state regulated industry and commerce for the purpose of enriching itself with precious metals, which could then be used to finance wars and expansion. Elizabethan England enacted a complex series of economic regulations, including wage and price controls, trade restrictions, governmentally enforced monopolies, and forced labor (including child labor).

The Massachusetts Puritans adopted the mercantilist worldview. During the seventeenth century, they made various attempts to impose wage and price controls, to establish monoply privileges, and to introduce other features of the mercantilist program.

Compulsory education was part of this worldview. It did not spring from a benevolent regard for the welfare of children. Far from it—mandatory labor was decreed for children along with mandatory learning. The governor of Massachusetts Bay declared that "no idle drones be permitted to live amongst us," and this ban on idleness applied as much to children as to adults. In 1640 the General Court (the legislative body) considered ways to teach children the spinning of yarn in order to increase the output of linen. In 1641 the Court, fearing that work habits were deteriorating, declared that "all masters of families should see that their children . . . be industriously employed." A 1642 act empowered the government to farm out as apprentices the children of parents who did not see to their "needful and beneficial employment." In 1646 the death penalty was authorized for any boy over sixteen who was "stubborn and rebellious" to his parents. A 1648 law stated the point clearly: children who became "rude, stubborn, and unruly" were to be taken from their families and placed under the discipline of a master who will "force them to submit unto government according to the rules of this order. . . ."

The Puritans did not disguise their view that children were natural resources to be exploited for the good of the community (as interpreted, of course, by the ruling oligarchy). There was no mushy romanticism here, no speculation about the "right to an education." State education was simply one facet of a comprehensive mercantilist program of social and economic controls.

The Puritans were a distasteful bunch, but it would be a mistake to suppose that their subordination of the child to the state was peculiar to them. In fact, this theme appears repeatedly throughout the history of American education. It was the ideological foundation of American public schools.

A national system of education was advocated by many American intellectuals during the late eighteenth century, and most of them left no doubt that this education was to serve state interests. "Let our pupil be taught that he does not belong to himself," wrote Benjamin Rush in 1786, "but that he is public property." A system of national education, argued Noah Webster in 1790, will "implant in the minds of the American youth . . . an inviolable attachment to their own country."

This theme also dominated the thinking of nineteenth-century educators. "There is one thing that we should have learned from the nations of Europe in respect to public education," declared an Illinois superintendent of schools, "all their systems, such as they are, are conceived, designed, and carried out with direct and persistent reference to the maintenance and stability of the existing political order of the government. And so it must be with us."

A New Hampshire State superintendent of public instruction argued that it is proper for the state to provide education "when the instinct of self-preservation shall demand it." "It is solely as an act of self-defense," he noted, "that the Government comes to the rescue of the schools." A U.S. commissioner of education argued that the individual "owes all that is distinctly human" to the state. Not surprisingly, therefore, he viewed state education as "a mere war measure, as a means of preservation of the State." The government should provide education, echoed a California superintendent, "as an act of self-preservation." Children, he maintained, "belong not to the parents, but to the State, to society, to the country."

The same principle has been enunciated many times in the present century as well. In 1902, the New Hampshire Supreme Court declared:

> Free schooling . . . is not so much a right granted to pupils as a duty imposed upon them for the public good. If they do not voluntarily attend the schools provided for them, they may be compelled to do so. While most people regard the public schools as the means of great advantage to the pupils, the fact is too often overlooked that they are governmental means of protecting the state from consequences of an ignorant and incompetent citizenship.

In a similar vein, a 1914 bulletin of the U.S. Bureau of Education stated: "The public schools exist primarily for the benefit of the State rather than for the benefit of the individual." Perhaps the most chilling description of the role of state education came from Edward Ross, a prominent American sociologist.

> To collect little plastic lumps of human dough from private households and shape them on the social kneading board, exhibits a faith in the power of suggestion which few people ever attain to. And so it happens that the role of the schoolmaster is just beginning.

The preceding passages are but a sampling of many similar passages that can be culled from the writing of American state educators. There has been general agreement that state education exists primarily to serve the goals of the state, rather than the goals of the child. This is the logic that justifies compulsory attendance.

Those who see government schools in America as child-centered often find it difficult to understand the reason for compulsory attendance. If the schools are intended as a boon to children and parents, if they are a great social service, then why must attendance be compulsory? Since when do "free" goods and services have to be forced upon consumers?

This reasoning is sound, but its premises are flawed. If the state schools were meant to be child-centered, then compulsory attendance is indeed an absurdity. But if, as we have seen, these schools exist "for reasons of State," then attendance at them (or state-approved equivalents) becomes not a privilege but a duty to be enforced by law. As more than one observer has pointed out, if the state may conscript adults into the military for a national purpose, then it may conscript children into school for a national purpose.

We are left with the conclusion that American public schools exist primarily to buttress the existing political order. Indoctrination is a feature common to all systems of state education, including the American system. The particular features of this indoctrination have changed throughout history, depending upon the values of the ruling class. (In the nineteenth century, for instance, "Americanizing" the flood of immigrants—i.e., imbuing the children of Irish Catholics with the values of Anglo-Saxon Protestantism—was a preeminent concern.) In general, however, state educators have sought to instill habits of loyalty and servitude to the powers that be.

When one is a member of a dominant social class, it is sometimes difficult to perceive indoctrination, because the values being imposed on others are often values of which one approves. This is why many Americans from a white middle-class background are blind to the extensive indoctrination in American public schools. A corrective for this blindness is to examine the reaction of minorities who have been subjected to forced "acculturation," as educators like to call it.

American Indians are a case in point. Not only were Indians slaughtered and driven from their homes, but they were subjected to the "benefits" of government education as well. The House Committee on Indian Affairs reported in 1818 that "in the present state of our country, one of two things seems to be necessary: either that those sons of the forest should be moralized or exterminated." Accordingly, a "Civilization Fund" was established in 1819 to educate the "savages." Indian education, under the control of the federal government, was used not only to eradicate vestiges of Indian culture, but to manipulate Indians into compliance with government programs such as the infamous massive Indian removals during the Jacksonian era.

Modern Indians have expressed contempt for their federally controlled system of education. A publication of the Indian Historical Press (1970) notes that the "only federally controlled educational system in this nation is that directed by the Bureau of Indian Affairs. . . ." Throughout history BIA schools have tried to "make good little white boys and girls of the Indian children," often with devastating results. The "bureaucratic control which is imposed on the people by governmental agencies" has consistently hindered the energy and creativity of the Indian people.

Bureau-directed schools "have the worst and most outdated textbooks and instructional materials. They permit Indian students to be subjected to the most outrageous research programs and psychological surveys." Standard texts used in BIA schools teach Indian children "that their grandfathers were savages, primitive people, unwashed and brutish"—stereotypes that fly in the face of historical facts. In a typical text, the killing of Indians by settlers who wanted their land is described as striking a blow "for freedom of the west," whereas the Indian defense of their land is described as "raids upon helpless frontier communities."

Through their many years of suffering and intimidation, Indians have learned that one pays a high price for "free" government education.

This is a lesson that all Americans would do well to remember.

16
Children's Rights in Political Philosophy

The plight of children throughout history has not, on the whole, been a happy one. Although their legal status has varied according to country and time, they have never enjoyed a legal status equal to that of adults. Rarely have children been permitted to control their own destinies; instead, they have been viewed as appendages of their parents or as property of the state.

Some ancient systems of law—Persian, Egyptian, and Roman, for example—permitted infanticide and the selling of children into slavery.[1] Infanticide was common among the Romans, and not until A.D. 374 was it punishable as murder.

> The conventional Roman attitude on fetal and infant life was strikingly callous. Seneca refers to the drowning of abnormal or weakly children at birth as a commonplace Roman phenomenon and as a reasonable kind of action. . . . Suetonius speaks casually of the exposure of children by their parents, with the implication that the act entirely depends on the will of the parents. . . .[2]

Although technically illegal, "the killing of legitimate children was only slowly reduced during the Middle Ages, and . . . illegitimate children continued regularly to be killed right up into the nineteenth century."[3]

Various brutal punishments have been deemed proper to inflict on children in the name of discipline—including severe whippings, prolonged confinement, and swaddling (i.e., wrapping children in cloth to render them immobile).[4] A thirteenth-century law cautioned that beatings should stop short of death: "If one beats a child until it bleeds, then it will remember, but if one beats it to death, the law applies."[5]

The severity of punishment varied according to the religious and cultural background of the parents. "For the Puritan," notes G. R. Taylor, "flogging was not just *a* method of discipline, it was *the* method which God had appointed."[6] The Quakers, on the other hand, placed less stress on physical punishment.[7] Illegitimate children have been especially victimized: "some medieval lawbooks treated them as almost rightless beings, on a par with robbers and thieves."[8]

The Romans sometimes castrated male infants for sexual purposes,[9] and such practices understandably disgust the modern reader. Yet we should remember that the American medical profession, during the late nineteenth century, sanctioned castration and clitoridectomies (as well as less severe surgical interventions) as "cures" for childhood masturbation.[10]

Children in Early Political Philosophy

Classical philosophers had surprisingly little to say about the legal status of children. They simply assumed that children, as dependent and immature beings, should not enjoy the same status as adults. The major question, therefore, became: who should have control of the child—the parents or the state?

Plato argues that children "belong to the state first and their parents second,"[11] and, following the Spartan example, he proposes an elaborate scheme of compulsory state education.[12] (During Plato's time, education in Athens "was optional and treated as a purely private affair.")[13]

Like Plato, Aristotle maintains that children "all belong to the state," and he criticizes Athenian education, where "every one looks after his own children separately, and gives them separate instruction of the sort which he thinks best."[14] The legislator "must mold to his will the frames of newly-born children,"[15] and Aristotle proposes a law whereby "no deformed child shall live."[16]

The father, according to Aristotle, enjoys "a kind of royal power"[17] over his children, "who live at the prompting of desire."[18] The relationship between father and child is analogous to chattel slavery—so, strictly speaking, a father cannot act unjustly towards his child:

> For there is not such thing as injustice in the absolute sense towards what is one's own, and a chattel, or a child till it reaches a certain age and becomes independent, is, as it were, a part of oneself, and no one chooses to harm himself; hence there can be no injustice towards them, and therefore nothing just or unjust in the political sense.[19]

Early English law apparently permitted a father to sell his son before the age of seven and even permitted the killing of newborns.[20] The law became less permissive over time, however, and restrictions were placed on this *patria potestas* (paternal power).

According to common law, the father could correct his child "in a reasonable manner," the father's consent was required for a marriage contract, and the father acted as "trustee" over his son's estate. These paternal powers, which ceased when the child reached twenty-one, could be transferred to another guardian at the father's discretion.[21]

Parental Power in Seventeenth-Century Thought

Theorists often regarded parental (and especially paternal) authority as important because of its relationship to political authority. Defenders of absolute monarchy grounded their arguments in paternal authority, and this became a major topic of debate in seventeenth-century thought.[22] The stage for this debate was set by the French philosopher Jean Bodin, a champion of absolute monarchy.

In his *Six Books of the Commonwealth* (1576), Bodin argues that the power of the father over his children is the origin and foundation of the sovereign's power over his subjects.[23] Nature requires a father to care for and educate his children, who in turn are obligated to obey without question. "This obligation is obvious, and founded in nature."[24]

Bodin notes that ancient laws gave fathers "power of life and death over their children," and he thinks this right "should be restored."[25] Bodin complains that fathers in his time have been deprived of their rightful authority; some of his contemporaries even suggested that a child should resist excessive coercion inflicted by the father—an idea that Bodin finds scandalous. Poorly disciplined children will grow up to defy the "authority of magistrates," so a well-regulated commonwealth must be based on well-regulated families.[26]

Bodin considers the possibility that a father might abuse the power of life and death over his children. He replies that the law must presume that if a father kills his child, he does so with just cause. Natural affection will prevent most cases of abuse. Moreover, "one cannot refuse to establish a good custom because certain ill consequences might occasionally ensue." No laws, Bodin points out, are risk free.[27]

Another important discussion of parental authority appears in the work of Hugo Grotius, a highly influential Dutch theorist of international law. In *On the Rights of War and Peace* (1625), Grotius argues that parents acquire authority naturally from having generated their child. Parental authority is valid during infancy, before the child reaches the "years of discretion," because "he who cannot govern himself must be governed by another; and the parents are the natural governors."[28] Parental authority can extend beyond the age of discretion as well, if the child remains within the family. This authority, which includes "the right of coercing" children to do their duty, lasts until children leave the family unit.[29]

Another seventeenth-century legal philosopher, Samuel von Pufendorf, also based parental rights and duties on natural law. Natural law requires parents to care for their children, and to assist in this task nature implanted in parents "the tenderest affection for their offspring." From this parental obligation, there flows the right of parents to direct the behavior of children "for their own welfare."[30]

Aside from the natural obligation of children to obey their parents, Pufendorf gives another (and somewhat novel) basis for obedience. Parental authority also rests on the "tacit consent" of the offspring.

> For it is rightly assumed that, if an infant had had the use of reason at the time of its birth, and had it seen that it could not save its own life without the parents' care and the authority therewith connected, it would gladly have consented to it, and would in turn have made an agreement with them for a suitable bringing-up.[31]

According to Pufendorf, a child owes primary allegiance to his father, and the father's authority continues until the child can fend for himself. Punishment is restricted to "moderate chastisement"—unless a child is habitually disobedient, in which case "he can be driven from the parental home and disowned."[32]

When children become capable of "mature judgment" but remain within the father's household, they are still obliged to follow the father's guidance. So long as a father provides support, he may require the child to "adjust himself to the circumstances of the father's household."[33]

Pufendorf sanctions the selling of a child into a modified form of slavery, if the child would otherwise die of starvation. This slavery agreement should be "endurable" and allow the father, when his financial condition improves, to repurchase his child. In no case, however, may a parent kill a child, e.g., through exposure. (Pufendorf also condemns abortion.)[34]

After a child leaves the paternal household, the father's authority "dissolves" (though children always owe respect). In extreme cases, as mentioned before, a father may drive a child from his household—

but the child may not leave without the father's permission.[35]

Grotius and Pufendorf agree that paternal authority lasts only as long as the child remains in the father's household, and both set limits to that authority. These notions were challenged by Sir Robert Filmer, whose most famous work, *Patriarchia*, is known more for the reply it elicited from John Locke than for its intrinsic merit.[36]

Patriarchal theory—where the authority of the sovereign is derived from the father's authority over his family—was popular among seventeenth-century defenders of absolute monarchy. Indeed, the Fifth Commandment, "Honor thy father and thy mother," was often interpreted as an injunction to obey the king—the "father" of his people.[37] According to Filmer, "If we compare the natural duties of a Father with those of a King, we find them to be all one, without any difference at all but only in the latitude or extent of them."[38]

Filmer denies that children attain freedom after leaving their father's house, because this would impose limits on paternal power and, by implication, on monarchical power. Fathers are "natural magistrates" whose natural authority cannot be alienated or transferred except with their consent.[39]

Filmer criticizes social-contract theorists, such as Grotius, who posit a state of nature where everyone is naturally and equally free. But if children are born in subjection to their parents, as Grotius conceded, then how can they be said to be naturally free? "Now for those that confess an original subjection in children, to be governed by their parents, to dream of an original freedom in mankind, is to contradict themselves. . . ."[40] Paternal authority comes from God, and only God can alienate it. "[T]he paternal power cannot be lost; it may either be transferred or usurped; but never lost, or ceaseth."[41] Therefore, "Every man that is born, is so far from being free-born, that by his very birth he becomes a subject to him that begets him: under which subjection he is always to live. . . ."[42]

Like his mentor Jean Bodin, Filmer recalls ancient systems of law that gave the father the power of life and death over his children, as well as the right to sell or castrate them.[43] This absolute paternal power was essential to Filmer's defense of absolute monarchy, for the right to impose death was seen as "the decisive attribute of sovereignty."[44] Thus, if political sovereignty was to be derived from paternal authority, it was necessary to defend the father's power of life and death, the ancient *patria potestas.*

The gauntlet thrown down by Filmer was taken up by John Locke (among others) in his classic work *Two Treatises of Government.* As part of his attack on Filmer, Locke elaborated on the nature and foundation of parental authority, and it is with this aspect of his theory that we shall be concerned.

Political authority and parental authority, according to Locke, are fundamentally different. Political authority arises from the consent of free and equal individuals to submit to a common authority and thereby secure their rights. Parental authority, on the other hand, derives from the "weak and helpless" nature of infants, who are "without Knowledge or Understanding." A person's natural freedom is made possible by the "Law of Reason." Reason tells us that true liberty is not a license to do as one pleases (which would include violating the liberty of others), but rather "is to be free from restraint and violence from others. . . ." True liberty, in other words, occurs within guidelines established by the rights of others. But in order to follow this "Law of Reason"—and thereby claim the freedom which it sanctions—one must have knowledge of the law. This knowledge can come only through the exercise of reason, so "he that is not come to the use of his *Reason,* cannot be said to be *under this Law.* . . ." And one who is not under the Law of Reason cannot be said to be free.[45]

Until the child reaches maturity and is capable of keeping his actions within the bounds that reason demands, he must be guided by the will of an adult. Natural law requires that parents "preserve, nourish, and educate" their children, and this gives parents authority over their offspring "during the imperfect state of Childhood . . . till Reason shall take its place. . . ."[46]

Locke argues that children are born free in the same sense that they are born rational. There is a potential for each that is realized at maturity. Natural freedom and the subjection of children to parents are therefore consistent. "A Child is Free by his Father's Title, by his Father's Understanding, which is to govern him, till he hath it of his own."[47] It is perhaps fair to say that, for Locke, a child enjoys vicarious freedom through his father.

Parental power differs "both as to time and extent" from political power. The jurisdiction of parents is temporary, and it lacks that essential "Mark of Sovereignty"[48]: the legislative power of life and death.[49] Parental authority is but a "temporary Government, which terminates with the minority of the Child."[50] And even here parental authority is severely limited. Locke is appalled by Filmer's insistence that a child is, in effect, a slave of the father. Ancient legal systems may have enforced the father's absolute power, but that is irrelevant. Historical precedents cannot render the unjust just. Cases cited by Filmer simply illustrate the "most shameful Action, and most unnatural Murder, humane nature is capable of."[51]

What, according to Locke, is the proper extent of parental jurisdiction? Like theorists before him, Locke is vague on this point. The basic obligation of parents is to care for and educate their children, and the parents have a "right" to the degree of "subjection" necessary to meet these goals. Parents have the "power of commanding and chastising" in order to direct a minor's behavior. Will parents abuse this power? Locke believes that natural affection is a sufficient safeguard in most cases.[52]

After children mature, they are no longer under the natural obligation of obedience. But the father may prolong the period of submission by threatening to withdraw the inheritance that his children would otherwise receive. He may be "sparing or liberal," depending on how well his children please him.[53]

The French Enlightenment

Eighteenth-century philosophers added little to the discussion of parental authority. With the demise of patriarchal theory, there was no longer a need to focus on the moral status of parents and children. When parental power is discussed in eighteenth-century works, it is usually presented in summary fashion and modeled after Grotius, Pufendorf, and Locke.

A significant shift in emphasis occurs in the mid-eighteenth century, however, particularly among French and German writers. There is perceptibly more interest in the relation between the *state* and the child than between the parent and the child. The rise of nationalist ideologies accounts for much of this change. With the rise of nationalism, more philosophers argued that the central purpose of education should be to "form valuable citizens to the state."[54] Children were seen as future citizens and patriots, whose education must be carefully supervised by the state to insure proper results. "Thus," wrote Charles Duclos in 1750, "it is patent that in Spartan education the first task was to form Spartans. In the same way, the sentiments of citizenship must be inculcated in every state; among us, Frenchmen must be formed, and in order to create Frenchmen, we must first work to form men."[55]

Baron de Montesquieu's *Spirit of the Laws* (1748) set the stage for a good deal of Enlightenment thinking about children, the state, and education. If a democracy is to survive, it must imbue its citizens with civic virtue—a "love of the laws and of our country," a love that elevates public interest above private interest.[56] Montesquieu praises Spartan education for its ability to produce virtuous citizens, and he leaves no doubt that this should be the central task of education in a republic:

> Everything therefore depends on establishing this love in a republic; and to inspire it ought to be the principal business of education. . . .[57]

Another formative influence on Enlightenment thought was J. J. Rousseau. In his essay on *Political Economy* (1758), Rousseau argues that the state should not "abandon to the intelligence and prejudices of fathers the education of their children, as that education is of still greater importance to the State than to the fathers."[58] Thus the state should supervise and regulate education.

> Public education, therefore, under regulations prescribed by the government, and under magistrates established by the Sovereign, is one of the fundamental rules of popular or legitimate government. If children are . . . imbued with the laws of the State and the precepts of the general will . . . they will learn to cherish one another mutually as brothers, to will nothing contrary to the will of society . . . and to become in time defenders and fathers of the country of which they will have been so long the children.[59]

Rousseau leaves no doubt that the primary function of education is to form citizens. Children should be taught "to regard their individuality only in its relation to the body of the State, and to be aware, so to speak, of their own existence merely as a part of that of the State. . . ."[60]

It was widely believed among the French *philosophes*—many of whom were determinists—that one's education (or lack of it) determines one's beliefs, moral habits, and actions. The French Enlightenment saw a strong reaction against monarchy and Catholicism, both of which were assailed during the French Revolution. If a democratic republic is to flourish, argued the *philosophes,* its citizens must be instructed so as not to fall prey to despotism amd superstition. Education, declared Baron d'Holbach (expressing the sentiments of the philosophes generally), "will best furnish the true means of rectifying the wanderings of mankind."[61] Holbach continued:

> A just, enlightened, virtuous, and vigilant government, who should honestly propose the public good, would have no occasion either for fables or for falsehoods to govern reasonable subjects; it would blush to make use of imposture to deceive citizens who, instructed in their duties, would find their interest in submitting to equitable laws. . . .[62]

The use of state education to form virtuous citizens was advocated by most of the French intelligentsia, including the physiocrats, the *philosophes,* and various liberal statesmen. When the Jesuit order was expelled from France in 1764, the loss of this mainstay of secondary schooling created an educational vacuum and thereby paved the way for an educational system that stressed nationalism and civic virtue.[63]

The major objections to Jesuit schooling were presented by Caradeuc de La Chalotais in an influential essay. The Jesuits, according to this Breton magistrate, should not be trusted as teachers, because they are loyal to the Pope, not to France. Moreover, the Jesuits offered free instruction in reading and writing to peasants and artisans. This endangers the French economy, because overly educated workers will be unsatisfied with mundane, tedious jobs. If, however, the French government were to control education, it could teach peasants and artisans only those limited skills needed to be satisfied with their station in life.[64] La Chalotais received considerable praise for his arguments, most notably from the great Voltaire.

After the French Revolution, calls for patriotic education became especially pronounced. Consider, for example, a decree passed by the National Convention in December 1793. Declaring that primary education shall be free, public, and compulsory, this decree requires that prospective teachers "produce a certificate of patriotism and morality"; that any teacher who "violates public morality . . . shall be denounced by the supervisors, and arraigned before the correctional police"; and that textbooks shall be selected by the "Committee on Instruction" that are "absolutely necessary for the training of citizens. . . ."[65]

Kant

Immanuel Kant was able to advocate liberty and individual rights in theory, while supporting unlimited obedience to existing states in practice. Although he sparked a pro-freedom trend among some German theorists (e.g., Wilhelm von Humboldt and a young Fichte), Kant's own approach "ended in a condition of virtual political paralysis."[66] This is to be expected of a philosopher who can declare, on the one hand, that every person has a right to freedom of action "so long as he does not infringe upon the freedom of others," and, on the other hand, that no citizen has the right to oppose any head of state in "word or deed."[67] And all of this within the span of one brief essay!

Kant elaborates on the rights of parents, children, and the state in more detail than most eighteenth-century philosophers. He considers the parent-child relationship within the context of rights, and he specifies that "all right is accompanied with an implied title or warrant to bring compulsion to bear on any one who may violate it in fact."[68] Parents have "the duty of preserving and rearing" their children, which implies a reciprocal right of the child to such care. This right of children—"which becomes immediately theirs by law, without any particular juridical act being required"—continues until they can maintain themselves, at which time they become their own masters.[69]

Kant bases the parental obligation on the fact that an infant "is brought without his consent into the world," which places the responsibility for care on the parents who entered into the procreative act as a matter of free will. The child is endowed with rights and thus cannot be regarded as property. Parents lack the right to abandon or destroy a child.[70]

Parental authority over infants is not based on contract, so after the child reaches the age of "emancipation" (the age at which it can support itself), all natural ties between parent and child dissolve. Parents lose their right to command, and children lose their right to support. Parents cannot demand further obedience as payment for previous support.[71]

When children attain their majority, they can remain in the household of their parents by contractual agreement.[72] At this point the relationship becomes one of master and domestic servant. The parent "*commands* as master," and the mature offspring "*obeys* as servant."[73] As a servant, the child belongs (in a sense) to the parent-master. That is, if the servant runs away, the master "is entitled to bring [him] again under his power by a unilateral act of his will."[74] But the master cannot treat the servant as property, because the master-servant relationship is contractual, and no person can contract himself into slavery. The contract, therefore, cannot be perpetual; it must be limited in time. During the "definite period" when the contract is in force, one party may intimate to the other that he wishes to sever the relationship. Presumably, then, after the initial time expires, so does the contract.[75]

From the preceding, we see that Kant posits a legal obligation by parents to care for their children, and he specifies education as one of these obligations. It follows, therefore, that the state has the right to enforce this parental duty. Unfortunately, Kant fails to specify criteria for adequate care and education, so we do not know when intervention should occur and what form it should take.[76] Nor does Kant seem particularly enthralled with state education. He regards the development of critical reasoning as an important aspect of education, and he argues that civic rights and duties should be taught, not by "officials appointed by the state, but [by] free teachers of right, i.e., the philosophers."[77]

Hegel

In the writings of G. W. F. Hegel (1770-1831) we see the glorification of the state carried to extreme limits. The state, for Hegel, "is the divine idea as it exists on earth." All "the worth which the human being possesses, all spiritual reality, he possesses only through the state."[78]

Hegel shares the common view that children have a right to maintenance at their parents' expense, from which is derived the parental right to demand obedience. Children "are not things and cannot be the property either of their parents or others."[79] This is because children are potentially free. Insofar as education is a parental concern, the object of education is to instill the proper ethical principles. The discipline imposed on children should promote this education, which has as its purpose "to break down the child's self-will." We cannot educate children through reasoning and benevolence. "If we advance reasons to children, we leave it open to them to decide whether the reasons are weighty or not, and thus we make everything depend on their whim."[80] Unless children are trained to be obedient and subordinate, they will become impertinent.

Hegel upholds the right of civil society (which he characterizes as a "universal family") to compel and provide for the education of children, because such education is necessary to prepare the child to become a member of society. "Society's right here is paramount over the arbitrary and contingent preferences of parents. . . ."[81] Many parents, Hegel points out, believe they have the right to control the educational destiny of their own children. Such parents have a "faddish dislike" of state education, but their resistance must give way to society's right "to compel parents to send their children to school. . . ."[82]

The Individualist Tradition

We shall now survey what some leading figures in the individualist tradition had to say about children, parents, and the state, beginning with Wilhelm von Humboldt's *The Limits of State Action.*

The Limits of State Action is a classic exposition of limited-government liberalism. Any "State interference in private affairs," argues Humboldt, "where there is no immediate reference to violence done to individual rights, should be absolutely condemned."[84] Humboldt opposes state education because he fears it will smother the diversity and individuality that is so essential to happiness.

> [I]f there is one thing more than another which absolutely requires free activity on the part of the individual, it is precisely education, whose object it is to develop the individual.[85]

The concept of justice developed by Humboldt is one of noninterference. One has the legal obligation to abstain from violating the rights of others, but one does not have positive obligations. This concept of justice, he points out, presupposes adults with mature faculties; it does not apply to children. Parents have the obligation to care for their children, and this obligation creates parental rights to say how their children shall be raised.

Thus far Humboldt is fairly traditional, but he now imposes

restrictions on parental power that go beyond what we have seen before. The rights of children (e.g., to life and property) cannot be abrogated by parents. Even the freedom of children cannot justifiably be limited, except insofar as is necessary to further their development. Restrictions on freedom cannot extend beyond the time required for a child's training, and children "must never be compelled to actions which extend in their immediate consequences beyond this period of development, or even over their whole life." This means that parents cannot dictate a child's marriage or career.[86]

Since the function of government is to protect rights, it follows that the state has the duty to protect the rights of children against their parents. The state must see that "paternal power does not exceed its limits, and must always watch closely over it." This supervision, however, should confine itself to maintaining the reciprocal rights and duties of parents and children; the state "must never seek to prescribe any positive rules for the definite training and instruction of the children by their parents. . . ."[87] Parents need not continually account for their actions to the state; it should be assumed that parental duties are properly discharged unless there is clear evidence of neglect or harm. Only then may the state intervene in family relationships.

According to Humboldt, the freedom normally granted to adults may be dangerous when exercised by children, and the duty to keep children out of harm's way falls primarily on the parents. But the state may assist by punishing adults who cajole or deceive children into harmful acts. Therefore, acts which are normally beyond the province of law, such as illicit sexual intercourse, can be prohibited by the state when they involve children.[88]

Bentham

Nineteenth-century English individualism had two distinct strains, one based on utility and the other based on natural rights. In the former category were Jeremy Bentham, James Mill, John Stuart Mill, and many other utilitarians. In the latter category were Thomas Hodgskin, Herbert

Spencer, Auberon Herbert, and a number of lesser-known figures. Mutual hostility was exhibited by these two schools on a number of issues. The utilitarians rejected the appeal to natural rights, and the natural rights camp attacked the utilitarians for their compromising attitude on state power. It is illuminating, therefore, to compare the treatment of children's rights by leading advocates of both schools.

Jeremy Bentham (1748-1832) had a far-reaching impact on political theory in general and on liberal thought in particular. Once viewed as a staunch individualist, modern scholars now see in Bentham the germs of later collectivism.[89] But the desire of Bentham to limit state power through an appeal to utility is unmistakable, and it heavily influenced his views on children.

According to Bentham, social measures should be judged according to their tendency "to augment or to diminish the happiness of the community." But a community is a fictitious body—only individuals exist—so we must understand what promotes the happiness of the individual before we can turn to the community, which is nothing more than an aggregate of individuals.[90]

Bentham justifies political freedom on the ground that the individual is most likely to know his own interests. Leaving the individual free to act on his own judgment, therefore, is the best way to maximize social utility. Specifically, human happiness depends on three things: knowledge, inclination, and physical power.

The individual is likely to have the best *knowledge* of how to achieve his happiness, argues Bentham; and he will have the strongest *inclination* to pursue it. "For who should know so well as you do what it is that gives you pain or pleasure?"[91] Both knowledge and inclination favor individual autonomy over direction by others—so even if another person had more power than oneself to bring about the conditions of happiness, this would not override the presumption that freedom promotes happiness better than direction by others.

According to Bentham, the basic relationship between parent and child is that of guardian and ward. A guardian exercises power over another person for the benefit of the ward, rather than for himself. The scope of the guardian's power is potentially unlimited; that is, he may direct the actions of the ward in any aspect of life, as long as this direction is needed to discharge the guardian's duties. The relationship between guardian and ward is that of a *trust*—the guardian must promote the ward's welfare—and it is this trust that imposes limitations on the power of the guardian. The "business of the [guardian]," states Bentham, "is to govern the [ward] precisely in the manner in which this latter ought to govern himself."[92]

Legislation, for the most part, is incompetent to direct the guardian in his activities. The conditions pertaining to the ward's interests are so diverse and variable that no law (which must deal in general terms) could possibly offer specific guidance. Therefore, state interference between a guardian and a ward should be minimal.[93]

The position of guardian imposes obligation on the parent. In order to discharge this obligation, the parent must be able to control the child and the child's property. From the obligation of the parent to provide care, therefore, there arises the obligation of the child to obey. From this perspective, the parent-child relationship is one of "master" and "servant."

Bentham thus sees the parent-child relationship as a compound condition of guardian-ward and master-servant. The parent has duties as a guardian and rights as a master; the child has rights as a ward and duties as a servant. The parent, in his role as a master, may set any rules for his child, limited only by the obligations imposed by his other role as a guardian. The child, in his role as a servant, must obey any commands of his master, limited only by the rights granted in his role as a ward.[94] Bentham's exposition of this complex theme constitutes one of the most thorough examinations ever written of the relationship between parents and children.

Spencer

Whatever their disagreements, most of the philosophers discussed thus far share certain common assumptions. From the parental duty to rear children, they derive the parental right to restrict the freedom of children when it is deemed necessary for their development. Some philosophers are willing to grant more discretion to children than others. Some attack parental authority, especially in educational matters, for the purpose of transferring that authority to the state. Nearly all discussions of children in philosophical literature are *future-oriented.* That is, they justify present subordination of children in the name of their future development, or in the name of their future value to society or to the state. Not until Herbert Spencer were these assumptions challenged. Spencer viewed children as essentially autonomous, and he rejected efforts to deny to children equal rights on the basis of their dependency. Spencer offered a more radical challenge to the conventional view of childrens' rights than had ever been attempted before.[95]

Herbert Spencer's opposition to state education is well known. What is sometimes overlooked, however, is that Spencer opposed all coercion of children, even that imposed by their parents. The legal system of his time that permitted parents to coerce their children in the name of punishment was condemned by Spencer as "vicious." The law of equal freedom—"every man has freedom to do all that he wills, provided he infringes not the equal freedom of any other man"—applies as much to children as to adults. Just as an adult requires freedom to exercise his faculties in pursuit of happiness, so "the child, too, has faculties to be exercised; the child, too, needs scope for the exercise of those faculties; the child therefore has claims to freedom—rights, as we call them—coextensive with those of the adult."[96]

Against those who say that children have no rights, Spencer points to the impossibility of specifying a precise time at which the child passes into the realm of adulthood and thereby acquires rights previously denied:

> [A]t what period does the human being pass out of the condition of having no rights into the condition of having rights? . . . Shall the youth be entitled to the rights of humanity when the pitch of his voice sinks an octave? Or when he begins to shave? Or when he ceases growing? Or when he can lift a hundredweight? Are we to adopt the test of age, of stature, of weight, of strength, or virility,

> or of intelligence? Much may no doubt be said in favor of each of these, but who can select the true one?[97]

To deny the rights of children, Spencer argues, is to sanction the legitimacy of their murder, robbery, or enslavement. "[I]f children have no rights, they cannot become the subjects of these crimes." What of the response that children have some rights (e.g., the right not to be murdered) but not other rights enjoyed by adults (e.g., freedom of choice)? Any proponent of this view, Spencer retorts, must explain precisely what rights are to be denied to children and why, from the principles of natural law, such rights should be denied.

Spencer next considers the traditional argument that because the parent is obligated to provide the child with the necessities of life, the parent thereby enjoys special rights over the child—rights that one adult cannot have against another adult. This does not follow, says Spencer. Parental support "establishes no title to dominion." If one man becomes benefactor to another man, this does not confer upon the first "the right to play the master over the other." Parental support cannot be used as an excuse to "trench upon the liberties of his child."[98]

The most plausible argument for ascribing fewer rights to children than to adults is based on the undeveloped faculties of children. Rights protect the exercise of human faculties; and because children's faculties are less developed than adults, they would seem to have fewer rights. Spencer responds to this argument as follows:

> The fullest endowment of rights that any being can possess is *perfect* freedom to exercise *all* his faculties. And if each of two beings possesses *perfect* freedom to exercise all his faculties, each possesses *complete* rights; that is, the rights of the two are *equal*; no matter whether their faculties are equal or not. For, to say that the rights of the one are less than those of the other, because his faculties are fewer, is to say that he has no right to exercise the faculties he has not got—a curious compound of truism and absurdity.[99]

Spencer was aware that his position was more radical than most people were willing to accept, but he maintained that his plea for the rights of children agreed with the requirements of education. Moral education strives to develop the power of rational self-control; and this power can be developed only through exercise. Education should teach children to be their own masters, and this it cannot do by making them submissive to others. Education should develop responsibility and self-control, yet coercive education denies to children the opportunity to practice and learn from mistakes. "No wonder that those who have been brought up under the severest discipline should so frequently turn out the wildest of the wild. Such a result is just what might have been looked for."[100]

If a child's future station in life is to be that of a slave, then enforced subordination might fit him to it. "But just to the degree in which such treatment would fit him for servitude must it unfit him for being a free man among free men."[101]

Notes

1. "The ancient Roman laws gave the father a power of life and death over his children; upon this principle, that he who gave had also the power of taking away." Sir William Blackstone, *Commentaries on the Laws of England*, ed. Thomas M. Cooley, 3rd ed. (Chicago: Callaghan and Co., 1884), vol. I, p. 295. Cf. James Kent, *Commentaries on American Law*, ed. George F. Comstock, 11th ed. (Boston: Little Brown and Co., 1867), vol. II, pp. 204-5.

2. John T. Noonan, Jr., *Contraception: A History of its Treatment by Catholic Theologians and Canonists* (Cambridge: Harvard University Press, 1966), pp. 85-6.

3. Lloyd deMause, "The Evolution of Childhood," in *The History of Childhood* (New York: Harper Torchbooks, 1975), p. 25. Despite its psychoanalytic perspective, this essay is the best overview of the cruelties inflicted on children throughout history. Another interesting essay on the history of childhood is J. H. Plumb, "Children: The Victims of Time," in *In the Light of History* (New York: Dell Publishing, 1972). The classic work in this field is Philippe Aries, *Centuries of Childhood: A Social History of Family Life*, trans. Robert Baldick (New York: Vintage Books, 1962). The central

theme of this book—that the concept of "childhood" was an invention of the early modern period and that it deprived previously happy children of their freedom and autonomy—has been challenged by deMause.

4. See deMause, "The Evolution of Childhood," pp. 25-50.

5. Ibid., p. 42.

6. Gordon Rattray Taylor, *The Angel Makers: A Study in the Psychological Origins of Historical Change, 1750-1850* (London: William Heinemann Ltd., 1958), p. 304.

7. See J. William Frost, *The Quaker Family in Colonial America* (New York: St. Martin's Press, 1973), pp. 64-92.

8. Edward Westermarck, *Christianity and Morals* (New York: Macmillan, 1939), p. 360.

9. See deMause, "The Evolution of Childhood," pp. 46-7.

10. See Ronald Hamowy, "Medicine and the Crimination of Sin: 'Self-Abuse' in 19th Century America," *The Journal of Libertarian Studies*, vol. I, no. 3 (Summer 1977), pp. 229-270.

11. Plato, *The Laws*, trans. Trevor J. Saunders (Harmondsworth: Penguin Books, 1970), p. 293.

12. For a good account of Plato's totalitarian tendencies, see Karl R. Popper, *The Open Society and its Enemies*, 5th ed. (Princeton: Princeton University Press, 1966), vol. I.

13. H. I. Marrou, *A History of Education in Antiquity*, trans. George Lamb (New York: Sheed and Ward, 1956), p. 69.

14. *Politica*, trans. Benjamin Jowett, rev. W. D. Ross, *The Works of Aristotle* (Oxford: Clarendon Press, 1921), vol. X, bk. viii.1.

15. Ibid., bk. vii.16.

16. Ibid.

17. Ibid., bk. i.13.

18. Aristotle, *The Nicomachean Ethics*, trans. H. Rackham (Cambridge: Harvard University Press, 1947), p. 185.

19. Ibid., p. 293.

20. See F. Pollock and F. Maitland, *The History of English Law Before the Time of Edward I*, 2nd ed. (Cambridge: Cambridge University Press, 1923), vol. II, pp. 436-7.

21. Ibid., vol. I, pp. 295-6.

22. For an excellent discussion of this subject, see Gordon J. Schochet, *Patriarchalism in Political Thought* (New York: Basic Books, 1975).

23. Jean Bodin, *Six Books of the Commonwealth*, trans. and ed. M. J. Tooley (Oxford: Basil Blackwell, n.d.), p. 6. For a brief discussion that places Bodin in his historical setting, see Quentin Skinner, *The Foundations of Modern*

Political Thought (Cambridge: Cambridge University Press, 1978), vol. II, pp. 284-301.

24. Bodin, p. 12.

25. Ibid.

26. Ibid., p. 13.

27. Ibid., p. 14.

28. Hugo Grotius, *On the Rights of War and Peace*, trans. William Whewell (Cambridge: Cambridge University Press, 1853).

29. Ibid., p. 94.

30. Samuel Pufendorf, *On the Duty of Man and Citizen* (1673), trans. F. G. Moore (New York: Oceana Publications, 1964), vol. II, p. 97. This is an abstract of Pufendorf's massive work on international law, *De Jure Naturae et Gentium* (1672).

31. Ibid. Pufendorf may have borrowed this argument from Thomas Hobbes. See *Leviathan* (1651), ed. Michael Oakeshott (New York: Collier Books, 1962), p. 152.

32. Pufendorf, p. 98.

33. Ibid., pp. 98-9.

34. Ibid., p. 99.

35. Ibid., p. 100. Pufendorf seems to say that the father's consent is necessary only before the child attains the age of reason, but this is not clear from the text.

36. *Patriarcha* was written during the 1630s but not published until 1680, long after Filmer's death, during a political conflict known as the Exclusion Crisis. This was an unsuccessful Parliamentary effort to exclude the Catholic Duke of York (later King James II) from the throne of England. Most scholars now believe that John Locke wrote the original version of his *Two Treatises of Government* during the Exclusion Crisis, which is why he devoted the entire *First Treatise* to rebutting Filmer.

37. See Peter Laslett's introduction to *Patriarcha and Other Political Works of Sir Robert Filmer*, ed. Peter Laslett (Oxford: Basil Blackwell, 1949), pp. 26-7. All quotations from Filmer are from this edition. Cf. Schochet, *Patriarchalism in Political Thought*, pp. 73-84.

38. Filmer, *Patriarcha*, p. 63.

39. Ibid., pp. 72-3.

40. "Directions for Obedience to Governments in Dangerous or Doubtful Times," in *Patriarcha and Other Political Works of Sir Robert Filmer*, p. 231.

41. Ibid.

42. Ibid., p. 232.

43. Ibid., p. 231. Cf. *Patriarcha*, p. 77.

44. See the discussion in M. Seliger, *The Liberal Politics of John Locke* (New York: Praeger, 1968), p. 213.

45. John Locke, *Two Treatises of Government*, ed. Peter Laslett, rev. ed. (New York: New American Library, 1965), pp. 347-8. One way that Locke attacks Filmer is to argue that the father has but "a joynt Dominion with the Mother" over their children (p. 216). The mother has "an equal Title" to parental authority, so it is more accurate to speak of "Parental Power" rather than paternal power (p. 345). Unfortunately, Locke sometimes fails to follow his own advice.

46. Ibid., pp. 347-50.

47. Ibid., p. 351.

48. Locke uses this phrase in ibid., p. 275.

49. Ibid., p 366.

50. Ibid., p. 354.

51. Ibid., p. 217.

52. Ibid., p. 355. For Locke's opinion on the physical punishment of children, see *Some Thoughts Concerning Education* (1693), ed. R. H. Quick (Cambridge: Cambridge University Press, 1892). Locke argues that parental praise and condemnation are sufficient in most cases to instill the proper habits in children (p. 34). Physical punishment is proper only in extreme cases: "Beating is the worst, and therefore the last Means to be us'd in the Correction of Children, and that only in Cases of Extremity, after all gentle Ways have been try'd and prov'd unsuccessful . . ." (p. 62). Parents who resort to violence have neglected to raise their children properly; to beat a child causes more harm than good (pp. 31-2).

53. Locke, *Two Treatises*, p. 357.

54. Baron d'Holbach, *The System of Nature* (1770), trans. H. D. Robinson (Boston: J. P. Mendum, 1889), vol. I, p. 131. On the rise of nationalism, see Hans Kohn, *The Idea of Nationalism* (New York: Macmillan, 1948), pp. 187-259. Cf. F. de la Fontainerie, *French Liberalism and Education in the Eighteenth Century* (New York: McGraw Hill, 1932).

55. Quoted in K. M. Baker, *Condercet: From Natural Philosophy to Social Mathematics* (Chicago: University of Chicago Press, 1975), p. 286. On the influence of the Spartan model, see Elizabeth Rawson, *The Spartan Tradition in European Thought*, (Oxford: Oxford University Press, 1969).

56. Baron de Montesquieu, *The Spirit of the Laws*, trans. Thomas Nugent (New York: Hafner, 1949), p. 34.

57. Ibid.

58. Jean Jacques Rousseau, *The Social Contract* and *Discourses*, trans.

G. D. H. Cole (London: J. M. Dent, 1913), p. 252.

59. Ibid.

60. Ibid., p. 251.

61. Holbach, *The System of Nature*, vol. I, p. 130.

62. Ibid., p. 131.

63. On the impact of the expulsion of the Jesuits in France and other countries, see R. R. Palmer, *The Improvement of Humanity: Education and the French Revolution* (Princeton: Princeton University Press, 1985), pp. 47ff. Cf. Dale Van Kley, *The Jansenists and the Expulsion of the Jesuits from France, 1757-1765* (New Haven: Yale University Press, 1975).

64. For an English translation of La Chalotais, *Essai d'education nationale*, see Fontainerie, *French Liberalism and Education in the Eighteenth Century*. For a discussion of La Chalotais, see Harvey Chisick, *The Limits of Reform in the Enlightenment* (Princeton: Princeton University Press, 1981), pp. 89-94.

65. *A Documentary Survey of the French Revolution*, ed. J. H. Stewart (New York: Macmillan, 1951), pp. 515-19.

66. Leonard Krieger, *The German Idea of Freedom* (Chicago: University of Chicago Press, 1972) p. 124. Krieger's discussion of Kant is illuminating.

67. Immanuel Kant, "On the Common Saying: 'This May be True in Theory, but it does not Apply in Practice,' " in *Kant's Political Writings*, ed. Hans Reiss, trans. H. B. Nisbet (Cambridge: Cambridge University Press, 1970), pp. 74, 83.

68. Immanuel Kant, *The Science of Right*, trans. W. Hastie, Great Books of the Western World (Chicago: Encyclopedia Britannica, 1952), vol. 42, p. 398.

69. Ibid., p. 420.

70. Ibid. Kant considers the "maternal infanticide" of an illegitimate child to be an exception to the rule that all murder should be punished with death. An illegitimate child, because it is born outside the laws that regulate marriage, "is thus born beyond the pale of constitutional protection of the law. Such a child is introduced, as it were, like prohibited goods, into the commonwealth, and as it has no legal right to existence in this way, its destruction might also be ignored." (Ibid., pp. 448-9.) Although Kant does seem to favor some punishment for this maternal infanticide, he regards it as homicide rather than murder. Homicide, unlike murder, may involve an honorable motive, such as the "womanly honor" that is preserved when a mother kills a child born outside of marriage. Cf. Huntington Cairns, *Legal Philosophy from Plato to Hegel* (Baltimore: Johns Hopkins, 1967), p. 456.

71. Kant, *The Science of Right*, p. 421.

72. Ibid. Kant notes that the master of the house contracts with his

children either "actually or virtually." Although Kant does not elaborate on this point, he would probably argue that children who attain the age of reason but remain in their father's house have tacitly agreed to obey the father.

73. Ibid., p. 422.

74. Ibid., p. 419. Kant also believes that a person should be able to force a runaway spouse to return "to the former relation, as if that person were a thing."

75. Ibid., p. 422. Kant is vague on the details of this supposed contract and exactly how it can be voided. Clearly, however, after the contract goes into effect, the servant-child cannot run away.

76. Ibid., p. 443. Kant thinks that government should care for "children exposed from want or shame, and who would otherwise perish," but he does not discuss the proper scope of government intervention in family affairs.

77. Kant, "The Contest of Faculties," in *Kant's Political Writings*, p. 186.

78. G. W. F. Hegel, *The Philosophy of History*, trans. J. Sibree, Great Books of the Western World (Chicago: Encyclopedia Britannica, 1952), vol. 46, p. 171.

79. G. W. F. Hegel, *The Philosophy of Right*, trans. T. M. Knox, Great Books of the Western World (Chicago: Encyclopedia Britannica, 1952), vol. 46, p. 61.

80. Ibid., pp. 134-5.

81. Ibid., p. 76.

82. Ibid., p. 140.

83. Wilhelm von Humboldt, *The Limits of State Action*, ed. and trans. J. W. Burrow (Cambridge: Cambridge University Press, 1969). After Humboldt finished this book in 1792, some chapters were printed in a German periodical. A complete German edition did not apear until 1852, followed by an English translation two years later. The English version influenced John Stuart Mill, who quoted Humboldt in the epigraph to *On Liberty*.

84. Ibid., p. 22.

85. Ibid., pp. 51-4. Humboldt's opposition to state education is ironic, considering his later job (beginning in 1809) as chief of education in the Prussian Ministry of the Interior. On this and on Humboldt's unfortunate drift toward Prussian nationalism in later life, see Krieger, *The German Idea of Freedom*, pp. 166-173; and Friedrich Meinecke, *Cosmopolitanism and the National State*, trans. Robert B. Kimber (Princeton: Princeton University Press, 1970), pp. 34-48 and 138-147.

86. Humboldt, *The Limits of State Action*, p. 122.

87. Ibid., p. 123.

88. Ibid., p. 124. Humboldt is aware of the problem in determining when a minor is competent to judge for himself, and he argues that the degree of guilt of an adult offender should be considered in relation to the maturity of the minor.

89. See J. Bartlet Brebner, "Laissez Faire and State Intervention in Nineteenth-Century Britain," *The Journal of Economic History*, Supplement VIII, 1948. Brebner casts doubt on Bentham's individualist credentials, and in so doing he criticizes A. V. Dicey's classic work, *Lectures on the Relation Between Law and Public Opinion in England During the Nineteenth Century* (first published in 1905). Brebner's attack was somewhat misplaced, however, as Dicey was well aware of the collectivist strain in Bentham's thinking. Indeed, in a chapter titled "The Debt of Collectivism to Bentham," Dicey notes "the tendency of Benthamite teaching to extend the sphere of State intervention"; and he maintains that the utilitarian rejection of natural rights "deprived liberty of one of its safeguards." (London: Macmillan, 1919), p. 309. Various articles about this controversy may be found in Peter Stansky, ed., *The Victorian Revolution* (New York: Franklin Watts, 1973), pp. 5-57. Cf. Elie Halévy, *The Growth of Philosophic Radicalism*, trans. Mary Morris (London: Faber and Faber, 1949). Halévy was a philosopher-turned-historian, and his book (first published in 1928) is perhaps the best account of British utilitarianism ever written.

90. Jeremy Bentham, *An Introduction to the Principles of Morals and Legislation* (1789), ed. Wilfrid Harrison (Oxford: Basil Blackwell, 1948), pp. 126-7.

91. Ibid., p. 371.

92. Ibid., p. 373.

93. Ibid., pp. 373-4.

94. Ibid., pp. 378-379.

95. It should be noted that Spencer argued for the equal rights of children in his first book, *Social Statics* (1851), but he later retreated from this radical position. In *Principles of Ethics* (New York: Appleton, 1893, vol II), pp. 167-173, Spencer denies that children have a right to "self-direction." Far from possessing equal rights, "the rights of children must have a nature quite different from that of the rights of adults."

96. Herbert Spencer, *Social Statics* (London: John Chapman, 1851), p. 172.

97. Ibid., p. 173.

98. Ibid., p. 174.

99. Ibid., p. 175.

100. Ibid., p. 186.

101. Ibid.

17

Justice Entrepreneurship in a Free Market

Modern libertarian thought is essentially deductive in character. Building from a foundation in natural law, libertarians derive the principle of nonaggression; and from this they deduce the standards of a just society. Consistency is the key word: what is permissible in the political sphere must be compatible with the principle of nonaggression.

On the extreme wing of libertarian ideology are the individualist anarchists, who wish to dispense with government altogether. The quasi-legitimate functions now performed by government, such as the administration of justice, can, the anarchists claim, be provided in the marketplace. Although this private administration of justice was defended by some nineteenth-century libertarians such as Gustave de Molinari and Benjamin R. Tucker, its greatest exponent has been Murray Rothbard.[1]

Many objections have been leveled at free-market justice, perhaps the most serious being that it is incompatible with the rule of law.

The original version of this paper was delivered at the Sixth Annual Libertarian Scholars Conference, October 1978, at Princeton University.

Critics of this theory envision a chaotic patchwork of competing agencies, each with its own set of procedures and standards. Without a government to impose a uniform system of (presumably) reliable and just procedures, these critics foresee various criminal bands imposing their wills in the name of justice.

The anarchists, of course, disagree with this projection. (Indeed they point out that the previous description applies to governments, past and present.) Specifically, the individualist anarchists do not oppose the rule of law. They argue that because the principles of justice are grounded in natural law, they thus fall within the province of human knowledge. Just as we do not require a government to dictate what is true in science or history, so we do not require a government to dictate standards and procedures in the realm of justice. We should look to reason and facts, not to government.

For example, the specific *content* of law in a libertarian society can be deduced with relative ease from a well-developed theory of property rights, including a theory of title, acquisition, and exchange. Similarly, the *formal* aspects of law—that it be clearly specified in advance, impartially applied, etc.—can be defended without recourse to government. Even the principles of restitution (the libertarian substitute for "punishment") are derived from libertarian first principles and have nothing intrinsically to do with government. Where, then, is the weak link that opens the door for a monopolistic government?

Recently the issue of procedural law has come to the fore in libertarian theory, largely as a result of Robert Nozick's *Anarchy, State, and Utopia.* Does a person have "procedural rights," such as a "right to a fair trial"? If so, can free-market agencies provide adequate protection for such rights?

Nozick's conception of procedural rights is the latch with which he opens the gate for his "ultraminimal state." Does a person charged with a crime have a right to have his guilt or innocence determined by a reliable epistemological procedure? Yet, says Nozick (though he fails to explain why), so "a person may resist, in self-defense, if others try to apply to him an unreliable or unfair procedure of justice."[2]

For Nozick it is not enough that a person be guilty before others have a right to punish him; those inflicting punishment must *know* that he is guilty. A person may in fact be guilty, but if no one can prove his guilt, no one has a right to punish him.

From this foundation, Nozick proceeds to argue that a dominant protection agency, in its effort to protect its clients from potentially unreliable procedures, may forbid that its clients be tried by other agencies using less reliable procedures. In thus establishing itself as an enforcer of legal standards, the dominant agency evolves through no morally impermissible steps into an ultraminimal state—the final arbiter of law in that society.

Essential to Nozick's argument is the assumption that legal procedures are *not* a matter of knowledge. If, for instance, it is possible to verify objectively that one procedure is valid whereas another one is not, then it does not matter who employs the procedures in question. If a dominant agency employs correct procedures, then it is morally right, but so is every other agency that employs correct procedures. If, on the other hand, the dominant agency employs incorrect procedures, then it is morally wrong, as is every agency that employs such procedures. Thus, if there is an independent verifiable standard by which to judge legal procedures, then Nozick's argument has no force whatever. That an agency believes in the reliability of its procedures has nothing to do with the alleged right of that agency to insist that other agencies conform to its standards. If the dominant agency uses what are *in fact* reliable procedures, then it cannot prevent other agencies from using reliable procedures as well. If, on the contrary, the dominant agency uses unreliable procedures, then to impose such procedures on other agencies would be manifestly unjust.

If we postulate objective procedures, therefore, the major issue becomes *what* procedures are employed, not *who* employs them. The dominance of a particular agency has nothing at all to do with this issue.

An interesting response to Nozick is contained in Randy Barnett's "Whither Anarchy? Has Robert Nozick Justified the State?" Adopting a hard natural-rights position, Barnett flatly denies the existence of "natural procedural rights." Whether we know a person's guilt or innocence

> . . . may be relevant as a practical problem or even a moral problem [but] I question its relevance to issues of rights. . . . If the nature and moral foundation of rights are what I alluded to earlier—a freedom to use property, created along with property ownership—then epistemic considerations cannot create or alter rights. The right of self-defense we contend is a direct result of an infringement on a property right. Its purpose is to protect and restore what is rightfully owned. Since it is ontologically grounded this right exists against an aggressor independently of whether we know who the aggressor is. Consequently we are entitled to take compensation from the actual aggressor whether or not we are sure of his guilt. That is, the actual guilt or innocence of the suspect as opposed to our subjective knowledge of his guilt determines if taking restitution from him is justified.[3]

I agree with Barnett that a Victim of invasion has the right to seek restitution from the Invader, and that the *actual* guilt of the Invader is the only germane issue (as far as the Victim is concerned). But Nozick raises an important issue of knowledge of guilt and its relation to the enforcement of justice. In adopting procedural rights, however, Nozick takes a wrong turn and fails to see the solution to his own problem. The important social relation that generates the whole question of reliable procedures is not that between the Victim and the Invader, but the relationship between the Victim and impartial Third Parties. *It is for his own safety, to prevent violent Third Party intervention in his quest for restitution, that the Victim must concern himself with matters of legal procedure.*

Much of this essay is concerned with the elaboration and defense of the above point. I shall attempt to deduce a theory of juridical procedure without recourse to the phantom of "procedural rights." Central to this discussion is the notion of justice entrepreneurship with its two essential ingredients: restitutive risk and the presumption of invasion.

If, as I shall argue, it is possible to derive specific legal procedures from the principle of nonaggression, then *procedural law may be classed as a branch of natural-law theory*. It shall be possible to speak of juridical procedures—methods of ascertaining guilt and innocence—as correct or incorrect, just or unjust. This has important implications for anarchist theory, for it presents to anarchism an objective standard by which to distinguish legitimate agencies from outlaw agencies in a free market. Even among those agencies which profess to uphold the libertarian principle of nonaggression, we shall be able to segregate those that employ invalid procedures and thereby condemn them on that basis.[4]

Moreover, we shall see that the entrepreneurial function of Justice Agencies—the source of profit for such agencies—provides a strong impetus for fairness and impartiality. The idea that there must be a "super-agency"—a state—to oversee lesser agencies is rejected totally. (Who, for instance, shall oversee the super-agency?) Just as consumer response provides a reasonably trustworthy mechanism in a free market to minimize fraud and deception, so potential Third Party response provides a built-in check to minimize deceit and unreliability by Justice Agencies.

(Throughout this chapter terms such as "Invader," "Victim," and "coercion" are employed constantly. The reader unfamiliar with the use of such terms in libertarian theory should consult the Appendix at the conclusion of this essay.)

Justice is often defined as "rendering to each man his due," and this is consistent with the libertarian theory of justice. Libertarian justice is concerned with rendering to the victim of invasion what is rightfully his—his property (or the equivalent in value), plus compensation for loss of time, suffering, etc. Libertarian justice is primarily a matter of *restitution,* not of punishment in the conventional sense. The Invader is liable for the loss he inflicts upon the Victim.

Before restitution can be accomplished, however, several preliminary issues must be settled. Did a violation of rights occur? If so, who was responsible? And what was the extent of the responsibility? These matters of fact must be decided before the subject of restitution is germane, and they are the first priority of a court of justice.

The first task of a court, therefore, is to settle an issue of *knowl-*

edge: Did or did not the accused commit the crime charged against him? A court, as an arbiter of guilt and innocence, is the personification of epistemological standards. It represents the social application of epistemological procedures, whose purpose is to assess the rational basis for a given knowledge claim—the charge of the plaintiff (the alleged Victim) against the defendant (the alleged Invader). The onus of proof is on the plaintiff to prove his case with certainty—i.e. "beyond reasonable doubt"—and the defendant is presumed innocent until proven otherwise.

A court works within a given system of law where its task is to apply general legal standards to specific situations. Its function is that of the minor premise in a deductive syllogism:

Major Premise: An Invader is legally bound to compensate his Victim for the loss incurred (a principle of libertarian law).
Minor Premise: Jones is an Invader (to be determined by the court).
Conclusion: Therefore, Jones is bound to compensate his Victim for the loss incurred.

Because libertarian law is concerned only with the prohibition of invasive actions, a libertarian Justice Agency will concern itself only with matters of alleged invasion. The first priority of a libertarian agency, to repeat, is to settle an issue of knowledge. Can the allegation be established with certainty? Implicit within the procedures of a court there lurks a theory of knowledge and certainty. The verdict of a court cannot be more reliable than the epistemological underpinning on which it is based.

A satisfactory account of free-market courts of law (hereafter referred to as Justice Agencies) must consider their *entrepreneurial* function—something that has been largely neglected in previous literature. A Justice Agency is more than a "hired hand" employed for the efficient prosecution and apprehension of criminals. Much of the Justice Agency's service is entrepreneurial in nature. Specifically, the Agency assumes the burden of risk that accompanies the use or threat of physical force in a free society. A client contracts with a Justice Agency not only because the Agency is more efficient in obtaining restitution, but also because the Agency is more likely to overcome public suspicion that the force used to obtain restitution is of an invasive rather than a restitutive nature. The degree to which an Agency can minimize this risk is a measure of its reliability and, ultimately, the source of its profit.

The risk referred to here stems from the right of Third Party intervention. Where there exists a coercive state of affairs (say, between two persons), a Third Party may forcibly intervene without the prior consent of the Invader. (The consent of the Victim is assumed throughout this discussion.) If A aggresses against B, a Third Party does not require the permission of A in order to come to B's defense. The coercive state of affairs initiated by the Invader creates a situation where a Third Party may violently intervene in behalf of the Victim in order to halt the invasive act.

The right of Third Party intervention is a corollary of one's right to use force in order to repel invasive acts, and it is a right which most libertarians defend. But problems arise when this right is applied to specific situations, particularly when a user of force fails to identify the *kind* of force he is using (i.e., whether or not it is restitutive). If a Third Party observes force or the threat of force, with no evidence that the force is justified, he will rationally conclude that he is witnessing an invasive act in which he has the right to intervene. And, as I shall argue later, the Third Party in this circumstance is morally justified in exercising his right of intervention. If an error is made—if a Third Party mistakenly intervenes with a true Victim seeking restitution—the responsibility for error rests with the *Victim* who failed to identify publicly his violent act as one of restitution.

This problem may be illustrated by considering Crusoe and Friday alone on an island. If Crusoe steals some of Friday's coconuts, and if there is no doubt in Friday's mind as to Crusoe's guilt, then Friday need not resort to the intermediary of a trial in order to take restitutive action against Crusoe. He may take immediate action, using force if necessary, to regain his property.[5]

Now consider the same situation with the addition of a Third

Party who is absent during Crusoe's theft. Suppose that Friday makes no attempt to inform the Third Party of Crusoe's deed, or that Friday charges Crusoe with the theft but provides no evidence to substantiate the allegation. (Crusoe, of course, denies the charge.) Friday proceeds to invade Crusoe's hut in an attempt to reclaim his coconuts (or the equivalent in value). Crusoe, in the meantime, screams that he is being aggressed against and solicits the aid of the Third Party to restrain Friday. The Third Party intervenes, using force to stop Friday.

Friday, acting on his knowledge, is morally justified in seeking restitution. But the Third Party, acting on *his* knowledge, is (as I shall argue) justified in coming to the "defense" of Crusoe, the apparent Victim. With the existence of a Third Party, Friday's act of restitution —when no effort is made to enlighten the Third Party as to the circumstances—becomes a high-risk activity. It exposes Friday to potential harm for which he has no legitimate redress. That is to say, if a Third Party, believing Friday to be the true Invader, injures him in the process of resisting his "invasive" act, Friday cannot then seek restitution from the Third Party. Friday's failure to provide public notice and proof of his claim against Crusoe, generates an inevitable clash between Friday and the Third Party—a clash, it must be noted, that Friday could have avoided but did not. The responsibility for this Third Party conflict, therefore, rests with Friday; and he undertakes private restitution against Crusoe at his own risk.

From the potential conflict of Friday and the Third Party, there arises a need for a "public trial" to ascertain Crusoe's guilt or innocence. This trial is required not because of special "procedural rights" supposedly possessed by Crusoe (such as the "right to a fair trial"), but because this public demonstration of Crusoe's guilt is the only way to eradicate or minimize the potential conflict between Friday and a Third Party. By allowing the Third Party to examine the basis of Friday's allegation against Crusoe, with the opportunity for Crusoe to respond, it is possible to harmonize the knowledge of Friday (that Crusoe is guilty) with the knowledge of the Third Party, so that the Third Party can cooperate (or at least not interfere) with Friday's quest for restitution.

The same principles apply to any society of three or more persons. Impartial Third Parties are not privy to the special experience of a Victim seeking restitution. Man's knowledge is limited—he is not omniscient—and individuals must act on the context of knowledge available to them. Friday may be a true Victim seeking restitution, but this fact may be inaccessible to others. Friday knows it, and Crusoe (presumably) knows it; but Third Parties do not. If Crusoe denies the charge of theft, and if Friday fails to substantiate it, then Third Parties are epistemologically obliged to view Friday as an Invader. Given their context of knowledge, there is no other rational option.

Thus, whoever employs *unidentified* force in a free society is engaging in a high-risk activity because of possible Third Party intervention. One who uses force, or threatens the use of force, is presumed by Third Parties to be the Invader unless there is evidence to the contrary. Although a Victim of invasion has the moral right to seek restitution from the Invader, and need not solicit the permission of others to do so, he faces the risk of violent Third Party intervention if he fails to verify his charge publicly. This potential conflict is a result of a "knowledge gap" between the Victim and innumerable Third Parties.

To put it another way (and as a lead-in to the subject of entrepreneurship), there is a *lack of coordination* between the knowledge of the Victim and the knowledge of Third Parties. Consequently, there is a potential lack of coordination between the *actions* of the Victim (force used to gain restitution) and the *actions* of Third Parties (force used to repel the apparent Invader). This absence of coordination creates a high level of risk for one who seeks restitution in a free society without prior verification of his claim in a public forum.

The major problem, therefore, confronting a Victim who desires restitution in a libertarian legal system, is as follows: How can the Victim regain what is rightfully his, by force if necessary, and avoid being branded in the public eye as a common Invader? How can he bridge the "knowledge gap" between himself and Third Parties? That is to say, how can the Victim coordinate his restitutive action with the action of Third Parties?

Here we must look to Justice Agencies on a free market. The Victim, by hiring a Justice Agency, transfers the risk discussed above (restitutive risk) from himself to the Agency. It is the business of an Agency to coordinate the knowledge of the Victim with the knowledge of Third Parties—the public in general—and thereby minimize the likelihood of public condemnation as an Invader when restitutive action is taken.

If an Agency successfully demonstrates, in a public forum, its client's case, then it may seek restitution from the Invader without fear of Third Party intervention. But if the Agency takes restitutive action without sufficient public verification, then it assumes the risk of Third Party intervention. In either case, the client is protected. He has contracted with the agency not only to effect restitution but to bear the risk of this activity. *This transfer of restitutive risk constitutes a major function of a Justice Agency, and this is the aspect that I have described as entrepreneurial.*

The concept of entrepreneurship has been developed by "Austrian" economists within the framework of catallactics, that branch of praxeology which studies "all market phenomena with all their roots, ramifications, and consequences."[6] Human action entails change (such as a shift in subjective value preferences); and change, coupled with man's "imperfect" knowledge, introduces uncertainty into the marketplace. This creates a role for the entrepreneur. As Ludwig von Mises puts it:

> The term entrepreneur as used by catallactic theory means: acting man exclusively seen from the aspect of the uncertainty inherent in every action. In using this term one must never forget that every action is embedded in the flux of time and therefore involves a speculation.[7]

Every action, because it entails some degree of uncertainty and hence speculation, has an entrepreneurial aspect. In the marketplace, however, we may identify professional entrepreneurs as those who *specialize* in risk and speculation for proft. No real economy ever achieves a state of perfect equilibrium—the "evenly rotating economy" of economic theory—and the disequilibrium of the market generates the demand for entrepreneurs.

In *Competition and Entrepreneurship*, Israel Kirzner elaborates brilliantly on the entrepreneurial function in the marketplace. He stresses less than Mises the speculative aspect of entrepreneurship and develops instead the notion of entrepreneurial *alertness*—the recognition "that an opportunity for profit *does* exist."[8]

A basic problem of the marketplace, Kirzner points out, is the coordination of many different bits and pieces of information among market participants. The conditions for a profitable exchange may exist, but if the potential participants do not *perceive* this opportunity, the exchange cannot occur. This is where the entrepreneur may profitably intervene.

> If A would be prepared to offer as much as twenty oranges for a quantity of B's apples, and B would be prepared to accept, in exchange for his apples, any number of oranges greater than ten, then (as long as A and B are each unaware of the opportunity presented by the attitude of the other) entrepreneurial profit can be secured by buying B's apples at a price (in oranges) greater than ten and then reselling them to A for a price less than twenty.[9]

Where A and B are unaware of the potential trade, Kirzner says, we have "an *absence of coordination*." The entrepreneur, alert to this opportunity, is able to coordinate the desires of A and B, and this "coordination of information ensures coordination of action."

The opportunity for entrepreneurial profit derives from the knowledge gap between A and B, both of whom desire to trade but are unaware of the possibility. There would be no entrepreneurial role in a world populated by omniscient beings. The absence of coordination Kirzner refers to is the result of man's limited knowledge. The entrepreneur thus functions as a conduit of information among market participants.

The manner in which I apply the entrepreneurial function to Justice Agencies should now be fairly apparent. Before proceeding, however, I must acknowledge the significant differences between entrepreneurship in the realm of voluntary exchange and entrepreneurship as I apply it to restitutive force. For one thing, catallactic risk differs from restitutive risk. The former entails the possibility of economic loss, unfulfilled expectations, or frustrated preferences. But the latter may lead to violence and a breach of justice.

Nevertheless, despite such differences, I believe there are sufficient parallels between market entrepreneurship and Justice Agencies to justify using the term in this context. I shall now summarize the entrepreneurial function of Justice Agencies, using the term "catallactic entrepreneur" to refer to the market entrepeneur of Mises and Kirzner, and the term "justice entrepreneur" to refer to my extension of this concept to free-market Justice Agencies.

Just as man's limited knowledge creates a function for the catallactic entrepreneur, so it creates a function for the justice entrepreneur. The knowledge gap between a Victim and Third Parties that will inevitably result in a violent clash opens the door for profit to one who can successfully bridge this gap. The justice entrepreneur, like the catallactic entrepreneur, seeks to coordinate disparate bits of information and thereby harmonize the actions of different individuals who operate from different contexts of knowledge.

As we have seen, for a market exchange to occur, it is not enough for the opportunity for exchange to exist. The potential participants must perceive this opportunity, and the success of an entrepreneur in transmitting information is a source of his profit. Similarly, for justice to be implemented in a free society, it is not enough for a Victim to know the justice of his cause. Because of restitutive risk, he is obliged to transmit his knowledge to the public at large; and the ability of a justice entrepreneur to fulfill this task is a source of his profit.

The entrepreneurial function of a Justice Agency provides a built-in safeguard to insure fairness and impartiality. It is not out of altruistic concern for the accused that an Agency strives to be scrupulously fair in its proceedings, but out of simple self-interest. An Agency can fulfill its entrepreneurial function of preventing Third Party intervention only if it is generally regarded as fair and reliable. If an agency conducts unfair or secretive trials, it would fail to gain esteem in the public eye and thereby defeat its own purpose. The Agency would be viewed as a common Invader, and any restitutive action on its part would be subject to legitimate Third Party intervention.

Unlike the catallactic entrepreneur, the "alertness" of a Justice Agency is its ability to recognize prospective cases involving restitutive risk where there is a reasonable chance to verify the client's allegation publicly. Its own public reputation—the vital key to its success as an agency—demands that it shun fabricated or poorly founded accusations. The fear of governmentalists that free-market Agencies will sell mock-justice to the highest bidder without regard for justice, objectivity, and reliable procedures is without foundation. That an Agency *claims* to be using restitutive force is not sufficient to prevent Third Party intervention. If an Agency employs force, then, like an individual, it is presumed to be an Invader unless there is proof to the contrary. For an Agency to use (allegedly) restitutive force without public verification is to brand itself an outlaw in the public eye.

Later in this essay we shall explore further how the entrepreneurial function of Justice Agencies generates objective standards with which to distinguish a legitimate agency from an outlaw agency. Moreover, we shall see that this notion of justice entrepreneurship dispenses with the problem of "procedural rights," as well as providing the basis to answer most of the objections raised by critics of free-market Justice Agencies. Before moving to another subject, however, we should consider briefly another way in which a Justice Agency functions as an entrepreneur.

We have thus far stressed the coordination aspect of justice entrepreneurship and neglected the speculative aspect mentioned by Mises in a previous passage. But justice entrepreneurship is speculative to a degree as well because man, a fallible being, may err even in the best of circumstances. A reliable Agency may find a man guilty of invasion and use restitutive force against him only to have evidence appear at a later time that establishes the man's innocence. In such a case, of course, the Agency is required to compensate the falsely convicted individual.

When an individual contracts with an Agency to seek restitution, he thus pays the Agency to perform two basic entrepreneurial functions:

1. The Agency assumes the burden of restitutive risk, and it attempts to minimize or eliminate this risk by coordinating the knowledge of its client (the purported Victim) with the knowledge of Third Parties, thereby avoiding the clash of violent Third Party intervention. The less conflict involved in restitutive action, the greater is the possibility of satisfying the client's desire to be compensated for his loss. Thus, it is in the Agency's interest to employ impartial, reliable procedures; and it is in the Victim's interest to seek out an Agency with precisely this reputation.

2. The agency assumes the burden of future uncertainty, where future information may overturn present knowledge. Again, it is to an Agency's interest to employ reliable procedures in order to minimize, to the greatest extent possible, the element of future uncertainty; and it is to the Victim's interest to seek out such an Agency.

We have seen that a major entrepreneurial function of a Justice Agency is to bear restitutive risk. An Agency's expertise is measured by its ability to negate this risk through public verification and dissemination of a knowledge claim—the allegation of the plaintiff against the defendant. This discussion of justice entrepreneurship obviously hinges on the notion of "restitutive risk"—the right of Third Party intervention when a purported Victim employs restitutive force without public verification of this claim. We shall now examine restitutive risk in more detail.

There are two issues to consider: first, the right of Third Party intervention itself and, second, the *application* of this right to particular situations.

As indicated previously, the right of Third Party intervention is a right to which most libertarians subscribe. Just as there is nothing in the principle of nonaggression that prohibits the use of violence in self-defense, so there is nothing that prohibits a Third Party using violence in defense of a Victim. If it is legitimate to use violence to counteract invasion, then any person may employ such violence whether or not that person is the Victim.

But a difficulty arises over the application of this right. The knowledge gap stressed earlier between a Victim and a Third Party is the rule rather than the exception. Unless a special effort is made to inform Third Parties, they rarely have access to the details of a dispute involving restitutive force. Of course it might be argued that the Third Party should ascertain relevant facts before exercising the right of intervention. If a Victim is morally authorized to seek restitution, he is right—period. Why must a Victim justify his restitutive violence for the benefit of Third Parties?

We must remember the purpose of public verification: it is not to *justify* the Victim's restitutive act morally, but to *identify* the *kind* of action he is taking. The potential misunderstanding between a Victim and Third Parties is factual, not evaluative. Violent acts do not bear external characteristics that enable one visually to distinguish between invasion and restitution. Invasion, for instance, may involve fraud without overt violence, in which case the Victim may be the first (and only) one to employ actual violence in his quest for restitution. The distinction between invasion and restitution can be drawn only with reference to property rights and property titles, and such particularized information is rarely accessible to Third Parties without deliberate effort.

In our previous illustration, Friday believes with good reason that Crusoe is an Invader. But the Third Party (who sees only Friday's violence against Crusoe) believes with equally good reason, given the context of his knowledge, that Friday is the Invader. This knowledge gap is caused by man's non-omniscience, and it gives rise to the key question: Who has the primary responsibility to bridge this gap, the Victim or the Third Party?

To maintain that the Third Party is obligated to know the relevant facts (who is the actual Victim, etc.) before he has the right to intervene in a coercive state of affairs is to erect what is in most cases an insurmountable barrier that effectively blocks any use of Third Party intervention whatever. Violent acts often occur suddenly, without previous warning; and to counteract the damage of violence usually requires a quick and decisive response. If a Third Party is required to investigate property titles before he intervenes in defense of the apparent Victim, the violent act will be concluded long before the Third Party reaches first base.

I contend that a contextual application of the right of Third Party intervention—an application that takes into account man's limited knowledge—places *major* responsibility upon the Victim. There is a principle operative here that I shall call the *presumption of invasion.* This principle states that *the person who is observed to initiate violence, or the threat of violence, is presumed to be the Invader unless there is evidence to the contrary.* If a Victim employs restitutive force, he assumes the burden of proof. As a user of violence in a free society, the presumption is against him; and he must overcome this presumption or face the consequences.

As a fulcrum for our discussion of this topic, consider another hypothetical example. B believes, rightly or wrongly, that C stole his wallet containing $100 at a party the day before. B sees C on the street, confronts him and demands his money back. C denies everything and an argument ensues. B then wrestles C to the ground and attempts to extract C's wallet so that B can regain what (he believes) is rightfully his. C calls for help, and an impartial Third Party—a passerby who knows neither B nor C—comes to C's aid. The Third Party fractures B's arm in an attempt to restrain him.

At this point, we do not know whether C did in fact steal B's wallet, so we cannot assess the validity of B's claim against him. Indeed, the Third Party in this example does not even know (as we do) of B's *belief* that C stole his wallet. He sees only B's physical assault of C, and he forms his judgment—that B is the Invader—on this basis.

If the presumption of invasion is correct, then we can state that the intervention of the Third Party is justified *regardless* of the validity of B's initial claim against C. The relation between B and C is one thing; the relation between B and the Third Party is another. And even if B does have a legitimate claim of restitution against C, this does not give B a blank check to gain restitution by any method he chooses. If B creates a situation that is bound to engender Third Party misunderstanding and intervention, then he must shoulder the risk of his action.

The alternative to the presumption of invasion is to hold that the Third Party was justified only if C was innocent of the original theft. If, on the other hand, C was guilty—if B was seeking legitimate restitution—then the Third Party's intervention, instead of being a defense of C, was in fact an act of *invasion* against B. In this case, the Third Party would be liable to compensate B for the injury inflicted upon him.

This latter interpretation requires virtual omniscience on the part of the Third Party and should be rejected on that basis. Any ethical or political theory must be grounded in the recognition that man is neither omniscient nor infallible. And since justice is concerned, at least in part, with a question of knowledge (guilt and innocence), a reasonable theory of justice can be derived only within a contextualist framework. We can no more require omniscience and infallibility in the sphere of justice than we can require them in other areas of knowledge.[10]

In maintaining that the onus of proof lies with B rather than the Third Party, we are asserting, in effect, that the Third Party cannot be held responsible for his lack of omniscience. True, B may have knowledge that the Third Party lacks—and in this sense B may be "right"—but B cannot reasonably expect others to have mystical insight into his private world of knowledge. B takes an action against C that would be regarded by any "reasonable man" as invasive. Overt violence is the most obvious and primitive form of invasive action. In a libertarian society, it is the most suspect activity in which one can engage. Although violence is not always invasive, it is presumed to be in the absence of contrary evidence. B, in opting for violence against C to effect restitution, automatically brings a wary public eye upon himself. He creates a situation where Third Party intervention seems appropriate. If things are not as they seem, then B must show *why* they are not. In the absence of public verification, Third Parties will regard B as the true Invader, and B assumes the risk of being so identified.

We have seen that the presumption of invasion lies with the apparent initiator of violence (or what we may term the "proximate" user of violence). This principle may be further illustrated by viewing the dispute between B and C from the perspective of the Third Party.

Prior to witnessing B's violence against C, the Third Party has no knowledge of B or C and no knowledge of a relationship between them. When the Third Party observes B's violence against C, he may infer with absolute confidence that a coercive relationship now obtains between B and C.

The proximate user of violence (B in our case) may be the Invader, or he may be the Victim seeking redress. In either case, B's violence establishes with *certainty* to any observer that a coercive state of affairs exists between B and C. His violence is a visible public announcement of this fact. By his action, B communicates a message to the public in general: he notifies them of a coercive state in which they have the right to intervene.

Thus far the Third Party has progressed from a condition of *tabula rasa* concerning B and C to the knowledge that he has the moral right to intervene *somehow* in the relationship. This is where his certainty stops, however, as he does not have knowledge of the total context in which the dispute occurred. And this is where the presumption of invasion comes into play.

The Third Party has two basic options at this point (assuming he does not ignore the situation altogether): (1) he may assume that B, the proximate user of violence, is the true Invader; or (2) he may assume that C, the apparent Victim, is actually the true Invader.

Given the Third Party's context of knowledge, (1) is rational thing to believe. Although the evidence against B is only partial (because the Third Party's knowledge is incomplete), the evidence against C, *by comparison,* is nonexistent. Even partial evidence is overwhelming when weighed against no evidence at all. The Third Party has reason to believe that B is the true Invader. It was B, after all, who used violence, so it was B who chose to announce the coercive state between himself and C. For the Third Party to speculate, contrary to appearance, that C is the Invader and B is the Victim would be totally arbitrary and hence irrational. In other words, C is presumed *innocent* until proven guilty. And if B's violence is based on a knowledge claim of C's guilt, then B has the onus of proof to demonstate his claim. Failure to do so leaves the presumption of invasion with B.

The presumption of invasion, therefore, is an extension of the principle that reasonable belief and action are based on evidence. And where there are two competing propositions, one with supporting evidence and the other without such evidence, the former proposition demands assent over the latter.

Another way to analyze the presumption of invasion—one that emphasizes more the obligation of a Victim to bridge the knowledge gap between himself and Third Parties—is to distinguish between *behavior* and *action*. Behavior, as I use the term here, refers to the outward, observable manifestations of human action. Action, on the other hand, is behavior viewed within a wider perspective of context and purpose.

The same kind of behavior may, in different circumstances, constitute different kinds of action. For instance, scratching one's head during a conversation may indicate nothing except that one's scalp itches. But if a baseball coach scratches his head during a game, it may be an important signal to a player. The behavior in these two cases is basically identical, but the purpose of the behavior, as well as the context in which the behavior occurs, are radically different. We are dealing with similar units of behavior but essentially different kinds of action.

The same is true of physical violence. Violence is an observable and easily identified unit of behavior in most cases. But violent behavior may, in different contexts, constitute different kinds of actions. Specifically, violent behavior can be either *invasive action* or *noninvasive action*. As far as moral and political theory are concerned, these are different kinds of actions altogether; they stand on opposite sides of the fence in regard to property titles.

When a Third Party sees B's violence against C, he observes the behavior of B, not the action of B. That is to say, the Third Party witnesses the outward manifestation of violence, but he cannot similarly witness the purpose and context that give meaning to B's behavior. The Third Party *infers* that B's violent behavior constitutes invasive action.

I maintain that the Third Party's inference is justified and, moreover, that B, in using unidentified violence, actually *communicates* through his behavior that he is an Invader. To defend this notion of behavioral communication adequately would require an essay in itself, so I can only outline the subject here.

Many kinds of behavior have conceptual significance within given societies. Behavior can convey a message as surely as words—indeed, language is itself a kind of behavior—and just as verbal communication is made possible by a common understanding about the meaning of words, so nonverbal communication is made possible by a common understanding about the significance of behavior. Within a certain society, for instance, a specific gesture may be generally understood to convey an insult. From an observable unit of behavior, individuals in that society will infer that an action of insult has occurred. This creates what we may dub a "presumption of insult." That is, anyone who uses this gesture in normal circumstances is presumed to be conveying an insult. The inferred link between the observable behavior and the presumed action is normal and natural within this society, so there is a *prima facie* case against anyone who engages in behavior of this variety. If the gesture-user does not wish to convey the commonly understood message, then the burden is with him to explain the extenuating circumstances. In lieu of this explanation, he cannot be surprised when others respond as if they have been insulted. Indeed, they have no reason to think otherwise.

The similarity between the presumption of invasion and the "presumption of insult" should be obvious. I am arguing that the inference from observed violence to invasive action is naturally to be expected, especially in a libertarian society. B, in using violence against C, sends a signal of "invasive action" through his behavior.

If this is not the true significance of B's behavior, then he has the burden to explain its true meaning. There is a *prima facie* case against the proximate user of violence, and it is up to him to convince Third Parties that things, in his case at least, are not as they seem.

A possible objection to the preceding argument is that it relies on conventional understanding about the significance of behavior. And where we rely on convention, we enter a problematic area where clear standards based on natural law rarely fare well.

In response to this, I must point out, as was mentioned previously, that language itself is conventional. If one argues that behavior has no particular conceptual significance, why not say the same for language? Suppose a man threatens to kill me, and I take action I deem appropriate to defend myself. The words, "I am going to kill you," signify a threat to me upon which I base my response.

But suppose my attacker later claims that "kill" does not mean the same thing to him as it does to me. Words, after all, are conventional, and where in nature is it written that "kill" must mean one thing and not another? "Kill," my attacker claims, does not signify a threat in his vocabulary; instead, it signifies something akin to worship and reverence. So my attacker's words really communicated his desire to worship and revere me.

What if I injure this man in my response to a perceived threat. If he can convince a judge and jury that "kill" does indeed signify "worship" to him, must I then compensate him for his injury? Am I now to be condemned as an Invader because I used violence in response to a misinterpreted threat?

In this case it is clear that I had good reason to believe I was going to be attacked, even if my understanding of the situation rested upon mere "convention." Perhaps I misinterpreted the intended meaning of my assailant's words, but he must bear the lion's share of responsibility for this misunderstanding. Although he was not technically an Invader, he cannot rightfully demand compensation from me for his injury.

Any approach to justice that ignores the contextual implications of language and behavior will, in the final analysis, create more problems than it solves. Suppose we cast aside contextualism and the presumption of invasion for a more absolutist approach to the problems of invasion and restitution. Enough of this talk about presumption and reasonable belief—let us consider only the facts. If a person violates property rights and property titles, he is an Invader—period. In our previous example of B seeking restitution from C, if C really is a thief, then B has a right to get his money back, by force if necessary. Hence, if a Third Party intervenes with B's restitutive force and injures B in the process, then the Third Party is an Invader *vis-à-vis* B and must compensate him for his injury.

One of the many problems with this approach is that it cannot deal adequately with *threats* of violence. A simple threat of violence is not a transgression of property titles; it expresses an *intent* to transgress. If a man walks up to me and points a gun at my head, I am not required to wait until he pulls the trigger before I have the right to use force against him. His behavior conveys a message—an intent to invade—and I have the right to use defensive violence. Let us say that I deliver a karate chop and send the attacker to the hospital.

But suppose that the attack was a joke. The gun was simply a toy, and my apparent assailant was actually hired by some friends of mine to play a prank. There was no real weapon and no intent to invade. And the prankster never stated his intent to harm me. He simply pointed a toy at me, which I misperceived as a real pistol, thereby inferring that his action was invasive in nature. *It is my mistake.* Does this mean that the prankster can rightfully demand compensation from me for his injury?

Yes, according to the absolutist approach. No, according to the contextualist approach. There was, in fact, no invasive action, so my violence against the prankster was, according to the absolutist theory, an act of invasion against *him.* (In objective terms, I violated his right to play a noninvasive joke.) The contextualist approach, on the contrary, maintains that my inference of invasion was justified, given the knowledge available to me; and that the prankster, in exhibiting behavior that ordinarily conveys invasion, must assume the risk of this behavior.

Even where a threat is genuine, an absolutist theory cannot justify defensive violence prior to the actual infliction of the invasive violence. Threats always entail communication and inference. One cannot *perceive* a threat per se; one *concludes* that a threat exists through a process of reasoning. And if we prohibit references to presumptions, reasonable expectations and contexts of knowledge, we destroy the very foundation that gives meaning to the concept of "threat" in the first place.

Having laid the foundation for restitutive risk, we shall now return to justice entrepreneurship and explore its ability to solve some problems facing a free-market legal system.

A major purpose of this essay is to derive legal procedures from the principle of nonaggression without recourse to special procedural rights. From one's own right to use violence to halt invasion, there flows the right of Third Party intervention. This right, when applied contextually, leads to the need for a public trial before a Victim employs restitutive force.

We have stressed that the foundation for juridical procedures does not lie in procedural rights of the accused. An alleged Invader will be presumed innocent in the public eye, regardless of his actual guilt or innocence, until his accuser proves the allegation in a public forum. Pretrial violence against the accused will be viewed as invasion and subject to Third Party intervention. Thus, it is not the accused's "right to a fair trail" that protects him but the presumption of invasion against anyone who uses force against him. The accused has the same basic right as everyone else—the right to be free from invasion—and this right is sufficient for his protection.

It is not the Victim-Invader relationship that generates the need for juridical procedures but the Victim-Third Party relationship. A Victim has a compelling but purely self-interested reason for submitting his grievance to a reputable Justice Agency for trial. This is the safest way to delegate restitutive risk and minimize the likelihood of Third Party intervention.

If my argument is sound, if the entrepreneurial function of a Justice Agency is to minimize restitutive risk by defeating the presumption of invasion, then we have a tolerably clear standard by which to gauge the legitimacy of an Agency in a free market. If the Agency must provide *public verification* of a knowledge claim, then we can deduce the minimum procedures a court must follow to avoid condemnation as an "outlaw agency." Full elaboration and defense of these procedures would require a separate essay; here we can only sketch an outline that will hopefully stimulate further discussion.

There are two aspects to court procedure: (1) the *public* aspect and (2) the *verification* aspect. We shall consider these two aspects separately.

1. The Public Aspect

A trial must be public. A secret trial, unless requested by the defendant, negates the entrepreneurial function of a trial and is invalid on this ground alone. There may be legitimate disagreements over the specifics that qualify a trial as public, but certain minimum requirements are, I think, beyond dispute.

(a) There must be public access to the trial itself. Interested Third Parties must be admitted to observe the proceedings (unless the defendant wishes to exclude them).

(b) The details of court procedure must be accessible to the public. Every Agency must have a "charter" wherein its rules and regulations are clearly specified.

(c) Careful records of every trial must be kept to permit Third Party examination and review of the proceedings. (The court, however, need not bear the expense of providing transcripts, although it may volunteer to do so for special review agencies in order to maintain its reputation.)

(d) A court must have a mechanism to disseminate its verdict to the public at large. This is where the reputation and integrity of an Agency play a major role. If a respected Agency wishes to serve public notice of a "guilty" verdict and an intent to use restitutive force, an announcement to this effect sent to other agencies (with an opportunity for them to challenge the verdict), combined with the implementation of restitution by uniformed, easily identifiable representatives of this Agency, will probably be sufficient to prevent Third Party intervention (or at least shift the presumption of invasion to the Third Party).

2. The Verification Aspect

In considering verification procedures, we must remember that the presumption of invasion places the onus of proof entirely upon the Justice Agency. And this onus pertains not only to specific verdicts but to the procedures themselves.

Suppose the "Lipton Agency" ascertains guilt and innocence by reading tea leaves, or the "Geller Agency" employs a professional psychic to read the accused's mind. Such agencies would have the responsibility to provide rigorous philosophical and scientific justification for their methodologies. Third Parties need not prove the unreliability of these procedures; rather, they are assumed to be unreliable until and unless the Agency employing them proves otherwise. Failure to do so will result in condemnation of the Agency as an outlaw.

(Incidentally, this underscores the vital importance of a general regard for reason among the members of a society. Juridical standards usually reflect the intellectual standards of a culture. For medieval jurists who believed that God would intervene in behalf of the innocent, trial by combat and trial by ordeal were quite logical. The evolution of rational standards within the common law tradition reflects a parallel intellectual maturation.)

Some of the specific verification procedures required from a Justice Agency are as follows:

(a) A Justice Agency may not employ force against a defendant prior to his conviction. The defendant is innocent until proven guilty. This means that a defendant, in effect, will be invited to attend his trial; and if he refuses he will be tried *in absentia*.

(b) An Agency does not have the right of subpoena unless by prior contractual agreement with those within its jurisdiction.

(c) An Agency must prove a defendant's guilt beyond "reasonable doubt." Anything less will not absolve it of the presumption of invasion.

(d) An Agency, in order to reinforce its good intentions and reputation, should provide a defendant with reasonable latitude in the choice of specific procedures. For example, the defendant may have a choice of a jury of up to, say, twenty members, composed of professional jurors or laypersons hired for the one occasion. Or the defendant may select a judge or panel of judges from an independent agency, thus separating the prosecution of his case from its resolution. There are many possible variations here, and in practice the reasonable options would be agreed upon in the legal profession, but the underlying principle must not be forgotten. *It is the Agency that must justify itself, not the defendant.* The fewer options provided by an Agency, the less willingness it displays to accommodate the reasonable requests of the defendant, the more its credibility will suffer. The self-interest of the Agency demands flexibility.

(e) The Agency must provide a defendant with defense counsel of his choice, within an established price range. If the defendant is found innocent, the Agency must absorb the cost (or pass it on to its client, per their contract). If the defendant is found guilty, the cost of defense and other court costs may be added to the restitution.

Of all the principles discussed thus far, this may seem the most doubtful. But it can be defended on epistemological grounds. To adequately test the procedures and conclusion of a specialized discipline requires a specialist in that field. A layman, for instance, usually lacks the knowledge and skill to investigate thoroughly the conclusion of a physicist or mathematician. And a professional who subjected his conclusions only to laymen, while avoiding the examination of his colleagues, would properly be held in low esteem.

We have a similar situation in the legal profession. There is good reason to believe that a libertarian legal system would be far less complex than what we have presently, but the areas of contract law and criminal jurisprudence would still have complex areas. There may be technical "gray areas" concerning the admissibility of lie-detector tests or "voice prints." Such topics would require one specially trained in the legal profession.

If a court is to reach a verdict with certainty, then, like any claim to certainty, its procedures must be capable of withstanding critical scrutiny. If a court convicts a defendant who, let us say, cannot afford to hire a defense counsel while refusing to furnish him with competent assistance, then the verdict of that court must be viewed with great suspicion. Subjecting its own procedures to independent, competent criticism is part and parcel of the Justice Agency's role of public verification.

In other words, if an Agency is to defeat the presumption of invasion, it must present the strongest case possible. And a trial without a defense counsel is certainly *not* the strongest case possible. This alone creates a serious doubt as to the Agency's integrity, and it may possibly lead to the Agency's condemnation in the public eye.

The preceding list is not intended to be exhaustive; rather, it is offered as a model of the procedures that may be derived from the principle of nonaggression. The important point here is not the procedures themselves, but the methodology used in deriving them. Using the concepts of justice entrepreneurship, restitutive risk, and the presumption of invasion, I have endeavored to bring the standards of procedural law into the realm of deductive natural law. I have tried to show that there are no serious gaps in the libertarian paradigm of natural law and noncoercion such that a monopolistic government must step forward to fill these gaps.

If, as I have claimed, juridical procedures can be deduced from the principle of noncoercion, then the procedures employed by a free-market Justice Agency can be judged as "correct" or "incorrect" using objective standards. It is not a matter, as Robert Nozick suggests, of the dominant Agency imposing its procedures upon lesser agencies in order to protect its clients from risky procedures. Rather, we may examine the procedures of all agencies—*including the dominant Agency*—in order to assess the validity of their procedures, as gauged by the entrepreneurial standard of public verification. If any Agency uses "risky" procedures (or, more accurately, invalid procedures), then that

Agency is an outlaw and subject to Third Party intervention when it employs force.

Appendix

For the purposes of this paper, we shall assume the libertarian theory of rights and property to be correct. Human interaction, according to this theory, may be divided into two broad categories: *invasive* and *noninvasive.* These categories depend in turn upon the identification of *property titles.* A title is a specification of ownership; to have a property title is to have rightful claim of use and disposal. For a person to use or dispose of property without the owner's consent is to violate the owner's property rights.

An invasive act involves the transgression of property titles. An *Invader* is one who so transgresses, and a *Victim* is the owner whose rights have been violated. A noninvasive action is any action that does not involve such a transgression.

Where two or more individuals interact with no violation of property titles, we have a *free* state of affairs. Where at least one person violates property titles, we have a *coercive* state of affairs. Coercion may involve overt physical violence, or it may not. Fraud, breach of contract—such actions, although they may be nonviolent, entail title violation and thus qualify as coercive.

Violence (physical force) may be invasive or noninvasive. Violence used to institute title violation is invasive. Violence used to counter an immediate threat (*defensive violence*) or violence used to restore rightful control over one's property or the equivalent in value (*restitutive violence*) are forms of noninvasive violence. (Throughout this essay, "violence," "physical force," and "force" are used interchangeably.)

It is important to note that the libertarian theory of justice is concerned not with the use of force per se but with the question of property titles. Libertarianism does not prohibit the use of force, or even the initiation of force. If, for instance, the force used is restitutive, then it is justified, even if force was not previously used by the Invader. Force is morally neutral: it can be used to initiate a state of coercion or to eradicate a state of coercion. As an example of the latter: if a thief retains his stolen property, then a state of coercion exists between the thief and the Victim so long as the rightful owner is denied control over his property. If the owner employs violence to regain his property, then that violence terminated the coercive state of affairs. (It must always be remembered that "coercion," as used in this essay, refers to a *state of affairs* that obtains among two or more persons when there is a violation of property titles.)

Notes

1. See G. de Molinari, *The Production of Security,* trans. J. H. McCulloch (New York: The Center for Libertarian Studies, 1977); and Benjamin R. Tucker, *Instead of a Book* (New York: Benjamin R. Tucker, 1893). One of the more elaborate discussions of justice agencies modeled after "insurance companies" is found in Francis D. Tandy's little known work, *Voluntary Socialism* (Denver: Francis D. Tandy, 1896), especially Chapter V. For Rothbard's presentation, see *For A New Liberty,* rev. ed. (New York: Macmillan, 1978), pp. 215–241.

2. Robert Nozick, *Anarchy, State, and Utopia* (New York: Basic Books, 1974), p. 102.

3. Randy Barnett, "Whither Anarchy? Has Robert Nozick Justified the State?" *Journal of Libertarian Studies* 1 (Winter 1977).

4. Some theorists deal with legal procedures in a libertarian society by stipulating that such procedures can be determined contractually beforehand between an Agency and its clients. Although this is a convenient way to deal with some problems, it skirts the "tough" problems confronting a free-market legal system, such as those arising when an Agency must try a person who was not previously a client.

5. For the purpose of illustration, I have used clear-cut examples throughout this essay, and I have avoided more complex cases involving, for instance, legitimate title contest between two parties, both of whom believe they are right.

6. Ludwig von Mises, *Human Action,* 3rd ed. (Chicago: Henry Regnery

Co., 1966), p. 233.

7. Ibid., p. 253.

8. Israel M. Kirzner, *Competition and Entrepreneurship* (Chicago: University of Chicago Press, 1973), p. 86.

9. Ibid., p. 216.

10. For discussions of contextualism, see the following: Richard I. Aaron, *Knowing and the Function of Reason* (Oxford: Oxford University Press, 1971); D. W. Hamlyn, *The Theory of Knowledge* (New York: Anchor Books, 1970); J. L. Austin, "Other Minds," *Philosophical Papers*, ed. J. O. Urmson and G. J. Warnock (Oxford: Oxford University Press, 1961); George H. Smith, *Atheism: The Cast Against God* (Los Angeles: Nash Publishing, 1974), pp. 130–140; Ayn Rand, *Introduction to Objectivist Epistemology* (New York: The Objectivist, Inc., 1967); Tibor Machan, *Human Rights and Human Liberties* (Chicago: Nelson-Hall, 1975); Douglas B. Rasmussen, "Austin and Wittgenstein on 'Doubt' and 'Knowledge,' " *Reason Papers*, no. 1 (Fall 1974), pp. 51–60.